Pedagogy of Resistance

Also available from Bloomsbury

Critical Pedagogy and the Covid-19 Pandemic: Keeping Communities Together in Times of Crisis, edited Fatma Mizikaci and Eda Ata
Critical Pedagogy for Healing: Paths Beyond "Wellness," Toward a Soul Revival of Teaching and Learning, edited by Tricia M. Kress, Christopher Emdin, and Robert Lake
Education, Equality and Justice in the New Normal: Global Responses to the Pandemic, edited by Inny Accioly and Donaldo Macedo
Education for Critical Consciousness by Paulo Freire
Education for Social Change, by Douglas Bourn
On Critical Pedagogy, 2nd Edition by Henry A. Giroux
Paulo Freire: A Philosophical Biography, Walter Omar Kohan
Pedagogy in Process by Paulo Freire
Pedagogy of Hope by Paulo Freire
Pedagogy of the Heart by Paulo Freire
Pedagogy of the Oppressed by Paulo Freire
Race, Politics, and Pandemic Pedagogy by Henry A. Giroux
Transnational Feminist Politics, Education, and Social Justice: Post Democracy and Post Truth, edited by Silvia Edling and Sheila Macrine

Pedagogy of Resistance

Against Manufactured Ignorance

Henry A. Giroux

BLOOMSBURY ACADEMIC
LONDON • NEW YORK • OXFORD • NEW DELHI • SYDNEY

BLOOMSBURY ACADEMIC
Bloomsbury Publishing Plc
50 Bedford Square, London, WC1B 3DP, UK
1385 Broadway, New York, NY 10018, USA
29 Earlsfort Terrace, Dublin 2, Ireland

BLOOMSBURY, BLOOMSBURY ACADEMIC and the Diana logo are trademarks
of Bloomsbury Publishing Plc

First published in Great Britain 2022

Copyright © Henry A. Giroux, 2022

Henry A. Giroux has asserted his right under the Copyright, Designs and
Patents Act, 1988, to be identified as Author of this work.

For legal purposes the Acknowledgements on pp. xiii–xiv constitute an
extension of this copyright page.

Series design by Charlotte James
Cover image © Jonathan Knowles / Getty images

All rights reserved. No part of this publication may be reproduced or transmitted
in any form or by any means, electronic or mechanical, including photocopying,
recording, or any information storage or retrieval system, without prior
permission in writing from the publishers.

Bloomsbury Publishing Plc does not have any control over, or responsibility for,
any third-party websites referred to or in this book. All internet addresses given
in this book were correct at the time of going to press. The author and publisher
regret any inconvenience caused if addresses have changed or sites have ceased
to exist, but can accept no responsibility for any such changes.

A catalogue record for this book is available from the British Library.

A catalog record for this book is available from the Library of Congress.

ISBN: HB: 978-1-3502-6949-1
       PB: 978-1-3502-6950-7
       ePDF: 978-1-3502-6951-4
       ePUB: 978-1-3502-6953-8

Typeset by Integra Software Services Pvt. Ltd.
Printed and bound in Great Britain

To find out more about our authors and books visit www.bloomsbury.com
and sign up for our newsletters.

For Rania
For Tony Penna
For Stanley Aronowitz

One must say Yes to life and embrace it wherever it is found—and it is found in terrible places.... For nothing is fixed, forever and forever, it is not fixed; the earth is always shifting, the light is always changing, the sea does not cease to grind down rock. Generations do not cease to be born, and we are responsible to them because we are the only witnesses they have. The sea rises, the light fails, lovers cling to each other, and children cling to us. The moment we cease to hold each other, the moment we break faith with one another, the sea engulfs us and the light goes out.

—James Baldwin, *The Fire Next Time*

Contents

Foreword: The Pedagogical Force of Fascism *Brad Evans*   viii
Acknowledgements   xiii

Introduction: Making Education Central to Politics in the
Age of Pandemics   1

Part 1 The Crisis of Democracy and the Deep Roots of Racial Terror
1   The Dictatorship of Ignorance and the Crisis of the Public
    Imagination   21
2   America's Nazi Problem and the Plague of Violence   55
3   Trumpism and its Afterlife   95

Part 2 The Crisis of Pedagogy
4   Fascist Culture and the Challenge to Critical Pedagogy   129
5   The Scourge of Apartheid Pedagogy   149

Part 3 From Hope to Resistance in the Age of Plagues
6   Rethinking Paulo Freire's *Pedagogy of Hope* in Dark Times   177
7   Towards a Pedagogy of Resistance   195

Notes   212
Index   261

Foreword: The Pedagogical Force of Fascism

The cover of *Pedagogy of Resistance* adorned with Isaac Cordal's haunting image speaks to an unfolding moment of peril, a creeping machinery of death that offers a view of education as a space of colonization, ethical abandonment, and a pedagogy of repression. Pedagogy has turned lethal, lost its innocence, and reveals its political dark side. The room in the image is a cavernous vortex of meditated punishment. The stench of oppression fills the barely breathable air. In the background, what look like students surveying the ruins of their own education appear dressed from head to toe in quarantine outfits which are cloaking them in a fabric that's less protective and more suffocating. They appear like educational lab rats, where they are the experiment. There is also a purity to the cloth's whiteness that's identifiable and yet disturbing. But what is the virus here? The students look at items, which seem like infected remnants from a disaster that's just happened. As they forensically survey these artefacts on neatly set out tableaus, the neat and linear organization of power is purposefully suggested. It's tempting to read this terrifying and yet all too familiar scene as politically revealing, seeing these items as books that can no longer be read on account of the fact that their contents are too dangerous to those in power. The now toxic thoughts of a Paolo Freire or Henry Giroux, held at a safe distance, as the students have been taught to look upon these items with alarm and profound suspicion. Meanwhile, a sinister skeletal figure looks down from on high, certain of his mastery and position. His watchtower an eery reminder of a past we misguidedly thought had been defeated. The students are already obedient, their allegiance to the nihilism of the present appears beyond question. They belong to a generation that's lived through some plague. They are the survivors, but now forced to live in a lockdown of a more terrifying kind. And just like in the times of Bruegel, what's triumphed is the triumph of death, even while people are still alive. But this is not about the spectacle that so haunted the Flemish artist. This is about a more mediocre and yet no less devastating violence. The brutalities of the fascism of the everyday.

Cordal's *The School* is a brilliant work that provides a perfectly fitting accompaniment to Henry Giroux's *Pedagogy of Resistance*. It offers a damning visual testimony to our times; one where new forms of fascism have been mobilized and where the importance of education has never been more crucial. It is suggestive to see Cordal's *School* as a warning. A dystopian vision wherein 'The dictatorship of ignorance,' as Giroux terms it, proves ultimately victorious. And yet, as Giroux shows, this nightmarish vision is not some distant promise or modelling for an alternative universe. Nor is it some phantasmic vision, which in any way stretches the imagination. If we can learn anything from Orwell, it is that dystopian visions like his 1984 simply didn't go far enough. Cordal's *School* then, as Giroux explains it, is symbolic of the perilous world currently being inhabited. A world where critical thinking is being surveyed like some dangerous relic from a considered past, and where the 'plague of violence' has liberated its deeply set germination patterns to now widely infect the political body. A world where the afterlife to fascism shows how futile it would be to simply reduce it to a single person such as the abhorrent Donald Trump.

Every book should be taken on its own terms. It should be read, and its intention understood. Yet it would be impossible to make sense of the importance of this book without reading Giroux's wider corpus. There is a need to recognize the author's tireless fight, from his earlier works that really changed how education was to be seen as a form of political intervention to recognizing the importance of culture and the demand to speak with multiple grammars. This would include his critiques of the Wars on Terror and the mobilization of war, which only stoked the xenophobic fires, to the way he provided such critical insight into the brutalities of the punishing state and its racialized violence. It would also include his concern with the politics of disposability and the ravages of neoliberalism, onto his anticipation of the arrival of Trump and how he merely accelerated in the most visible ways many terrifying dynamics already on play. Giroux's *Pedagogy of Resistance* is not, therefore, simply an isolated cry for a better world. It is the latest volume in a meticulous and always enriching mapping of history and its many devastating trajectories. It is also the latest life chapter in his personal fight to have us find reasons to believe in this world.

If there is a singularity to this text, I would suggest it reads something like this: *While the forces of fascism may seem insurmountable, there is always hope in a pedagogy of resistance.* In the face of death, this is a book whose intention is to put itself on the side of life. It invokes an affirmative sense of what resistance might look like, and how another world might be reimagined. Still, nothing is certain here. Fascism remains a formidable enemy which, as Giroux shows better than anyone, must be also understood as a pedagogical force. There is then a reason why the university matters, Giroux explains. For education is on the frontlines to this battle. A battle that has only been accelerated and become all the more pronounced following the global lockdown.

I could spend a considerable amount of time here explaining more fully what Giroux brings to our understanding of fascism and why a pedagogy of resistance is so important in these perilous times. But that's better left for Giroux. What I will say is that this is not a book that will please orthodox social scientists or any academic who believes in the idea of some neutral or objective basis to research and enquiry. And it's all the better for it! Fascism is never neutral, although its effects are often neutralizing. Fascism is never objective, although it so often objectifies as it destroys. Passivity in the face of a system that seeks to colonize the very language of the viral and the toxic in order to harness its terrifying energy and turn it back upon itself is a world where everyone is already co-opted. Mindful of this, Giroux presents more than a troubling diagnostic of our times. He gives us a powerful manifesto for how education can be harnessed in the presence of the death-driving machines whose educational toxicology seeks to kill off the critical in thought.

It is worth also pointing out here that Giroux never simply provokes in order to calculate pithy affects. Invoking the terms 'fascism' and 'apartheid pedagogy' is done with the utmost respect for the meaning of language. And as this book also shows with such ethically sensitive detail, it is done with an acute appreciation of history. Unlike so many, Giroux doesn't make historical comparisons lightly, nor does he revel in the type of shock statements which have sadly become the hallmark of careerist academics so eager to simply be known (often without anything meaningful to say). Hence, my earlier point about understanding Giroux's wider corpus is crucial. While having his finger on the pulse of the critical present better than anyone I know, Giroux is also a living testament to the power of educational awareness that comes with lived experience and a sustained intellectual commitment that spans generations and is seldom matched. This is so refreshing from an author who constantly fights for the rights of disenfranchised youth, and yet would be deeply mindful of the ageism that's also cast its brutal watch over the present. If Giroux's conceptual acumen thus demands our attention, it is because he remains true to the spirit of both Freire and his unrequited belief in the power of education, along with Walter Benjamin who knew the importance of questioning the time in which we live—a time, we might add, where the spectre of fascism and its nihilistic demands are more present than ever.

I would like to end here with a brief comment on friendship. If this book is about hope, then it is my hope that through these pages you will find the ability to recognize that fascism is never absolute, and its success can only really be fulfilled if it co-opts us into believing its divisions and violence is inevitable. If the dead thoughts of nihilism infect the body such that it comes to desire its own oppression, forcing us to actively participate in a world that is already set for its own ruination, so these very forces can be unlearned and the future steered by educators in a new direction. This takes courage. But a courage that must be based upon trust, mutual understanding and respect for one another. It is a courage which then takes us back to the earliest understandings of political and philosophical enquiry, seeking in the very same movement the love for knowledge and the love for the types of friendship this journey will hopefully permit. Fascism thrives on enmity. The antidote to breaking its infectious hold, as Giroux tells, is a pedagogical togetherness that is unwavering in its demand to put friendship central to politics.

So, as I write this short foreword, I too am reminded of the love and friendship I have for an immeasurable public intellectual truly worthy of that name. But don't take my word for it. Take hold of the book, feel the weight of its historical reckoning in your hands, reflect for a while on the terrifyingly resonant image on the cover, consider whether this school and its dead leaders are already directing your insight, then venture into the depths of the nihilism alert to the need for an educated escape. Perhaps then, like myself, you will also find a critical friend in Henry Giroux.

Brad Evans
Professor of Political Violence & Aesthetics
University of Bath, UK

Acknowledgements

I write alone, but my work is always informed by the presence, ideas, and the help of others both living and dead. First there was James Baldwin, who gave me a lesson in the power of the written word, infused with passion and commitment. Second, the Beats broadened my understanding of the cultural revolution and the mixing of the personal and the political. Third, Marxist and critical theory forced me to think far beyond my capabilities and offered me a language for the long journey against oppression. The Frankfurt School saved me from falling into the trap of political orthodoxy and uncompromising purity—a curse for so many intellectuals today. My friends Paulo Freire, Stanley Aronowitz, and Zygmunt Bauman were my lifelong mentors. Carol Becker always came through for me and was always a voice of deep insight and compassion. Donaldo Macedo and I have been in dialogue about personal and political issues for over forty years. Brad Evans has greatly enlarged my understanding of violence, critical theory, and what it means to be a working-class intellectual. This book builds on their work and aims at offering a language and set of ideas in which higher education can be seen freshly and differently as a crucial site for educating young people and others to be critical, responsible, engaged citizens. In other words, to learn how to fight over and struggle collectively for a real democracy.

I want to thank Rania, my wife and partner, for her enormous help in pushing me to think through a number of the ideas that shape this book. She has been an invaluable source of emotional strength and intellectual insight. Maya Sabados, my assistant, has been enormously helpful in reading different chapters, always with a keen editorial eye for errors. Tony DiMaggio kindly edited with great insight a crucial chapter of the book and made it much better. Bill Moyers has always been there to support my work and he never held back with his honesty and courage. Thanks to Robin D. G. Kelley for his support over the years. He is one of the most humble and brilliant intellectuals of his generation. Many thanks to Oz, Oscar Zambrano, for reading and commenting on my work whenever it appears. I am indebted to Gustavo Figueiredo, my Brazilian friend, for the many conversations we have had over the years and for his generous help with translations and publishing opportunities he provided for me speaking to a Latin American audience. Tony Penna has been supportive in a way in which there is no adequate language to thank him. Ken Saltman is a dear friend and I have learned a great deal from him over the years. Thanks to Ray Seliwoniuk for his friendship and advice. Dean Birkenkamp was always there for me as an editor and friend. I am grateful for having the luxury of a number of individuals who have made friendship and solidarity a lived and nourishing experience. My lifelong friend Bill Reynolds is always in my thoughts in his final days in the sunset. We had a great ride together. I also want to thank a number of dear friends who publish my work: Maya Schenwar and Alana Price at Truthout, Michael Lerner at Tikkun, Jeffrey St. Clair at *CounterPunch*, Rowan Wolf at UncommonThought, David M. Arditi at Fast Capitalism, Andrew O'Hehir at Salon, and Michael D. Yates at *Monthly Review*. Thanks to Rise Up Times, which has reprinted much of my work and to which I am deeply grateful. I am thankful to a select number of Deans, Provosts, and Presidents at McMaster who supported my work and gave me the space and encouragement to work at McMaster. Finally, I am incredibly grateful to Mark Richardson, my editor at Bloomsbury, who has given me enormous encouragement and support in publishing my work. He is an editor who goes far beyond the normal interventions and help.

A number of the ideas in this book appeared in different forms in Truthout, *CounterPunch*, Social Text, Social Identities, and Salon.

Introduction: Making Education Central to Politics in the Age of Pandemics

Henry A. Giroux

It is certain, in any case, that ignorance, allied with power, is the most ferocious enemy justice can have.

—James Baldwin

I. Making the Pedagogical More Political

In this introduction, I outline how this book is organized around diverse themes and sections and in doing so summarize its key points. This forecast is intended to provide a general theoretical scaffold and narrative that makes it easier for the reader to understand how the different sections of *Pedagogy of Resistance* interact as part of a broader and more comprehensive political, pedagogical, and cultural narrative. In an age of medical and political plagues, neither critical education nor democracy has fared well. As the value of education declines as a public good, democracy is emptied of any substance. Shared fears now replace shared values, conspiracy theories proliferate, civic culture declines, and the aptitude for informed judgement gives way to the collapse of standards necessary to distinguish between not only truth and falsehoods, but also good and evil. At a time when all vestiges of critical thought are being purged from public schools, women's reproductive rights are under attack, and tyranny translates into increasing levels of violence, the collapse of conscience, social responsibility, and justice proceeds at an alarming pace. As the forces of conformity, anti-intellectualism, and authoritarianism gain ground globally, people increasingly lose their capacity to think critically and act responsibly, if not courageously. As the forces of anti-democratic populist revolts grow, critical modes of agency wither, opening a space for both oppressive forms of education and the tyrants that benefit from them.

Under such circumstances, democracy is cast as the enemy of politics, and critical education is viewed as the nemesis of freedom. Nihilism and despair shred both politics and education of its democratic visions and, in doing so, transform education on the broader cultural front into a script for reproducing diverse forms of right-wing ideology. Increasingly, right-wing legislators view teaching the truth as the enemy of education and in doing so mandate what teachers can say and teach in the classroom. Teaching about race, racism, sexism, and social justice and diversity now generates McCarthy-type forms of represssion on the part of right-wing ideologues. As public and higher education are increasingly defined by the logic of white nationalism, instrumentalized, techno-scientific methodologies, and regressive forms of managerialism, authoritarian neoliberalism reasserts itself with contempt for democratic politics and increasingly displays complicity with the emerging forces of racism and white supremacy. Censorship, discipline, and obedience become the mechanisms to produce pedagogies of repression while matters of understanding, truth, critical thinking, and the knowledge and skills needed to address pressing social, economic, civic, and political problems are discouraged.[1]

Education for critical citizenship and civic practice gives way to corporatized and marketed notions of education in which managerial models of education are being coupled in many states with alarming forms of censorship regarding America's racist past and present. [2] As a culture of fear sweeps over many states and school districts, teachers are threatened with not only insults and diverse forms of harassment by right-wingers, but also by reactionary legislators who threaten to take away their licences or fire them. A malevolent poverty of spirit and cruelty has now joined hands in the culture wars with a maligned form of pedagogical repression. Across the United States, educational reform is now being defended by right-wing extremists, intent on stripping it of its democratic and critical values.

In the current historical moment, education becomes nothing more than a propaganda machine and a training centre for global capital. Education has become a site of struggle for the reproduction of anti-democratic tendencies. This becomes clear as public and higher education default on their role as democratic public spheres, dedicated to creating educated and socially responsible citizens. Across the globe, the political and educational conditions that give rise to an updated form of fascist politics are being strengthened. In an age marked by the withering of civic culture, the erosion of any sense of collective citizenship, and the emergence of regressive forms of hyper-individualism, democracy is both destabilized and enfeebled. In this case, the ideas, agents, and civic institutions necessary for a democracy begin to disappear.

I think it is fair to argue that higher education no longer emulates the struggles that took place in the 1960s. Given the full-fledged attack on faculty and the rise of short-term contracts and an adjunct labour force, faculty now fight merely to survive in university jobs that are as precarious as they are labour-intensive. Faculty powerlessness breeds repression and represents a direct attack on academic freedom. Sedated by fear, loneliness, rootlessness, anxiety, and the rise of the punishing state, artists, writers, researchers, educators, and other cultural workers are compelled to withdraw into their respective disciplinary silos, pressured to look away, and willingly abandon their sense of social and ethical responsibility.

Compelled to conform and adjust to existing pedagogies of repression, part-time academics are pressured into becoming gated intellectuals, dissuaded, if not coerced, into refusing to use their classrooms or other cultural sites to address grave social problems such as the threat of nuclear war, ecological devastation, and the sharp deterioration of democracy worldwide. Under such circumstances, academics often engage in a form of self-sabotage by either withdrawing from public life or becoming complicit with the neoliberal forces that want to destroy democracy in their relentless pursuit of capital. On the other hand, tenured faculty in the ensuing years have become tame, quiet, lost in their irrelevancy, and disconnected from the horrors of a medical, political, and ideological plague that killed between 600,000 and 800,000 Americans.[3] Neoliberalism works hard to make academics dysfunctional, both undermining control over their labor and downgrading them to either agents of corporate interests or driving them to the abyss of academic irrelevance. As the connection between education and the public good and its diverse social problems decline, irrelevance, if not complicity, become defining features of higher education.

Collective consciousness, with its potential for mass resistance and broad coalitions united for social change, is weakened under the pressure of the capitalist spectacle with its obscene language in the service of violence, bigotry, and white nationalism. Commodities now enslave critical thought, turning citizens into consumers overburdened by market-based choices. The public is now reduced to the role of marketed commodities, all the while ensuring that the responsibilities of citizenship are reduced to an advertisement or an act of conformity. The mall now replaces traditional public spheres as a site of engagement and social interaction. Political power is now exercised by zombies who relentlessly attempt to pacify any sense of critical thought and agency while promoting a politics that thrives in creating zones of social abandonment and social death. The aftermath of Trump's presidency has given birth to an army of zombie politicians, particularly in the Republican Party, who are creating a dystopian social order for those marginalized by class, race, gender, and religion—all those populations considered non-white and non-Christian. Zombie is an avatar for death and cruelty and refers to the walking dead who suck the life out of democracy, public values, and the common good.

Zombie economics and its political followers separate economic activity from social costs and, in doing so, eliminate any sense of moral and social responsibility from politics. This dystopian universe is not simply about dread, pessimism, and 'objectively terrible things… it is about losing control over your life.… it is about right-wing crazies subverting democracy even as they claim to revere it'.[4] America is in deep trouble and the moral reckoning now facing it is whether or not it wants to promote and sustain the promise and reality of a substantive democracy or allow the country to tip over the abyss into a full-fledged notion of authoritarianism.

Authoritarianism does not tolerate doubt, critical inquiry, or knowledgeable judgements. Instead, it thrives on modes of education geared towards certainty, rigidity, unquestioning loyalty to authority, cultism, and instrumental reason.[5] The pandemic has worsened the authoritarian tendencies driving education across the globe. In addition, the recurrence of instrumental logic sweeps matters of political and moral responsibility under the carpet, setting the stage for more ominous repressive measures to emerge against any viable notion of higher education as a crucial site for learning the knowledge, skills, and body of literature students need to participate in a strong and participatory democracy. Lost here is the mission of preparing young people for the trials and struggles necessary for democratic citizenship.

The pandemic has wreaked havoc on many higher education institutions trying to survive financially, given student tuition loss. Increasingly, courses are geared to providing jobs and linked directly to the labour market. One consequence is that faculty and academic fields that don't translate immediately into the needs of a business culture are being eliminated. As I mentioned earlier, this is happening at a time when many right-wing state legislators under cover of the financial crisis and the perilous state of higher education are passing laws prohibiting faculty from teaching about racial injustice, addressing systemic racism, and injecting what they call 'an anti-racist mind-set into campus life'.[6] Under the guise of 'patriotic education', matters of justice, ethics, equality, and historical memory now vanish from the classrooms of public and higher education, and from powerful cultural apparatuses and social media platforms that have become the new teaching machines.

Increasingly, public schools are being defunded, teachers are losing control over the conditions of their labour, and unions are relentlessly undermined in the ability to work for the rights of teachers and students. Neoliberal modes of governance have turned higher education into an adjunct of corporate logic, saddling both faculty and students with what Thomas and Meg Young call 'manic managerial' demands that prevent faculty from becoming serious scholars and students from becoming informed citizens. Faculty are now removed from policy making and relegated to the status of over-stressed and overworked "semi-academic factory workers." Faculty research is now driven by corporate priorities and the need for massive grants; disinvestment in higher education has become the order of the day. Adding to this nightmare, grantsmanship has become a singular force for getting an academic promotion, gaining tenure, and increasingly being hired in higher education.

Overburdened by out-of-control tuition, crippling debt, and large classes (or online classes), students have become cogs in an academic culture in which material self-interest and instrumentalism occupy a privileged place in defining the student experience. Any vestige of a humanistic culture designed to prepare students to be socially responsible and committed citizens has been undermined by the neoliberal yardstick of profit and corporate values.

Liberal arts and the promise of an expanded and literate public are no longer part of the mission of higher education. Training has now replaced educating people for democratic citizenship. The mission of the university is now built around developing human capital—its mission is vocational, 'oriented entirely around the market logic of job preparation'.[7] In the age of gangster capitalism, higher education appears to be entering a death spiral. Gone is the age of the academic as a public intellectual whose academic work and public interventions were a model for enriching public life and addressing staggering forms of economic inequality, needless wars, and class and racial injustices.

Gone are the diverse teachers and academics who worked tirelessly to inspire individuals and social movements to unleash the energy, insights, and passion necessary to keep alive the spirit, promises, and ideals of a radical democracy. As Khalid Lyamlahy argues, it almost seems quaint to talk about an age when educators produced research that focused on 'silent questions and neglected connections', produced a language that generated a 'more active affinity between people', and engaged in pedagogical practices and cultural work that highlighted a politics that refused 'to divorce itself from social institutions and material relations of power and domination'.[8] No longer able to take on the role of border crossers, too many academics are reduced to short-term contracts and temporary work that both undermines academic freedom and reduces them to part-time clerks trying to survive.

This is an especially difficult time for educators, some of whom have pushed back against the utter degradation of teaching and learning that has gone on with full force since the 1980s in the United States.[9] The pandemic has further weakened education as it has substituted the language of method, instrumental rationality, and technological mastery for substantive questions about the role of education in a time of rising exclusionary nationalism and economic populism. Increasingly, it has become easier for a corporatized version of higher education to insist on the importance of training in what Gayatri Spivak once called 'a time of legitimized violence'.[10] What has been forgotten by the proponents of neoliberal education is that the first casualties of authoritarianism are the minds that oppose it.

Jim Crow is back without apology, suffocating American society in a wave of voter suppression laws, the elevation of racist discourse to the centres of power, and the ongoing attempt by right-wing politicians to implement an apartheid pedagogy in which important social issues that challenge the racial and economic status quo disappear. The cult of manufactured ignorance now works through disimagination machines engaged in a politics of falsehoods and erasure. The spectacle of Trumpism and its brew of white supremacist ideology and disdain for the truth undergirds the further collapse of democratic visions in higher education, made even more evident by the obsession with methodologies and the reign of instrumental reason, which has returned on the educational front with a vengeance.

Educators need a new language, vision, politics, and renewed sense of solidarity. They need to wage a full-fledged fight against the neoliberal university and in doing so connect it to the broader struggle for a substantive democracy. They need to bring the truth out of the shadows and create a space for critical thought and civic action, while pushing at the frontiers of the social imagination. Most of all, they need to acknowledge and fight for the centrality of education in shaping modes of agency, identity, values, social relations, and visions of the future.

This is especially true at a time when language has been hijacked and used in the service of dehumanization, hatred, and violence. Language is never innocent, and history teaches us that language that begins with hate often ends with violence. Can educators and other cultural workers work towards developing a politics capable of both operating and challenging a society defined by the menace of market values and the growing registers of a fascist politics? Toni Morrison was right in observing that the work of teachers, public intellectuals, and other cultural workers 'is more indispensable than ever before because the world is more dangerous than ever before'.[11] Their role is crucial in educating informed citizens while shining a light on injustice. In what follows, I want to explore these sentiments by examining education, pedagogy, and teaching and learning in the broadest terms and in relation to the multiple places in which it occurs.

I: Making the Political More Pedagogical in the Age of the Image

The architects of a new breed of fascist politics increasingly dominate major cultural apparatuses and other commanding political and economic institutions worldwide. Their nightmarish reign of misery, violence, and disposability is legitimated, in part, through their control of a range of knowledge-producing settings that construct a vast machinery of manufactured consent. This reactionary educational formation includes the mainstream broadcast and social media, digital platforms, the Internet, and print culture, all of which participate in an ongoing spectacle of violence, the aestheticization of politics, the legitimation of opinions over facts, and an embrace of a culture of ignorance. In a system that generates human needs that it cannot satisfy, pedagogies of distraction and diversion now dominate politics and culture. These oppressive educational practices suppress the underlying causes of staggering inequality, massive misery, and a politics of disposability, offering the false promises and seductions of demagogues instead.

It is hard to imagine a more urgent moment for taking seriously the call to make education central to politics. The rule of authoritarianism is imposed less and less by military coups than through elections subverted by the force of oppressive forms of education that extend from the schools to social media and other cultural apparatuses. The educational force of the cultural sphere is now amplified by the merging of power and new instruments of culture that have produced powerful sites of struggle to normalize and legitimate dominant ideas, values, and social relations. Politics is now visual, image-based, and dominated by the workings of an image culture and its proliferating spectacles. This is evident in the unprecedented power of social media platforms such as Facebook, Google, Twitter, Tik Tok, and Instagram. As Jeffrey Edward Green argues in *The Eyes of the People*, politics has become ocular, strongly shaped by an image culture that redefines the undertakings of citizenship through the power of the spectacle and spectatorship rather than through the traditional registers of decision-making and shared dialogue and close engagements.[12] In the age of surveillance and rising authoritarianism, social media has become the twenty-first-century version of George Orwell's all-seeing TV screen depicted in *1984* as the omniscient screen that enables Big Brother to watch everyone. Jean Seaton captures the resemblance between *1984*'s Big Brother mode of surveillance and today's social media. She writes:

In *1984* television screens watch you, and everyone spies on everyone else. Today it is social media that collects every gesture, purchase, comment we make online, and feeds an omniscient presence in our lives that can predict our every preference. Modelled on consumer choices, where the user is the commodity that is being marketed, the harvesting of those preferences for political campaigns is now distorting democracy.[13]

People are more prone to engage in politics by watching and listening to those who control the media rather than participating directly in the process of shaping the forces that bear down on their lives. This notion of ocular politics and its appeal to raw emotion was evident in the ways in which former President Donald Trump used the educational force of social media and the power of the image to keep his audiences in a constant state of agitation. He used social media to marshal popular feelings by accentuating and mobilizing a revolting ecstasy of fear, hate, resentment, and vindictiveness. Visual messaging for Trump was not only a direct way to reach his followers, but it was also a medium for waging political warfare and expanding the culture wars. In doing so, he influenced the political culture of the United States dramatically through a relentless spectacle of emotional ferment, lies, and distraction waged on Twitter and a range of conservative media outlets, all the while further legitimating right-wing insurgencies across the globe. The domain of authoritarian culture has never been as powerful as it is today, moving the world closer to the edge of the abyss, which is now in sight.

Social media is turbocharging right-wing political movements, further weakening the cultural and educational foundations shaping the public imagination. As democratic institutions and political culture are undermined and hollowed out, emotive rants undermine reason, truth, and evidence. Rituals of expressive emotional catharsis are mobilized through mass rallies of hate, which Trump conducts long after his election defeat. Social media, within dominant constellations of power and control, has become a war machine relentlessly reproducing a culture of propaganda and dehumanization. Educators, liberal politicians, and journalists that operate in a social order wedded to instrumental rationality and the accumulation of profits often fail to address how media empires connect knowledge and power through language and an image culture that dumbs down civic culture, while undermining the critical faculties necessary to create enlightened citizens. Orwell's *1984* has a lesson about language and propaganda that is as relevant today as when it was published in June 1949. In Orwell's dystopian novel, we get a glimpse of Trump's 'systemic stripping of meaning out of language'. Echoing Big Brother, the Trump regime 'aim[ed] to eradicate words and the ideas and feelings they embody. Its real enemy is reality—[attempting] to make understanding the real world impossible: seeking to replace it with phantoms and lies.'[14]

As democracy wanes, community is reduced to a cult-like allegiance to the strongman reinforced by emotional and simplistic appeals and hollow and simple-minded language, which fuels conspiracy theories, manufactured paranoia, and the fictional worlds of misinformation reproduced in right-wing disimagination machines. In this subversion of language, there is the spectre of terror, that is, 'the terror of a world where people have fewer and fewer words to use and whose thinking is distorted by ideologies'.[15] At this point, education becomes the breeding ground in various cultural apparatuses for transforming 'democratic citizens into totalitarian subjects'.[16]

Making education crucial to politics means addressing the cultural forces shaping policies and society to create a formative culture in the service of democratic modes of agency, desires, and identities. If education is going to work in the service of democracy, it needs a new vision and language in which the call for real change resonates with the concrete needs, desires, values, and modes of identification that working-class people of every stripe can understand and relate to critically. Education needs to be meaningful in order to become critical and transformative. In part, this suggests providing narratives in which people can recognize themselves, place their problems in a wider context, exercise their critical faculties, and develop strategies to challenge the conditions that oppress them.

a plague of manufactured ignorance was and continues to [...] by Trump and his media and political operatives as part of [...]ons campaign. One consequence of this is the production of a se[...]ned helplessness among many Trump supporters, which easily morphs into a form of manufactured ignorance and alienation. Roger Berkowitz touches on the sense of loss and meaning to which Trump and his allies appeal. He writes that 'For an existentially lonely and purposeless citizenry who have lost their identities in classes and traditions, there is a profound need for a story that makes the world make sense, that tells them that they matter.'[17] Over 74 million people voted for Trump in the 2020 election, testifying that the corridors of loneliness and solitude now fill a massive deindustrialized landscape of poverty, precarity, and despair, all made worse by a shrinking welfare state and globalization.

Democracy as a fragile institution is no longer in the mission statements of most universities wedded to providing labour for the global workforce. If we are going to develop a politics capable of awakening our critical, imaginative, and historical sensibilities, it is crucial for educators and others to create a political project infused with a language of critique and possibility, apprised by the crucial notion that there is no substantive democracy without learned citizens. Such a language is necessary to enable the conditions to forge a collective international resistance among educators, youth, artists, and other cultural workers in defence of not only public goods, but also a democracy with the guarantee of not only civil and political rights, but also economic rights that ensure both dignity and a meaningful sense of agency.[18]

In an age of social isolation, information overflow, a culture of infantilization, consumer glut, and growing white supremacist and re-branded fascist movements, it is all the more crucial to take seriously the notion that a democracy cannot exist or be defended without citizens who are critical, knowledgeable, and willing to act on their insights and values. Education cannot be reduced to training or treated as merely a commodity or tool of propaganda. As Leon Wieseltier has argued, the promise of higher education lies in its 'nonutilitarian character, so that individuals can know more than how things work, and develop their powers of discernment and judgement, their competence in matters of truth and goodness and beauty, to equip themselves adequately for the choices and the crucibles of private and public life'.[19]

Moreover, education cannot be reduced to schooling in an image-based culture. It must be broadly understood as taking place in various locations and defined, in part, through its interrogation on the claims of democracy. As Ariel Dorfman argues, it is time to produce cultural institutions and empowering pedagogical conditions in multiple places extending from the mainstream press to the online digital world in order 'to unleash the courage, energy, joy and, yes, compassion with which rebellious millions [can] defy fear and keep hope alive in these traumatic times'.[20] Such sites are important in the efforts to engage education as a political force. Pierre Bourdieu rightly observes that 'important forms of domination are not only economic but also intellectual and pedagogical and lie on the side of belief and persuasion [making it all the more] important to recognize that intellectuals bear an enormous responsibility for challenging this form of domination'.[21] This is an especially crucial demand at a time when the educational and pedagogical force of the culture works through and across multiple places. Schooling is only one site of education, while movies, television, books, magazines, the Internet, social media, and music are incredibly significant forces in shaping world views, modes of agency, and diverse forms of identification.

At a time when truth has become malleable, and people are being told that the only obligation of citizenship is to consume, language has become shallower, and more individualistic, detached from history and more self-oriented, all the while undermining viable democratic social spheres as spaces where politics brings people together as collective agents willing to push at the frontiers of the political and moral imagination. Too many people across the globe have forgotten their civic lessons, and in doing so, cede the ground of history to the purveyors of lies, militarism, and white supremacy. Under such circumstances, the horrors of the past are forgotten, making it difficult – as Primo Levi, an Auschwitz survivor, once warned – to recognize that "Every age has its own fascism."[22] Terror comes in many forms and one powerful expression is when people become too fearful to develop a language in which they can both understand and challenge the world in which they live. Not only does such linguistic deprivation fail to ward off the plague of propaganda, but it also contributes 'to an annihilation of the self and the destruction of the capacity to recognize the real world'.[23] As educators and intellectuals, it is crucial to remember that there is no genuine democracy without the presence of citizens willing to recognize the real world, hold power accountable, engage in forms of moral witnessing, break the continuity of common sense, and challenge the normalization of anti-democratic institutions, policies, ideas, and social relations.

Making education fundamental to politics suggests that as academics, researchers, and artists we ask uncomfortable questions about what Arundhati Roy calls 'our values and traditions, our vision for the future, our responsibilities as citizens, the legitimacy of our "democratic institutions," the role of the state, the police, the army, the judiciary, and the intellectual community'.[24]

In opposition to pedagogies of oppression aligned with fascist politics, which I call apartheid pedagogy, education has the crucial task of creating situations in which people develop a collective sense of urgency that prompts and enables them to learn how to govern, rather than merely learn how to be governed. Education for empowerment means creating informed and critically engaged social movements willing to fight the emotional plagues, economic inequality, human misery, systemic racism, and collapse of the welfare state caused by neoliberal capitalism and other forms of authoritarianism. Democracy's survival depends upon a set of habits, values, ideas, culture, and institutions that can sustain it. Democracy is both precarious and always unfinished and its fate and future are not only a political issue but also an educational one.

Once again, there is no democracy without a knowledgeable public and no justice without a language critical of injustice. Democracy should be a way of thinking about education, one that thrives on connecting pedagogy to the practice of freedom, learning to ethics, and agency to the imperatives of social responsibility and the public good. Moreover, it is crucial to acknowledge that capitalism and democracy are not the same thing. Against the reign of neoliberal capitalism, there is a need to embrace a radical notion of democracy, that is, a form of democratic socialism with its emphasis on not only personal and political freedoms but also economic rights. This is a crucial project that must inform any radical vision of the future. In the age of nascent fascism, it is not enough to connect education with the defence of reason, informed judgement, and critical agency; it must also be aligned with the power and potential of collective resistance. Consequently, there is an urgent need for more individuals, institutions, and social movements to come together in the belief that the current regimes of tyranny can be resisted, that alternative futures are possible, and that acting on these beliefs through collective resistance will make radical change happen.

Global neoliberal capitalism reproduces pedagogical 'death zones of humanity' that undermine the capacity for people to speak, write, and act from a position of empowerment and be responsible to themselves and others. Against this form of depoliticization, there is the need for modes of civic education and critical literacy that provide the bridging work between thinking critically and the possibility of interpretation as an intervention. Such bridging work is committed to the realization that there is no resistance without hope and no hope without a vision of an alternative society rooted in the ideals of justice, equality, and freedom.

The greatest pandemic we face in the world today is the pandemic of ignorance, white Anglo-Saxon supremacy, authoritarian nationalism, militarism, and the willingness to surrender power as individual and social agents to those who write the past and present in the scripts of domination. Pedagogy has never been more valuable as a political tool that can offer the resources to challenge the ideological, educational, and militant practices deployed by the emerging right-wing and fascist groups. Pedagogy is crucial for understanding how power shapes and is reinvented with respect to questions of culture, sexuality, history, and political agency. The great Marxist theorist, Antonio Gramsci, was right in noting that culture deploys power and that such power is always pedagogical. Moreover, in the current age culture is a crucial site and weapon of power and has assumed an unparalleled significance in the structure and organization of agency, identities, knowledge, social relations, and in deciding who inhabits the public sphere and who doesn't. As a political project, pedagogy is the struggle over those public and private spaces in which people's everyday lives are aligned with particular narratives, identities, cultural practices, and political values.

Critical pedagogy is the essential scaffolding of social interaction and the foundation of the public sphere. It is a crucial political practice because it takes seriously what it means to understand the relationship between how we learn and how we act as individual and social agents; that is, it is concerned not only with how individuals learn to think critically but how they come to grips with a sense of individual and social responsibility. It is the essential component in the realm of visibility, the realm of appearance, the realm of acknowledgement. At issue here then is the crucial political question of what it means to be responsible for one's actions as part of a broader attempt to be engaged as a responsible and critically informed citizen who can expand and deepen the possibilities of democratic public life instead of condemning life to the unknown and often hidden and suppressed chapters of disposability. Human agency is inseparable from the formative cultures and pedagogical practices that create the possibility of a mobilized citizenry and radical change.

A politics of the spectacle now shapes politics as pure theatre meant merely to deflect, misrepresent, and sabotage the mundane realities of human suffering, hardship, and violence. The current spectacle shaping mainstream politics functions largely to separate the past from a politics that in its current form has turned deadly in its attack on the values and institutions crucial to a functioning democracy. In the post-Trump age, Trumpism has become the dominant ideology among more than 43 million of Trump's hard-core followers. This is an anti-democratic politics that is anti-truth, anti-rule of law, and has little regard for social justice.

For a large part of the population in the United States in the post-Trump era, the politics of disappearance and disposability continues to thrive given that democracy is still in crisis. Trump may have lost the election, but his influence is everywhere, and one consequence is that public values are continually denigrated and undermined by the politicians who slavishly endorse his malignant politics and authoritarian worldview. Again, without contradiction, in this instance,

Trumpism harbours the echoes of a fascist past that remains hidden, whose traces are unseen or purposely ignored. Such fascist passions appear before us like the harrowing depths of Chantal Meza's *Mirrors of the Void*, which while difficult to determine, slowly reveal the most monstrous, brutal, and devastating of faces. The brilliance of Meza's work is to show how the violent traces of the past tear into the present, mapping what she calls Fragments of Catastrophe, the accumulation of disasters which layer history. But for memory to be effective, as Meza shows, it is not enough for historical remembrance to be merely stated or acknowledged. It, too, needs to be imaginative, equipped with a resistive defiance in the face of those forces that continue to annihilate humanity and its courage to reveal and fight for the truth.

The violence of disappearance surrounds us today. It is a prison with and without cells; it is the pit where the dead bodies of journalists and poets are buried; it is the police who come in the night to arrest dissidents; it is the deep grammar of a social system at war with democracy. The ghosts of resistance, like Meza's Apparitions, are everywhere. They wait for memory to come alive, for moral witnessing to hold power accountable, and to give voice to the dead whose presence is a reminder that one can never look away in the face of barbarism. They move in the menacing shadows of the present and serve as an early warning system for illuminating the darkest moments of history. Humankind is in the midst of a crisis in which it is crucial for individuals to critically engage and resist the pandemics of injustice that undermine the capacities for critical thought, dialectical thinking, and the desire for a democratic alternative to neoliberal capitalism.

Educators need to develop a politics infused with the notion that history is open and that it is necessary for people to think otherwise to act otherwise, especially if we want to imagine and bring into being alternative democratic futures and horizons of possibility. At stake here is the need to develop a vision infused with a mix of justice, hope, and struggle, a task in the age of pandemics that has never been more important than it is today. Moreover, in the face of the emerging tyranny and fascist politics that are spreading across the globe, it is time to merge a sense of moral outrage with a sense of civic courage and collective action. At the very least, education is a central part of politics because it provides the foundation for those of us who believe that democracy is a site of struggle, which can only be encountered through an awareness of both its fragility and necessity.

Pivotal to this struggle is the necessity to rethink and relearn the role that critical education and civic literacy have and can play in producing a collective anti-capitalist consciousness. There is no democracy without an educated public and there is no educated public without the support and existence of institutions that define education as a public good, and as a crucial public sphere. Educators, artists, intellectuals, and other cultural workers have a moral and political responsibility to put into place those pedagogical sites and practices that enable the critical agents and social movements willing to refuse to equate capitalism and democracy and uphold the conviction that the problems of ecological destruction, mass poverty, militarism, systemic racism, staggering economic inequality, and a host of other social problems cannot be solved by leaving capitalism in place. Education in its multiple sites and expressions once again must do justice to democracy and the conditions that make it possible by writing the future in the language of struggle, hope, equality, compassion, and the fundamental narratives of freedom and equality.

Part One

The Crisis of Democracy and the Deep Roots of Racial Terror

1

The Dictatorship of Ignorance and the Crisis of the Public Imagination

The most tragic form of loss isn't the loss of security; it's the loss of the capacity to imagine that things could be different.

—Ernst Bloch

Rethinking the Ghosts of the Past

William Faulkner's prescient observation that 'The past is never dead. It's not even past' is more relevant today than ever. In its updated version, we live at the present moment not only with the ghosts of genocidal mass violence, but also with the ghosts of fascism. America lives in the shadow of a genocidal history inflicted on Native Americans and Black slaves, the horrors of Jim Crow, the incarceration of Japanese Americans, the rise of a race-based carceral state, and the violence of a persistent racism that continues to touch every aspect of the lives of people of colour.[1]

Democracy has always been fragile in the United States, but at the present moment it has moved from being imperfect to collapsing under the rubric of a failed state.[2] The threat of authoritarianism is no longer on the horizon. It has arrived, forecasting a bleak future haunted by the death-bearing spectres of a poisonous past. And while we live with the ghosts of our past, we have failed to fully confront its implications for the present and future. To do so would mean recognizing that updated forms of fascist politics in the current moment are not a rupture from the past but an evolution.[3] This evolution is evident as Rick Perlstein observes in 'an insurgency against democracy with parliamentary and paramilitary wings'.[4] The first refers to the attempts by Trumps' political allies to overthrow a 'free and fair election' through legal means and the second consists of a mix of right-wing individuals and far-right militia groups that 'mobbed the Capitol seeking traitors to lynch'—this was a violent insurrection bolstered by a long authoritarian history 'that has been coded into conservative politics for a long time'.[5] The third is evident in the vigilante lawlessness being waged by right-wing politicians and mob rule against women's reproductive rights, undocumented immigrants, and people of colour.

Unsurprisingly, language is now thinner, detached from history, colonized by the shredding vocabulary of market fundamentalism. This is a language that contributes to a political and civic illiteracy wedded to the forces of racism, neoliberal capitalism, anti-intellectualism, militarism, consumerism, sexism, cultism, and the corporate state.[6] The United States has reneged on the demands of morality and the imperatives of critical citizenship. America now behaves like a fortress under siege. Gangster capitalism has emerged as a secular religion reproducing vast and unacceptable inequalities across a range of categories that extend from race to class to gender. There are few institutions left that enable a collective consciousness capable of developing a critical stance, engaging history, and holding power accountable. With the rise of right-wing disimagination machines, cultural institutions have turned toxic, producing a large segment of the public living in what Max Boot calls 'hermetically sealed disinformation machines'.[7] The dark cloud of manufactured ignorance and ethical somnambulance now shapes the collective consciousness of millions of Americans who cannot envision a future that does not imitate a present plagued by an ascending authoritarianism.

While many theorists have rightly commented on the profound emptiness at the heart of American culture, what is often ignored is how this crisis is normalized and experienced as a personal failing.[8] Feelings of isolation and loneliness are at the heart of a capitalist neoliberal order that isolates people in a world that shreds the foundations of community, eradicates democratic values, and confines them to the dreary, individualizing logic of privatization and unchecked individual responsibility. This constitutes not only a political catastrophe but also a crisis of subjectivity, agency, and what Dmitri N. Shalin rightly labels 'the all-too-common failure of civic imagination [and] the reluctance to acknowledge a shared humanity and [willingness to] reach out to the oppressed still struggling to gain full citizenship in a society plagued with prejudice and injustice'.[9]

Under neoliberalism, the logic of insidious individualism organizes society around a series of exclusions that produce an aching sense of precarity and insecurity, reinforced by the notion that all problems, however systemic, are a matter of personal responsibility and the result of individual failures. As John Douglas Macready argues, gangster capitalism cuts 'the ties that bind people together... isolates [them] from fellow citizens... and prepare[s] them for despotism'.[10] In this logic, both the isolated individual and the public imagination are rendered superfluous. At work here is a crisis of political culture and depoliticization that is more dangerous than the damaging public policies that emerged in the United States since the rise of neoliberal capitalism in the 1970s. The neoliberal political subject ceases to be political and serves mainly as a source of consumption in a world in which buying and selling are the only obligations of citizenship.[11] Erich Fromm is right in arguing that the atomization and loneliness that comes with capitalism has devastating psychological consequences. He writes:

> the average man feels insecure, lonely, depressed, and suffers from a lack of joy in the midst of plenty. Life does not make sense to him; he is dimly aware that the meaning of life cannot lie in being nothing but a 'consumer'. He could not stand the joylessness and meaningless-ness of life were it not for the fact that the system offers him innumerable avenues of escape, ranging from television to tranquilizers, which permit him to forget that he is losing more and more of all that is valuable in life ... We produce machines that are like men and men who are like machines.[12]

Equally alarming is the fact that the crisis of neoliberal capitalism has not been matched by a crisis of ideas, even as the United States has increasingly been organized on fascist principles for the last few decades.[13] Under such circumstances, depoliticized and alienated subjects lose their sense of critical agency and increasingly invest in cult-figures and become more and more willing to believe that social problems can only be solved by aggression, hatred, and violence. Cultural apparatuses enhanced by new technologies that trade in disinformation and combine propaganda and a flight from social responsibility have a new reach, intensity, and power and have become the new far-right disimagination machines.[14] They are about more than combining kitsch, entertainment, and the spectacle. They not only produce a culture of lies, paranoia, irrationality, and manufactured ignorance, they also wage a full-fledged assault on the public imagination and the intellectual capacities and identities that give life to historical memory, struggles for social justice, and economic democracy.[15] Mimicking the viciousness normalized in Trump's reality-TV show *The Apprentice*, the language of humiliation, dehumanization, and disparagement has become a source of mass entertainment while fuelling a culture of cruelty.

Robert Lipsyte goes further in indicting the corporate-controlled digital media by arguing that 'News Corporation, the Fox News empire, and a gang of broadcast imps will ensure that a lasting plague of misinformation, propaganda masquerading as journalism, and plain old fake news, will be our inheritance.'[16] A proliferating number of cultural outlets and the new/digital communication technologies now poison and dumb down our discourse with unprecedented speed and volume. Klaus Marre rightly refers to these outlets as 'the conservative outrage-industrial-complex', which is more than willing to stir 'up discontent and [poison] the minds of gullible Americans because it is good for business… It is based on lies, embellishments, and the careful selection of stories that will keep [their audience] angry at "others" in perpetuity'.[17]

These conservative and right-wing misinformation technologies and media outlets are the new face of a repressive educational apparatus undermining the society's political and ethical forces used to fight the erosion of democratic ideals such as equality, popular sovereignty, and social justice. Fabrications extending from climate change and the false claim that Trump won the 2020 election to lies promoted about the alleged dangers of immigrants on the southern border have become normalized through the workings of corporate-funded think tanks and the digital media ecosphere, all aligned with conservative politicians.[18]

As large corporate behemoths profit by removing traditional gatekeepers (journalists) that filter information for the public, they allow the rampant spread of propaganda and disinformation with a 'friendly' face, mostly within peer networks and among people that individuals trust and find solace in. The pernicious pedagogical influence of the conservative social media was exceptionally pronounced prior to Biden's election as president. In part, this was evident in the role they played in the spread of rampant COVID-19 disinformation and the proliferation of wild conspiracy theories disseminated by the neo-fascist QAnon movement, which paved the way for the January 6 insurrection.[19]

Within this climate of ignorance, irrationality, and misinformation, Trumpism has gained the support of millions who embrace a rigid anti-intellectualism in a society in which larger members of the public have not only stopped questioning themselves but are willing to support the violent mobilizing passions of a white nationalist, fascist politics. The unapologetic mass psychology of manufactured stupidity practiced by the Trump administration and endemic to Trumpism echoes an earlier period in history. As Victor Klemperer points out in his *The Language of the Third Reich* written in 1947, 'With a great insistence and a high degree of precision right down to the last detail, Hitler's *Mein Kampf* preaches not only that the masses are stupid, but also that they need to be kept that way and intimidated into not thinking.'[20]

Matters of ethics and social responsibility have fallen prey to the sordid values of a market-driven society that has abandoned any concern for the public good. Memories of a fascist and genocidal racial past now disappear or are rewritten in cultural apparatuses marked by an almost unimaginable ignorance echoing what Richard Rodriquez once called 'an astonishing vacancy'.[21] As Thomas Klikauer and Nadine Campbell observe, we live in a world of disinformation that is deliberately 'created and disseminated with the express purpose to cause harm'.[22] James Baldwin was right in claiming that America harbours 'an extraordinary capacity for denial, even when confronted with evidence and logic'.[23] Such denials in the age of Trumpism have resulted in an enormous capacity for evil and violence.[24] Ignorance has turned lethal and threatens to produce what John Dewey once called the eclipse of the public.[25]

The Crisis of the Public Imagination in the Age of Trumpism

As Drucilla Cornell and Stephen D. Seely observe, the public imagination is a form of collective consciousness that is constructed around shared meanings, ethical horizons, and complex social relations that affirm 'a rich collective imagination and democracy itself'.[26] A democratic public and collective imagination grows out of those public spaces that 'allow us to be affected by, and imagine, others in new ways. This, in turn, demands the widest form of participatory democracy among ourselves'.[27] The public imagination emerges out of those public spaces where people exercise a sense of solidarity and develop the capacity to 'challenge economic structures [and] change the way we live together socially'—outside of the dictates of neoliberal capitalism and a 'nostalgia for white supremacy'.[28]

In the age of Trumpism, critical thought, if not reason itself, appears to have taken flight, immune to sustained analysis and informed judgement. Intellectual skills and critical distance both atrophy and are the objects of disdain, especially in a society deeply immersed in all manner of spectacles that reproduce the theatrics of celebrity culture, rumour mills, and game shows. The United States has become a country that hides the obscenity of the profit motive partially behind the language of therapy and the emotional uplift provided by a regressively self-centred and bloated notion of individual happiness and resilience.

American society is intoxicated with celebrity culture. It sells, entertains, fixates on the lives of movie stars, revels in billionaires,

Twitter and Facebook celebrities, and infamous porn stars such as Stormy Daniels. It constructs entertainment as a spectacle that trades in civic illiteracy, commercial relations, and sensationalism. As the horizons of the political shrink, politics takes on the model of pro-wrestling and game show. Social problems are relegated to the dustbin of a visual and messaging swamp that delights in producing verbal grenades, racial panics, fear-mongering, spectacularized violence, and endless stories narrating the lives of the rich and famous. Celebrity culture blunts the edge of a society in decline, offering manufactured ignorance and a culture of shock, callousness, and immediacy as a script for infantilizing under the pretence of entertaining large segments of the public. War culture trades off this infantilization, offering scripts for producing militarized forms of toxic masculinity in which wannabe Rambos dress up as soldiers, draped in deadly weapons, while defiantly weaponizing their own identities.

As disimagination machines choke the oxygen out of democracy, thinking becomes dangerous along with the institutions that nurture it while turning civic literacy and historical memory into their opposite. Despite the pandemic crisis, which revealed the inability of the market to address the crisis in public healthcare and a host of other social issues, there has been little outcry against neoliberal capitalism, with its celebration of market and business values that attack the welfare state, public goods, public values, and civic culture. While the centrist Biden administration is rolling back some of the most regressive policies produced under the Trump administration, there is no movement towards eliminating the structural and ideological forces that sustain neoliberal capitalism. What has not become clear to an increasingly besieged public is that neoliberalism produces forms of civic decay, moral irresponsibility, and political corruption while legitimating and rewarding ignorance, commodification, privatization, and crass selfishness over those values that generate trust, cooperation, critical thinking, compassion, social responsibility, and the common good.[29]

The right-wing disimagination machines both disregard and undercut a history of dangerous memories while rewriting it in ways that reproduce a conservative, if not a reactionary, white nationalist narrative of the country's past. Right-wing disimagination machines are part of a pedagogy of oppression and erasure that writes marginal populations, if not collective resistance, and the horrors of a savage capitalism, out of the script of democracy. This is a pedagogical machinery that cancels out the future for many young people and people of colour. Instead of affirming a common set of standards supporting shared standards of truth and justice, this diverse cultural apparatus plays to the public's need to be entertained, especially through a culture of banality, cruelty, and violence. Right-wing media have been enormously successful in garnering attention and bringing to the centers of power an image-based culture marked by a putrid call for a racially pure world.

With the rise of the new digital, aural, and visual technologies and social media as dominant pedagogical forces, violence has become performative, functioning as a prominent feature of social and political power, and packaged to mimic the unbridled monopolization of pleasure now associated with extreme and sensational images of brutality and heartlessness. Part of the Trump legacy is a culture of shocks and outrages presented as either legitimate sources of entertainment or as part of a survival-of-the-fittest ethic endemic to neoliberal spectacles of misery, dehumanization, and corruption.[30] Under the reign of these emerging cultural apparatuses and pedagogical tools, connections are ignored among the conditions that produced, for instance, the armed racist and xenophobic mob that attacked the Capitol, the toxic presence and defence of white supremacists in the Congress, and the gaggle of crooks, convicted felons, hucksters, and US war criminals pardoned by former President Trump.[31]

Pedagogical Plagues and the Shaping of Collective Consciousness

Since the 1980s, with the emergence of predatory neoliberalism, there has been a radical shift in consciousness, one that undermines the public imagination and wreaks havoc on civic institutions and culture.

Caught in the power of all-encompassing market values, Americans no longer live as citizens with shared public values, but as individualized consumers, increasingly indifferent to the fact that matters of solidarity, care for the other, and freedom itself are a collective endeavour vital to a meaningful democracy. The public's collective relationship to history, each other, and the planet itself appear in serious disrepair. Education as a cultural force, operating pervasively in multiple spheres, has become the handmaiden to a culture of lies, dizzying inequality, privatization, deregulation, and racism. Education now renounces its critical function and becomes a tool 'to abandon individual freedom, civil liberties, and human rights'.[32]

How does one explain the conservative media's willingness to reproduce the values and endless misrepresentations of a Republican Party that embraces white supremacy and white nationalism as integral to its political identity? How to explain a conservative media apparatus that spreads lies about the election and debunks crucial public health measures that prevent people from dying from COVID-19? This is a media apparatus that includes Fox News and supports Republican Texas Governor Gregg Abbott's reckless decision in March 2021 'to completely open establishments… and lift a face mask mandate for public areas, retreating from the vital measures needed to fight the coronavirus pandemic'.[33] This is not just bad policy. Abbot's decision put thousands of people's lives at risk. Dr Kavita Patel highlights the seriousness of this morally reckless act of non-governance. He writes: 'Abbott has purposefully injected a new infection into the state in the form of irresponsible policies that will promote unnecessary infection, hospitalization and death.'[34] How else to explain a right-wing media sphere that supports Abbot's decision to use $250 million, taken from a natural disaster fund, to complete Trump's border wall in Texas while a strained Texas power grid needs urgent upgrading? This is a media apparatus in the service of not just violence but the death of democracy and the rise of an authoritarian politics. Of course, the conservative media are not alone in such an endeavour. One might add that the mainstream media has been relatively silent on the related fascism question, and only recognized the impending crisis of fascism once the Washington Capitol was stormed on January 6.

There is more at work here than an educational and cultural apparatus that harbours a contempt for truth, civic literacy, and democracy. This is a pedagogical machinery that functions as a mask of nihilism, embraces the fog of civic illiteracy, and serves the needs of the financial elite and tyrants. Not only does it wage war against the public imagination, but it also infantilizes and depoliticizes, dismantles the possibilities for self-reflection, and normalizes the unthinkable. Normalizing the unthinkable is evident in the presence of a former president, conservative politicians, and their followers who align themselves with right-wing extremist groups such as the Oath Keepers, the Three Percenters, and the Proud Boys. These groups share 'with neo-Nazis, the neo-Confederate Ku Klux Klan affiliates, the esoteric fascists and white separatists' the belief that 'Whites are undergoing extermination, liberal ideology is a form of White self-hatred, and that Jews are at the centre of this agenda.'[35]

There is also the shameful practice on the part of the conservative media to downplay, if not defend, Trump's blizzard of lies and his bungling handling of the pandemic, including his support for the genocidal notion of 'herd immunity', which largely discriminates against the working class, the poor, and poor men and women of colour who are at the front lines of the service industry risking their lives. The stakes could not have been higher given the more than 600,000 dead because of such policies and the lies that legitimated them. Salmon Rushdie captures succinctly the notion that when it came to Trump's miserable failure in dealing with the pandemic, 'nothing was unthinkable, no matter how low he and his followers sank'. He writes:

> the virus (like everything else) was politicized, minimized, called a Democrat trick; the science was derided, the administration's lamentable response to the pandemic was obscured by a blizzard of lies, wearers of masks were abused by wearers of red hats, and the mountain of the dead went on growing, unmourned by the self-obsessed charlatan who claimed, in the face of all the evidence, that he was making America great again.[36]

Amid the lies, cover-up, disregard for science, and the stupidity circulated by the right-wing media, acts of violence in the public imagination were associated with people of colour rather than systemic problems that are the result of an economic system that produces massive inequalities in wealth, power, income, accountability, and social justice. As the public imagination becomes impoverished, the nation is constructed through the lens of a white muscular nationalism rooted in an unforgiving politics of exclusion and disposability. This is an aggressive nationalism whose endpoint is a dehumanization of others along with a politics of cruelty, exploitation, and disposability.

The Republican Party as the New Face of White Supremacy

The Republican Party no longer hides its racism and boldly engages in widespread voter suppression.[37] As of May 2021, a slew of Republican lawmakers in forty-eight states have introduced restrictive voting bills.[38] As Robin D. G. Kelley has argued, Republicans have made clear that they endorse the white supremacist notion that 'the United States [should] be a straight, white nation reminiscent of the mythic "old days" when armed white men ruled, owned their castle, boasted of unvanquished military power, and everyone else knew their place'.[39] It is crucial to mention that these bills are also aimed at preventing youth from voting as well. Closing polling stations, restricting student ID as a form of voter identification, and restricting absentee voting to people over 65 or older automatically eliminate young people from voting by mail.[40] All of these issues are a stumbling block for young voters, whose changing demographics scare the party of the Confederacy. Republicans have also argued openly that voter suppression policies are meant to enable permanent minority rule for them, the endpoint of which is a form of authoritarianism.[41]

Fascist politics feeds on paranoia, and the Republican Party under Trump's leadership indulges in a form of paranoid style that translates into a conspiracy-laden politics that is used as a protective shield to promote what economist Paul Krugman calls lethal madness, reinforced by a combination of ignorance and fear. He writes 'One of our major political parties has, quite simply, gone mad. This madness will kill thousands of Americans in the next few months, because politics is by far the best predictor of who is still refusing to get vaccinated. But COVID-19 deaths may be only the beginning of the deadly effects of the triumph of the paranoid style.'[42]

This contemporary appropriation of the tools of a fascist politics is exacerbated by the undermining of a public vocabulary and modes of civic literacy capable of critically addressing the profound structural changes produced by neoliberalism's practice of deregulation, privatization, devaluation of the welfare state, and deterioration of public goods such as the educational system, the healthcare system, and the welfare state. At its core, gangster capitalism is about the politics of exclusion, disappearance, and disposability. Authoritarian neoliberalism in this instance reveals its fascist values given the violent nexus between the carceral state and what has been called racial capitalism with its long history of 'colonial dispossession and racial slavery'.[43]

The threat of violence once associated with fringe extremist groups has found a home in a Republican Party that now endorses the political, ideological, and social conditions that have given rise to several violent white supremacist and neo-Nazi groups.[44] Racialized violence has become a central feature of American society, moving from the margins of American society to its endorsement at the highest level of government, especially under the Trump regime. Moreover, it becomes even more pernicious in a society in which guns, forceful encounters, and visual representations of violence dominate screen and popular culture. The latter makes it all the easier, as Vincent Brown argues in the *Los Angeles Review of Books*, 'to think that violence is the solution to nearly everything'.[45] For the Republican Party, violence is now sanctioned as a pathway to political power. The GOP's increasing use of the language of violence is part of a larger culture of threats, dehumanization, and attacks on anyone who disagrees with their right-wing supremacist doctrines and the Trump-sanctioned ecology of serial lying. Ruth Ben-Ghiat provides some recent examples:

> An anchor on the One America News Network calls for the execution of 'tens of thousands' of 'traitors' who stole the election from Trump. A sitting Congress member, Rep. Matt Gaetz (R-Fla.), tells Americans that they 'have an obligation to use' the Second Amendment, which is not about recreation but 'the ability to maintain an armed rebellion against the government if that becomes necessary.' Lara Trump, former president Donald Trump's daughter-in-law, suggests that people who live on the border with Mexico 'arm up and get guns and be ready… and maybe they're going to have to start taking matters into their own hands.'[46]

As Ben-Ghiat makes clear, America now inhabits a 'politics that depends on force'.[47] Vital to such a politics is a level of zealotry and culture of violence that devalues human life, militarizes society, and 'produce[s] the ideal public for an authoritarian society'.[48] It also accelerates and intensifies assaults on the public imagination, constitutes an attack on historical memory, civic culture, public education, and undermines the democratic institutions that support them. Public space has become contaminated with a form of fascist politics that represents a fusion of racial cleansing, life-draining forms of competition, and the abandonment of social responsibility. It also aligns itself with cruel austerity policies, hyper-militarism, xenophobia, a culture of disposability, social atomization, grotesque inequalities, and massive impoverishment, all of which 'are not just [considered] possible, they are welcomed'.[49]

The Scourge of Historical Amnesia

As the boundaries of the unthinkable become normalized, historical consciousness is replaced by manufactured forms of historical amnesia and ignorance. As white supremacy becomes entrenched at the highest levels of power and in the public imagination, the past becomes a burden that must be shed.[50] Disparaging, suppressing, or forgetting the horrors of history has become a valued and legitimating form of political and symbolic capital, especially among the Republican Party and conservative media. Not only have history's civic lessons been forgotten, but historical memory is also being rewritten, especially in the ideology of Trumpism, through a sordid affirmation of the racist history of the Confederacy, American exceptionalism, and the mainstreaming of an updated form of authoritarianism.[51]

Theodor Adorno's insights on historical memory are more relevant than ever. He once argued that as much as repressive governments would like to break free from the past, especially the legacy of fascism, 'it is still very much alive'. Moreover, there is a price to be paid with 'the destruction of memory'. In this case, 'the murdered are… cheated out of the single remaining thing that our powerlessness can offer them: remembrance'.[52] Adorno's warning rings particularly true at a time when two-thirds of young American youth are so impoverished in their historical knowledge that they are unaware that six million Jews were murdered in the Holocaust.[53] On top of this shocking level of ignorance is the fact that 'more than one in 10 believe Jews caused the Holocaust'.[54] Historical amnesia takes a particularly dangerous turn in this case, and prompts the question of how young people and adults can even recognize fascism if they have no recollection or knowledge of its historical legacy.

The genocide inflicted on Native Americans, slavery, the horrors of Jim Crow, the incarceration of Japanese Americans, the rise of the carceral state, the My Lai massacre, former President Bush's torture chambers, and black sites, among other historical events, now disappear into a disavowal of past events made even more unethical with the emergence of a right-wing political and pedagogical language of erasure. For example, the Republican Party's attack on the teaching of critical race theory in the schools, which they label as 'ideological or faddish', both denies the history of racism as well as the ways in which it is enforced through policy, laws, and institutions. For many

Republicans, racial hatred takes on the ludicrous defence of protecting students from learning about the diverse ways in which racism persists in American society. For instance, Republican Governor Ron DeSantis of Florida stated that 'There is no room in our classrooms for things like critical race theory. Teaching kids to hate their country and to hate each other is not worth one red cent of taxpayer money.'[55] Mitch McConnell reintroduced the 'Save American History Act' to limit federal funding to schools that use material or resources from the *New York Times's 1619* project on slavery. It appears that DeSantis and McConnell want to save students from discovering the existence and practice of slavery in American history. In this updated version of historical and racial cleansing, the call for racial justice is equated to a form of racial hatred, leaving intact the refusal to acknowledge, condemn, and confront in the public imagination the history and tenacity of racism in American society. This is not merely wilful ignorance masquerading as educational reform, it is a full-fledged attack on a certain element of fearlessness that comes with critical thinking, holding power accountable, speaking truth to power, and standing up for one's convictions. What is it about critique—raising the bar on making the world a better place by aligning ideals with the messy reality—that reveals the good and bad of history, that threatens the Republican Party and their media acolytes? This is not only a measure of civic illiteracy and ignorance; it is also a form of moral cowardice and a shameless form of political opportunism in the service of a fascist politics.

Bolstered by a former president and a slew of Vichy-type politicians, right-wing ideologues, anti-public intellectuals, and media pundits deny and erase events from a fascist past that shed light on emerging right-wing, neo-Nazi, and extremist policies, ideas, and symbols. The threat of a fascist politics looms large in America given the fact that 74 million people voted to re-elect Trump.[56] America's Nazi problem was also evident in former President Trump's response to the neo-Nazi march in Charlottesville, Virginia when he stated that 'you also had...

very fine people, on both sides'. Shamefully, Trump revealed his own white supremacist ideology by making a political and moral equivalence between fascists spreading hate and those opposing racism and white supremacy. He has also defended preserving Confederate monuments and their noxious past and gave support during a presidential debate in 2020 to the Proud Boys, which emboldened them and similar alt-right groups.[57] He also incited the attempted coup on the Capitol on January 6 by a motely band of neo-Nazis and other far-right extremists.[58] It gets worse. John Kelly, Trump's former chief of staff, reportedly insisted that Trump on a visit to Europe to mark the 100th anniversary of the end of the First World War, claimed that 'Hitler did a lot of good things', pointing explicitly to the economic recovery under Hitler.[59] For Trump, economic recovery and growth erased the Nazi crimes of genocide, war, and violence unleashed on the world under Hitler. It gets worse. General Mark Milley, Chairman of the Joint Chiefs of Staff, who served under Trump, told two *Washington Post* reporters, Carol Leonnig and Philip Rucker, that 'Trump's attempt to overturn the 2020 election results put him in the same camp as Nazi leader Adolf Hitler'.[60] According to their book, *I Alone Can Fix it*, Milley is reported to have said that Trump's lies about the election were spreading 'the gospel of the Fuhrer' and that Trump's supporters were comparable to 'Nazi Brownshirts', a violent group of paramilitary thugs who threatened those who opposed Hitler's rise to power.[61]

America's infatuation with fascist politics is also visible in the growing acts of domestic terror aimed at Asians, undocumented immigrants, and people of colour. Trump's language of hatred played no small role in inciting such violence. It is also visible in the normalization of and tolerance for the rise of extremist groups who increasingly resort to intimidation and violence as a threat to those politicians, critics, journalists, and others who reject the Trumpian worldview. Ben-Ghiat is useful in pointing to the fascist politics at work in what she calls 'the culture of threat', which builds on a long history of racial injustices, police violence, threats against the political opposition ('Lock her up') and state terror against non-whites. She writes:

This culture of violence and threat builds on histories of racial persecution and on policing used as an instrument of terror against non-whites. When the everyday murder of one group has been normalized, it is easier for the public to accept state-sponsored violence around political events, like elections, as necessary to 'save the country'.... The culture of threat is also facilitated by a tolerance for the activities of extremist groups: even a militia march on the Michigan statehouse in May 2020 didn't overly alarm many. And it builds on the consequences of allowing civilians to own hundreds of millions of lethal weapons. The devaluing of human life and the desensitization to harm and loss that come with mass shootings (2020 saw 611 such events in the U.S., a 47% jump from 2019) produce the ideal public for an authoritarian society.[62]

Historical amnesia also finds expression in the right-wing press and among media pundits such as Fox News commentator Tucker Carlson, whose addiction to lying, unrelenting investment in a frenzy of irrationality, and advocacy of white supremacy create an echo chamber of misinformation that normalizes the unspeakable, if not the unthinkable. How else to explain what Juan Cole calls Tucker Carlson's 'tin foil hat conspiracy theory of "'replacement,'" the notion that that sinister forces (often alleged to be Jewish) were deliberately swamping the US with immigrants so as to replace hard to control free white people with docile, poorly paid brown immigrants'.[63] Carlson has also attacked the Black Lives Matter movement, suggesting that their involvement in racial justice protests intimidated the jury in the Derek Chauvin trial to convict him of murder and manslaughter charges. In other words, the jurors were not swayed by the testimony of more than three dozen witnesses or the almost unwatchable video of George Floyd pleading for his mother, who had been dead for two years, claiming all the while that he could not breathe. Instead, their verdict was based on fear of reprisals by those fighting for racial justice.[64]Carlson's demagoguery appears to have no bounds as is evident in his claim that the fall of Afghanistan in August 2021 to the Taliban was due in part to the country's rejection to the growing rights of women who, among other things, served in government roles, proving that the Afghan people did not want to adhere to a grotesque acceptance of gender studies.

This follows earlier comments by Carlson and Rush Limbaugh, who appeared to revel in the news that COVID-19 disproportionately affected African Americans. Limbaugh said he was 'waiting for the racial component',[65] and Carlson later mimicked this racist view, indicating it was time to focus on 'how to improve the lives of the rest, the countless Americans who have been grievously hurt by this, by our response to this. How do we get 17 million of our most vulnerable citizens back to work? That's our task.'[66] This is unadulterated white supremacy and racial cleansing without apology. Equally alarming is the fact that *Tucker Carlson Tonight* is the highest-rated programme in US cable news history and has an average nightly audience of 4.33 million viewers.[67]

The influence of right-wing demagogues like Matt Drudge, Ben Shapiro, Sean Hannity, Glen Beck, and Tucker Carlson on social media platforms such as Facebook is enormous. Some critics claim that Facebook has become a 'right-wing echo chamber', especially in the US.[68] Rational responses now give way to scripted theatre, hyped emotions, and racist ideologies fuelled by lies whose power are expanded through their endless repetition. Joan Donavan, the chief of research at Harvard's Shorenstein Center, claims that right-wing news outlets such as One America News Network, Blaze TV, and Fox News package 'footage designed to overwhelm the sense-making capacity' of their audience while inspiring far-right extremists, vigilantes, and militias to 'live out fantasies of taking justice into their own hands'.[69]

Right-wing hosts such as Hannity and Carlson appear to take delight in making racist comments, which resonates with and further normalizes the bigoted narratives that they pitch to their audience. Yet, such displays of overt, unapologetic racism are not new; rather, they are part of a long legacy of manufactured ignorance that informs the political and media culture of the US. Truth has collapsed under the weight of visceral, raw emotion. William Rivers Pitt argues that Carlson has become unhinged politically and morally given his support for the endless falsehoods and right-wing conspiracies he peddles on

Fox News. Pitt touches on Carlson's fascist politics, largely endorsed by Trump's followers, claiming that he promotes not only baseless lies, but also furthers white supremacist doctrines. Pitt writes:

> Trump loyalists want us to believe the election was stolen by Italian satellites, the Capitol was sacked by FBI agents dressed in their finest MAGA gear, and all of it is controlled by a cabal of cannibal pedophiles who run Hollywood and the Democratic Party. These theories are bizarre, wild and baseless, to be sure, but they are also dangerous, grounded in white supremacy and a deep disdain for democracy.[70]

One of Tucker's bizarre suggestions is that the FBI was responsible for the attack on the Capitol. In this instance, he joins Trump's former chief of staff, Mark Meadows, who, in an email sent to former acting Attorney General Jeffrey Rosen asking him 'to examine… an array of baseless conspiracies that held that Mr. Trump had been the actual victor. That included a fantastical theory that people in Italy had used military technology and satellites to remotely tamper with voting machines in the United States and switch votes for Mr. Trump to votes for Joseph R. Biden Jr.'[71] Carlson is squarely in the company of a group of serial liars, racists, and anti-Semites such as Marjorie Taylor Greene, Paul Gosar, and Matt Gaetz. Lying is only one visible trait of their authoritarian proclivities, they also are unapologetic about the support they get from far-right groups. For instance, Gosar has openly appeared and is publicly endorsed by Nick Fuentes, a leader of a white nationalist group who has spread the groundless theory that the FBI may have been behind the insurrection at the Capitol on January 6. Gosar has ties to the America First movement, which 'aims to preserve white, Christian identity and culture'.[72] Catie Edmondson, writing in the *New York Times*, places Gosar's association with far-right groups in a larger context. She writes:

> His is unapologetic association with [racists] is perhaps the most vivid example of the Republican Party's growing acceptance of extremism, which has become apparent as more lawmakers espouse and amplify conspiracy theories and far-right ideologies that figure prominently in the belief systems of fringe groups.[73]

In this case, I think it is fair to re-examine Theodor W. Adorno's claim that 'Propaganda actually constitutes the substance of politics' and the right-wing production of an endless stream of lies and denigration of the truth. These tsunamis of manufactured ignorance are not merely delusional but endemic to a fascist cult that does not answer to reason but only to power while legitimizing a past in which white nationalism and racial cleansing become the organizing principles of social order and governance.[74] In the era of post-truth, right-wing disimagination machines are not only hostile to those who assert facts and evidence but also supportive of a mix of ruinous ignorance and the plague of civic illiteracy. The latter requires no effort to assess the truth and erases everything necessary for the life of a robust democracy. From the Murdoch media empire to the Sinclair Broadcast Group, right-wing media has become, as Denis Muller recently stated, a 'propaganda operation masquerading as a news service'.[75]

The pedagogical workstations of depoliticization and manufactured ignorance have reached new and dangerous levels amid emerging right-wing populisms.[76] It is not surprising that we live at a time when politics is largely disconnected from echoes of the past and justified on the grounds that direct comparisons are not viable, as if only direct comparisons can offer insights into the lessons to be learned from the past. We have entered an age in which thoughtful reasoning, reflective judgements, and critical thought are under attack. This is a historical moment that resembles a dictatorship of ignorance, which Joshua Sperling rightly argues entails:

> The blunting of the senses; the hollowing out of language; the erasure of connection with the past, the dead, place, the land, the soil; possibly, too, the erasure even of certain emotions, whether pity, compassion, consoling, mourning or hoping.[77]

It is clear is that we live in a historical period in which the conditions that produced white supremacist politics are intensifying once again. How else to explain former President Trump's use of the term 'America First', his labelling immigrants as vermin, his call to 'Make America

Great Again'—signalling his white nationalist ideology—his labelling of the press as 'enemies of the people', and his numerous incitements to violence while addressing his followers. Moreover, Trump's bid for patriotic education and his attack on the *New York Times's 1619 Project* served as both an overt expression of his racism and his alignment with right-wing white supremacists and neo-Nazi mobs. Historical amnesia has become racialized. In the rewriting of history in the age of Trump, the larger legacy of 'colonial violence and the violence of slavery inflicted on Africans' is resurrected as a badge of honour.[78]

America's long history of fascist ideologies and the racist actions of a slave state, the racial cleansing espoused by the Ku Klux Klan, and an historical era that constitutes what Alberto Toscano calls 'the long shadow of racial fascism' in America are no longer forgotten or repressed but celebrated in the age of Trump.[79] What is to be made of a former president who awarded the prestigious Medal of Freedom to a blubbering white supremacist, ultra-nationalist, conspiracy theorist, and virulent racist who labelled feminists as 'Feminazis'. In this case, one of the nation's highest honours went to a man who took pride in relentlessly disparaging Muslims, referred to undocumented immigrants as 'an invading force' and an 'invasive species', demonized people of colour, and recycled Nazi tropes about racial purity while celebrating the armed insurgents that attacked the Capitol as 'Revolutionary War era rebels and patriots'.[80] Under the banner of Trumpism, those individuals who reproduce the rhetoric of political and social death have become celebrated symbols of a fascist politics that feeds off the destruction of the collective public and civic imagination.

Education as a Depoliticizing Machine in the Age of the Spectacle

What these events in capsule form suggest is that an updated right-wing pedagogical machine has become a bullhorn for revitalizing the coma of depoliticization while resuscitating an erasure of historical consciousness about former fascist regimes and their underlying powers of persuasion and repression. Anthony DiMaggio is right in stating that right-wing pundits have succeeded in not only embracing neo-fascist political rhetoric, but have also produced and rely on 'a staggering historical ignorance of their audiences, whom they correctly believe know little about classical fascism, and will not notice that they're smuggling into programs extremist discourse, even as their followers come to embrace neo-fascistic political ideology'.[81] When not rewritten in the interests of the powerful, history becomes a workstation of repression, a tool of power to further what Marc Auge calls, in another context, forms of 'oblivion' that erase 'memory traces'.[82] In this context, Trumpism becomes synonymous with a form of historical amnesia in which the necessity for remembering the horrors of the past is denied, if not repressed. Memory is forgotten and the process of learning from the past is defined as a destructive pedagogical task.

In the age of fascist politics, memory loses its potential for remembrance, vigilance, and moral witnessing. It becomes dangerous. Americans are now urged to forget history to remain loyal, happy members of a cult that celebrate demigods and embrace a politics that is as violent as it is racist. Such problematic and deplorable advice can even be found among prominent historians such as Richard Evans, who states, given his denial that a fascist politics can emerge in the current era in the United States, 'You can't win the political battles of the present if you're always stuck in the past.'[83] It should be noted that Evans later rescinded this position claiming that in light of the January 6 assault on the Capitol edged on by Trump that he had crossed the line and should now be considered a fascist.

White supremacy, overt racism, and shocking instances of nativism were on full display during the January 6 insurrection. Racist code words and dog whistles gave way to supporters carrying the Confederate Flag while others supported sweatshirts emblazoned with 'Camp Auschwitz'. Notwithstanding this horrifying expression of white supremacy, support for the bigoted lies that informed the Trump regime appeared undiminished, even though it was reminiscent of an older racist spirit demonstrated in the film, *Birth of a Nation* (1915).

This overt display of white supremacy was further illustrated and defended most dramatically by a larger number of Republican Party Congressional representatives and, without hesitation, just hours after the January 6 assault on the Capitol and the ensuing deaths and injury to numerous police officers. More than half of the House GOP and seven Republican Senators refused to certify the election results, making clear their support for minority party rule at any cost. In addition, House Republicans refused to censor Marjorie Taylor Greene, an avowed QAnon believer, an inane advocate of conspiracy theories, and shockingly ignorant anti-Semite who peddled the foolish claim, among others, that Jewish Space lasers caused the 2018 California Camp wildfires and that Democrats traffic and cannibalize children and drink the blood of babies. Soon after Rush Limbaugh's death, the endless praise he received by right-wing pundits and conservative media members brought into focus the proto-fascist educational and racist ideological rot at the core of most of America's media outlets.[84] There is more at stake here than simply the tired mainstream argument that the GOP has 'surrendered to extremism'.[85] What Americans may be facing is a choice between either a fascist theocracy or a social democracy.[86]

Ignorance has become death-dealing in the United States. Millions are infected with the COVID-19 virus, and over 678,000 people have died as of September 2021 in part because of the Republican Party and conservative media's disdain for science, evidence, experts, and the public good. The pandemic revealed the utter failure of neoliberal capitalism in the United States in dealing with public health policies and staggering levels of inequality. As Richard D. Wolff points out, 'Today's declining U.S. capitalism can no longer repeat its previous bland celebrations of private enterprises and free markets. Too much is going wrong, provoking criticism, and deepening divisions across U.S. society.'[87] Yet, such failures were rarely connected to 'decades of neoliberal austerity [and] cuts in health and education'.[88] Neoliberalism breeds elements of a fascist politics, as was evident when under the

Trump regime, children were separated from their parents and put into cages modelled after prisons and harking back to the era of concentration camps.[89] Racial capitalism breeds more than ignorance. Under gangster capitalism, Black people have been increasingly subject to police violence while the police enacted such violence on the assumption that they could do so with both encouragement and impunity.

Violence is now mobilized and legitimated through the language of individual freedom. Freedom has become risk-free, a defining feature of citizenship, unmoored from any notion of social responsibility. Under gangster capitalism, freedom is deregulated, removed from any notion of the common good, and wedded to notions of self-absorption and consumerism bereft of strong support for the social contract. Deregulated freedom finds expression in the age of the pandemic among thousands who refuse to wear masks during the plague. Others embrace a gun culture and paramilitary aesthetic at rallies and demonstrations, dressed in uniforms and armed with all manner of military-grade weapons to signal their allegiance to freedom from government rules and to make clear their membership as cult members in the army of Trumpism. Individual freedom is now legitimized through a reactionary language that without apology operates in the service of violence. In this context, symbolic violence harbours the threat of real violence while becoming the primary mode of communication through which right-wing extremists publicly express their militarized identities and aversion to democratic values and rights. In a culture saturated with market-driven needs, culture turns cold and hard, and loses its sense of empathy and social values.[90]

Neoliberal fascism has created a society and culture that Achille Mbembe describes as a form of necropolitics. This is a society in which those who have power define whose lives matter and those whose lives don't. Under a regime of necropolitics, people of colour, the elderly, undocumented immigrants, Muslims, and those others removed from the axis of power and privilege are considered disposable. Or, as Mbembe puts it: 'The calculus of life passes through the death of the Other.'[91] Blood drips from the death-dealing institutions of the United

States. Its institutional and structural violence is rarely connected to historical analogies of an earlier era of racial lynching and systemic racial terror. Also dismissed are the histories and lessons to be learned from the earlier authoritarian societies that emerged in Europe in the 1930s and 1940s.

Moral bankruptcy now functions as the backdrop for forms of social and historical amnesia that produce and legitimize the plague of depoliticization and its normalization of state violence, setting the stage for the emergence of updated forms of fascist politics. Language functions as a vehicle for violence, and ideology degenerates into an unabashed rationale for force. Imagining alternative futures gives way to an intellectual coma fuelled by a culture and collective consciousness steeped in the ethos of consumerism, self-absorption, corruption, manufactured ignorance, and spectacles of deception, barbarism, and violence.

What is starkly evident is that the current crisis has deeper roots beyond the media emphasis on the bizarre beliefs of QAnon and other extremist groups. The spectacle of violence pathologically embraced by right-wing military groups, the stupidity and lies underlying ever-growing conspiracy theories touted by many Trump supporters, and the growing hate symbols in American society suggest that fascism did not suffer an irreversible historic defeat in the 1940s. Yet, it is much easier for the media to focus on the bizarre notion that Democratic leaders are paedophile Satanists who drink the blood of young children than to address the underlying causes that have given rise to a form of fascist politics.

It is important to re-emphasize that under the Trump regime, theatre defined politics and was reproduced and exacerbated by a corporate-controlled media dominated by right-wing cable networks, talk radio, and other cultural apparatuses of ignorance wedded to celebrity culture, game shows, and reality-TV shows. Far from being simple forms of entertainment, these cultural apparatuses are teaching machines that enable the pedagogical conditions that produce a crisis of mass consciousness, agency, identity, and literacy at work in American politics today. The habits of consumption and the attack on civic culture that have long eroded the crucial habits of critical thinking and citizenship have now morphed into the ruinous consuming seductions of ignorance.

The Crisis of Education and the Public Imagination

The current crisis of politics is more than a crisis of mass anxiety, national identity, and capitalism itself. It is also a crisis of education, the public imagination, and the conditions that make a radical democracy possible. Collective insecurity caused by massive degrees of immiseration, economic collapse, and uncertainty provides the grievances that feed a collective turn towards all manner of authoritarian politics. The emptiness, despair, and cynicism that defines the current historical crisis can also be traced to the collective political demobilization of traditionally Democratic constituencies in an era of deindustrialization, rising inequality, and mass insecurity, which cleared the way for the empowerment and mobilization of Trump's increasingly white nationalist base.[92]

The crisis of the moment demands not only a new energy, but also a new language and understanding of the fundamental conditions that have created a collective consciousness among the American public that normalizes white supremacy, authoritarian nationalism, a white homeland, and the laws and pedagogy of neoliberal capitalism that function to disempower people. Catastrophes are no longer unexpected or merely the source of mass anxiety; they are now normalized in a culture that undermines the capacity for criticism while serving 'as the seedbed for a resurgent fascism'.[93] Thoughts of a future that embraces justice and economic equality have morphed under the aegis of Trumpism into an enfeebled politics in which moral outrage and anger are heaped upon an 'internal enemy'. The latter fuels the paranoid and violent fantasies of right-wing extremists whose targets are those 'others' who do not uphold the legacy of white nationalism,

American exceptionalism, and an allegiance to the unrestricted notion of individual freedom.

Fascist politics has emerged out of a form of neoliberal capitalism that does more than engage in privatization, deregulation, and commodification in the interests of financial markets. It also shapes the identities, values, and subjectivity of individuals. No longer merely blinded by the seductions of an all-encompassing consumerism, the public imagination is now infected with the normalizing ethos of a fascist politics whose aim is to purge democracy of both its promises and ideals. What roles do the dominant educational forces under the sway of neoliberal capital—from Hollywood and the universities to talk radio and social media—play in marking the boundaries of dangerous ideas, unsafe nonconformist discourses, memories of resistance, and critical thinking itself? How might we understand the role of culture as a form of domination, whose function is at least as important as economic and political domination and whose power, as Pierre Bourdieu has observed, rests on the side of belief and persuasion?[94] How do we grasp culture as a political and educational force that both deploys and reflects power?

Rather than focus on the spectacles produced by right-wing populism with its slogans, spectacularized violence, lies, and conspiracy theories—all made for a reality-TV media that trades in shocks and entertainment—while not unimportant, it is more useful to look at the underlying set of institutions that constitute those formative cultures that employ forms of symbolic violence and shape particular notions of agency, identity, and social relations in the present historical moment.

A crucial challenge for progressives is to counter the underlying conditions that cause the collective consciousness to incorporate elements of fascist politics. This would mean interrogating the ensemble of institutions, meanings, ideologies, and pedagogical practices that create those formative cultures that promote a mix of intersecting fundamentalisms. Such a task is crucial for rethinking and reclaiming definitions of power, education, and politics that are necessary for the creation of a 'new sensibility' capable of embracing a public imagination synonymous with the imperatives of democratic socialism.[95]

At stake here is recognizing the power of consciousness and education both in shaping who we are and how we relate to others within a range of unsuspecting assumptions, sanctioned notions of common sense, dominant notions of reason, and forms of tacit knowledge that turn politics and subjectivity into a pathology. What I am suggesting is that for education to become an agent of change that can lead people to self-reflection and collective action, it is crucial to understand the underlying dominant fundamentalisms with their respective formative cultures that limit who we are and what we can become. Spectacles produced by the conservative media machines provide comforting if not reassuring entertainment for many of the white supremacists, economically disenfranchised, those harbouring anti-immigrant sentiments, and followers of Trump who believe that whites have replaced Blacks as the primary victims of racial discrimination in American society. But they do more, as they also divert attention away from the underlying conditions and vitriol of a fascist politics that furthers a crisis in democratic culture. Instead of laying bare the conditions at work in Trumpism and its underlying ideology and wrecking policy machines, media spectacles and disimagination machines leave 'people feeling anxious, alienated, and resentful'.[96]

Fundamentals of Neoliberal Fascism

Three intersecting formative cultures or fundamentalisms have strongly shaped the emergence of a new political formation that I call neoliberal fascism. These three fundamentalist formative cultures normalize the unthinkable and create the conditions for morally compromised lives willing to become complicit with the ugliness of cultural formations steeped in an authoritarian politics of disposability and a racialized form of neoliberal capitalism.[97] The first of these formative cultures is a free-market fundamentalism that functions educationally to rewrite politics and define the requirements of citizenship through the ethos of consumerism, reduces all social relations to commercial exchanges, defunds public goods such as schools, and separates economic activity from social costs. Moreover, free-market fundamentalists wage a full-fledged attack on the social contract and the welfare state, and in doing so, limit the scope of agency for millions to what can be called the politics of survival. Under such circumstances, people spend their daily lives fighting for the bare necessities of life. Under neoliberal capitalism, American society has entered a dire nightmarish period in which, as Salman Rushdie has argued, 'People are too busy trying not to die.'[98]

One consequence is a mode of agency in which time is a liability rather than an enabling force for developing one's capacity to be a critically engaged and informed participant in a democracy. All personal, political, and social relations are now defined in market terms, rendering matters of meaningful agency, identity, and dignity subject to the market's totalizing rule. As Naomi Klein points out, human dignity expressed as the right to 'basic security in your job... some certainty that you will be taken care of in old age [and not] be bankrupted by illness, and that your kids will have access to the tools they need to excel' have been dismissed by many conservative politicians and pundits as privileged policies for 'welfare queens' and freeloaders rather than as human rights.[99] Of course, the real issue here is the political and ethical aversion on the part of neoliberals, centrists, and conservatives to redistribute wealth and restructure power in order to address real problems caused by inequality.

As Wendy Brown has noted: 'casting markets and market conduct as appropriate for all human and organization—neoliberal reason has a specific antipathy to politics, and even to democratic power-sharing (apart from voting). It treats politics and democracy as at best ruining markets and at worst leading toward tyrannical social justice programs and totalitarianism'.[100] In a society marked by staggering inequalities, people cannot define their lives outside of the market's limited boundaries. Undermining all notions of the social, neoliberalism has become the enemy of democracy and social justice and must be resisted at all costs.

The second cultural formation that functions as a toxic pedagogical force in American culture is a brand of religious fundamentalism that 'has turbocharged the support among Trump loyalists, many of whom describe themselves as participants in a kind of holy war'.[101] Largely made up of white evangelical Christians and other Christians, this form of religious fundamentalism has become a solid mainstay of the Republican Party as it has moved into an ideological position that is aligned with extremist authoritarian policies, values, and practices. For example, many conservative evangelicals 'advocate voter suppression as a way to keep Republicans in power, even if most Americans don't support them'.[102] Not only do right-wing evangelicals collapse the line between religion and the state, but they also advocate a theocratic model of politics that Chris Hedges has labelled as an American form of fascism.[103] The most extreme elements of the white-evangelical movement embrace a militaristic ideology that is key to radical extremists groups such as the 'boogaloo' boys, who view themselves as participants in a holy war. Former Assistant Secretary for Threat Prevention and Security Policy at the Department of Homeland Security Elizabeth Neumann argues that Christian nationalism has become pervasive among white evangelicals. She states that increasingly, large segments of this group view:

> America as God's chosen nation [and] believe the United States has a covenant with God, and that if it is broken, the nation risks literal destruction—analogous to the siege of Jerusalem in the Hebrew Bible. In the eyes of these believers, that covenant is threatened by cultural changes like taking prayer out of public schools and legalizing abortion and gay marriage.[104]

This extremist religious movement functions as an educational and political force that legitimizes the worst forms of bigotry, wages war on reproductive rights and same-sex marriages, pushes creationism in the schools, is anti-science, and perpetuates a rigid moralism and messianic view of the world that promotes a disdain for critical thinking and progressive forms of education. At the same time, it has played a crucial role in supporting Trump's toxic policies, which include putting immigrant children in sordid detention centres, imposing a reign of terror on people of colour, bungling the COVID-19 response, and supporting the intersection of anti-intellectualism, anti-Semitism, and systemic racism.[105] This is a conservative movement that lives in circles of certainty, and adherents believe that they are fighting a war between the forces of evil and good. This is more than a perilous binary; it is also a prescription for a dangerous form of ignorance that supports both a form of Christian nationalism and a white nationalism aligned with the toxic notion of 'blood and soil'. Hedges makes a compelling case in labelling white Christian leaders as fascists by pointing to their call to make 'America a Christian state', the cult of personality that they support, their authoritarian denial of equal rights to non-Christians, and their belief in the 'cleansing power of apocalyptic violence'.[106]

The third cultural formation is a form of manufactured ignorance and militarized illiteracy that works through numerous registers to empty language of meaning and eliminate the standards for distinguishing right from wrong, historical memory from historical amnesia, and social responsibility for ethical and political irresponsibility. As Karen J. Greenberg makes clear, the suppression of history, memory, and language opens the doorway to fascism and a 'state of unparalleled heartlessness and greed'.[107] The ongoing refusal of Americans to confront what James Baldwin once called 'the algebra of their history' has become 'a kind of universal obscenity'.[108] Suppressing or whitewashing history erases those echoes of the past that should shed light on and sound the alarm bells when select groups are dehumanized and treated as unknowable and undesirable. Under the Trump regime, a culture of lying normalized a world where truth was not only undermined but lost its legitimacy. In the age in which the truth is relegated to fake news, 'everything that matters is denied and everything that embodies evil is reinvented'.[109] This was a form of illiteracy sanctioned at the highest levels of the former Trump administration and is the outgrowth of a society inundated with a militarized culture of commands, ignorance, consumerism, and immediacy. Post-truth is a conceptual signifier that operates in the service of violence against the ethical imagination and the standards at work in producing civic literacy and the institutions that support it. Increasingly, meaning has been emptied out of its critical and moral referents and subjected to the dual vocabulary of the market and war. This is a language that reduces people to commodities and feeds a society of the spectacle through a language that trades in violence, a friend/enemy distinction, and rewrites history in the discourse of the powerful; that is, a discourse of white supremacy.

The signposts for a cultural formation of ignorance are evident in the long-standing attack on public schooling, teachers, and unions, with 'education' being reduced to the market imperatives of neoliberal capital. Defunded and turned into testing centres and efficiency mills, public schooling as a democratic public sphere has been privatized, degraded, and broken, furthering a culture of ignorance and illiteracy. Market values instrumentalize education and find critical thinking dangerous. In a culture dominated by corporations and the profit motive, political passions and moral convictions have become a liability. Moreover, the United States is now hostage to a culture of immediacy driven by social media. Knowledge now begins with tweets, Facebook postings, and endless streams of selfies on Instagram. Many Americans no longer read, choosing instead to scan selected bits of information, disconnected from broader narratives.

Under the rule of corporate-controlled power, social media apparatuses have stripped knowledge of any substantive context and accelerates time at a pace that prevents both contemplation and experience from crystallizing into a politics of thoughtfulness and responsibility. Ideas, values, and ideologies that offer a sense of critical agency and civic and social imagination have no room in a society in which reason, truth, science, and meticulous judgements are viewed with contempt. Destabilized perceptions and normalized fictions have now become the dominant currency of politics. Bill Russo, a former campaign advisor for Biden, goes further and argues that social media, especially Facebook, has a toxic influence on society and has:

> twisted and distorted our world and our politics into something barely recognizable, where conspiracy theories and disinformation

run rampant. This is not a feature of our society that we must simply accept. It is a choice to create an algorithm that feeds the distrust and polarization that are tearing us apart.[110]

Russo may have underestimated how toxic and damaging Facebook is. Francis Haugen, a whistle-blower who appeared on CBS's '60 minutes', argued that when it came to public safety, Facebook chose profits over the public good. For instance, they did little to stop endangering young girls whose eating disorders and thoughts of suicide worsened while using Instagram. A warning that was revealed in its own research. Moreover, Facebook did almost nothing to prevent right-wing extremists from fanning the flames of racial hatred; it largely ignored human trafficking organizations using its platform; and it was complicit in its enabling on its various platforms of the widespread dissemination of conspiracy theories, misinformation, and poisonous propaganda. As the capacity for political speech withers, there is a breakdown of shared values and the widening gulf of malignant normality, moral depravity, and civic illiteracy. Under the reign of market values, ignorance thrives in a society in which all matters of responsibility are individualized. Under neoliberal capitalism, human connections give way to an ethos of misguided libertarian individualism that views all problems as personal failings. In this discourse freedom is tied to self-interest and a rejection of any notion of social responsibility—evident in the rejection of mask-wearing as more important than saving lives and respecting the common good. Gangster capitalism celebrates 'wealth, privilege, and power' with little or no regard for social costs, and 'invents reality' as it sees fit.[111] Neoliberal dogma constitutes a war on the ethical imagination as individuals, increasingly under the onslaught of neoliberal capitalism, become prisoners of their own experiences.

Max Horkheimer was right in 1939 when he suggested that it was impossible to talk about fascism without talking about capitalism, especially as it works relentlessly 'to transform democratic citizens into totalitarian subjects' through what he and Theodor Adorno called the culture industry.[112] Moreover, the educational force of neoliberal culture now prepares its willing subjects from the inside, moulding their desires, anxieties, and identities through psychological domination. The misery created by neoliberal capitalism bears down not only on the body but colonizes the mind through the force of a formative educational apparatus that emerges out of the crisis of democratic institutions, civic values, and political culture. We live at a time when it is impossible to talk about capitalism without talking about fascism. As America moves closer to adopting a fascist politics, the words of Bertolt Brecht resonate with the times. He writes: 'how can anyone tell the truth about Fascism unless he is willing to speak out against capitalism, which brings it forth?'[113] With America on the brink of fascism, it is time to talk about the potential end of democracy as we know it, however imperfect, and what it might mean to struggle to imagine and bring into being a future in which democracy can thrive rather than be imperilled.

2

America's Nazi Problem and the Plague of Violence

Fascism was... something that came to life in the course of a powerful social development. Language provides it with a refuge. Within this refuge a smoldering evil expresses itself as though it were salvation.

—Theodor W. Adorno

Democracy in Crisis

Democracy across the globe is in free fall, gasping to breathe again. According to a report by Freedom House, a pro-democracy think tank, the decline in global freedom has been getting worse over the last fifteen years. According to the report:

> The impact of the long-term democratic decline has become increasingly global in nature, broad enough to be felt by those living under the cruelest dictatorships, as well as by citizens of long-standing democracies. Nearly 75 percent of the world's population lived in a country that faced deterioration last year. [Moreover] as a lethal pandemic, economic and physical insecurity, and violent conflict ravaged the world in 2020, democracy's defenders sustained heavy new losses in their struggle against authoritarian foes, shifting the international balance in favor of tyranny.[1]

Under the guise of addressing the spread of the coronavirus, an increasing number of societies have produced a pandemic of human rights abuses.[2] Not only has the spread of the virus exposed the brutal systemic inequities in the fabric of the global social order, imposed massive suffering, and pushed millions into poverty, it has also gutted civic space with a wave of repressive policies that have included jailing dissidents, journalists, health care workers, doctors, educators, and others who have been critical of failed government responses to the public health crisis.[3] Under former President Trump, white nationalism, a politics of lawlessness, a culture of brutality, a powerful and approving right-wing propaganda machine, and a systemic attack on the social state enabled the rise of neoliberal fascism in the United States. This slide into authoritarianism also emboldened a 'second coming of fascism [included] India (the largest democracy in the world) and Brazil (the largest democracy in Latin America)' as well as in Turkey, Hungary, the Philippines, and other countries across the globe.[4]

Holding power accountable by shining a light on government mismanagement, corruption, and state violence has come at a heavy cost for critics and opposition political parties.[5] Exposing the ravages of gangster capitalism has made visible the latter's false appeal to democracy to cover up a mythical, if not deceitful, notion of the American dream. Instead of a narrative of American exceptionalism, which furthers the fairy-tale notion of the United States as the moral and enlightened leader of the alleged free world, we are left with a society that has relinquished its power to a Republican Party that has become the vanguard of white supremacy. Columnist Frank Rich got it right in 2018 when he stated, 'the Republican Party has proudly and uninhibitedly come out of the closet as the standard-bearer for white supremacy in the Trump era'.[6] More Recently, Patrick Cockburn has argued that the most dangerous threat facing the world today is 'the transformation of the Republican Party in the US into a fascist movement' and cites those elements of the Republican Party which echo a fascist politics. He writes:

> It is worth listing the chief characteristics of fascist movements in order to assess how far they are now shared by the Republicans. Exploitation of ethnic, religious and cultural hatreds is probably the most universal feature of fascism. Others include a demagogic leader with a cult of personality who makes messianic but vague

promises to deliver a golden future; appeals to law-and-order but a practical contempt for legality; the use, manipulation and ultimate marginalisation of democratic procedures; a willingness to use physical force; demonising the educated elite—and the media in particular; shady relations with plutocrats seeking profit from regime change. One by one these boxes have been ticked by the Republicans until the list is complete.[7]

And the list goes on. In its latest incarnation, the forces of authoritarianism have actively supported a tsunami of police violence against Black people, embraced conspiracy theories over science and rational reason, conflated patriotism with an attack on critical thinking, drawn from the poisonous well of anti-intellectualism while venerating 'a masculine gun culture, Hollywood movies, and mass consumption'.[8] The racist and state violence that had been growing in the United States since the Reagan administration was accelerated under Trump's racist, white nationalist government and exploded with the January 6 attack on the Washington Capitol. The Capitol rampage was led by Trump loyalists, carrying Confederate flags, Nazi symbols, and a slew of white supremacy regalia. The immediate aim of the Trump-inspired right-wing insurgents was to invalidate certification of the election results and destroy the constitutional basis of the American democratic experiment. Trump's rise to power and his presidency proved that fascist politics was on the march in the US. The violent siege of the US Capitol on January 6 'rendered visible the plague of homegrown white neofascism'.[9]

Put in a broader historical context, the attack on the Capitol was an act of political terrorism made in the name of white supremacy. It echoes a sordid history that includes the violence against Blacks that took place in Tulsa a hundred years ago. Tulsa was destroyed because of white supremacist violence and over 300 Black people were killed. That was an act of political, domestic, and economic terrorism. What is often missing from the recent accounts of the Tulsa accounts of mass violence and terrorism is that 'it was part of a long and shameful pattern in which White mobs used murderous violence to erase African

American prosperity'.[10] Today, economic and political terrorism are unified and drive a Republican Party that is relentless in its destruction of the rights of Black people and its willingness to destroy democracy as well. Politics in American society has become an extension of racial violence. This is a fascist politics that no longer hides in the shadows or margins of society and has become a governing principle of the Republican Party. Under Trump, the Republican Party was no longer uncomfortable about its authoritarian politics, and as Rick Perlstein adds, 'dropp[ed] the pretense altogether'.[11] This is evident in the language of hard-core former President Trump's supporters, such as his former national security director and top advisor, Michael Flynn. Appearing at a QAnon Memorial Day conference in Dallas, Texas, Flynn endorsed the notion that a violent military coup, like the one that happened in Myanmar, could and should happen in the United States. Referring to a question from the audience as to why what happened in Myanmar could not happen in the US, Flynn replied, 'No reason. I mean, it should happen here. No reason.'[12] According to Mary Papenfuss of *HuffPost*, Flynn's remarks were met 'with wild screams of approval'.[13] America's slide into fascist politics with its undercurrent of white supremacy has been acknowledged even by President Joe Biden in speeches he delivered marking both the Tulsa race massacre and Memorial Day.[14] Using a language long associated with leftist critics, Biden warned that US democracy was not only in danger but that Americans had to recognize and challenge the 'deep roots of racial terror'.[15]

Sarah Grillo flushes out Biden's warning stating that racism for Republicans is the issue to adopt as a winning political strategy. She writes: 'the Republican strategy for the 2022 elections and beyond virtually assures race—and racism—will be central to political debate for years to come.... Republicans see this most divisive issue as either political necessity or an election-winner—including as it relates to voting laws, critical race theory, big-city crime, immigration and political correctness.'[16] This is a strategy that provided the political, educational, and cultural backdrop for creating the conditions that gave rise to the attack on the Capitol.

As the white supremacists and far-right groups pillaged the Capitol, shouting 'Fight for Trump! Fight for Trump! Traitor, traitors, traitors!' they attacked police officers with clubs, chemical spray agents, metal barriers, fire extinguishers, and any other object they could turn into a weapon. They vandalized several offices, including the offices of House Speaker Nancy Pelosi (D-CA). Over 140 police officers were injured in the riot, and one Capitol police officer, Brian D. Sicknick, was killed. Close to 238 officers and National Guard personnel deployed to the Capitol to protect it 'tested positive for the coronavirus or were exposed to it'.[17] This egregious and almost unprecedented slide into violence to overturn an election made clear that America was at war with itself.

The violence of the attack on the Capitol gave way to another kind of domestic terrorism in which the Republican Party refused to establish a formal commission to investigate the attack. No doubt such a commission ran the risk of revealing Republican Party complicity in both extending the logic of the big lie of a stolen election and efforts to rewrite its history and the role it played in inciting the mob's violent insurrection against the Capitol. Chauncey DeVega goes further and argues, 'by refusing to investigate Donald Trump's coup attempt and the Capitol attack, today's Republican Party has shown itself (again) to be a terrorist organization'.[18]

As it built walls that functioned as a global symbol of nativism, separated the children of immigrants from their parents, and used the military to crush peaceful protests against police violence, corruption, and systemic racism, America lost all pretence to being a democracy. The savagery of neoliberal capitalism and its culture of ruthlessness have now merged with elements of a fascist politics. As the United Nations secretary-general António Guterres points out, the wrecking machine of neoliberal capitalism has done more than propagate the false myth of American exceptionalism and set the stage for an emerging fascist politics worldwide, it has also increased the global criminalization of dissent, engineered economic devastation, and caused the virus to thrive in countries such as Brazil and India. He writes:

because poverty, discrimination, the destruction of our natural environment and other human rights failures have created enormous fragilities in our societies.... Human rights defenders, journalists, lawyers, political activists—even medical professionals—have been detained, prosecuted, and subjected to intimidation and surveillance for criticizing government responses to the pandemic. Pandemic-related restrictions have been used to subvert electoral processes and weaken opposition voices.[19]

The United States has suffered a steep decline in democracy over the past few years, especially under the Trump regime. According to The Freedom Report, the US has experienced an 11-point decline in freedom since 2020, 'making it one of the 25 countries to suffer the steepest drops over the 10-year period'.[20] The US now ranks 'closer to countries such as Romania and Panama than western European partners such as France and Germany'.[21] The Freedom House report was not alone in assessing the decline of democracy in the United States. The Economists' Intelligence Unit cited the US as a 'flawed democracy' and ranked it 25th out of 167 countries analysed as democratic nations.[22]

The length and breadth of the struggle in the United States to close the gap between its ideals, promises, and reality has reached a vanishing point. America's penchant for violence abroad has now turned inward. The Trumpian call for 'law and order' encouraged dictators across the globe and accelerated a politics of disposability connected to updated forms of racial cleansing, white nationalism, and white supremacy. Authoritarian nationalism increasingly finds its counterpart in forms of cultural triumphalism and the proliferation of state violence, now largely waged by Republican-controlled state legislatures. Authoritarian nationalism is also aligned with a historical politics of erasure and terror whose endpoint is the hidden burial ground of 'los desaparecidos'—the disappeared in a land of social abandonment.

America's collective desire for a democratic future has not simply been diminished; it appears to have become irrelevant, if not an object of scorn by both the Republican Party and the legion of Trump followers. America is haunted by apocalyptic yearnings camouflaged in the promise of a white public sphere and society cleansed of those populations considered expendable. Essential to this bigoted and nativistic social formation is a racially infused notion of citizenship, an atomized notion of personal liberty, and an unmitigated defence of individualism and selfishness free of any pretence of social responsibility.[23] To paraphrase Zygmunt Bauman, visions have now fallen into disrepute, and what once produced shame, many Americans are now proud of.[24]

America's Nazi Problem

We live at a time in which the conditions that produce authoritarian societies are with us once again. America has 'a Nazi problem', evident not only in the 74 million people who voted for a white supremacist presidential candidate in 2020 but also in the attack on the Capitol by Trump's followers whose 'minds [were] waterlogged with conspiracy theories [took] lies as truth, spread hate and bigotry, [and wrapped] themselves in several flags—American, Confederate, Blue Lives Matter—and [who] use the Bible as a weapon of violence and repression'.[25] This is not to suggest that the United States, especially under the Trump regime, replicated precisely Hitler's Nazi Germany. Trump is not Hitler, nor is Trumpism a precise replica of Nazi ideology. Robert Jay Lifton is right in arguing that the United States may not be 'headed inevitably for an authoritarian society or Nazi-like society [but] there are parallels. And they're dangerous. You know, the Nazis didn't do away with the major institutions of Germany.'[26] Trump, his incorrigible followers, and the Republican Party as a whole have unleashed elements of an authoritarian irrationality, which is the dark and menacing underside of a racist, anti-democratic politics and psychology. What we are witnessing is a society plunging into a society where politics that operates in the service of violence has become the norm.

The Black Lives Matter movement has made clear that America is reproducing alarming echoes of the past. It has exposed the mobilizing passions and ideological discourses of fascism evident in Trumpland. At a different time in history, Cedric Robinson identified this American form of fascist politics as racial capitalism.[27] According to Robinson, America had its own home-grown version of fascism, which did not simply emulate the fascist European movements of the 1920s but reached back to the era of Jim Crow and the rise of the Ku Klux Klan in the United States.[28] Fascism was no longer viewed as simply an import from Europe. The historical manufacture of fascism was acknowledged as dating back long before its rise in Europe at the beginning of the twentieth century. Its roots in the United States began with the era of settler-colonial racism and evolved into 'the violent nexus between the carceral state and racial capitalism', which became the new site of fascism.[29]

The collective institutions and public spheres capable of resisting the logic of neoliberal capitalism and the emerging fascist politics—from schools and unions to the courts and independent media—are either under attack or being dismantled. In this neoliberal dystopian dreamscape, democratic hopes have been privatized, and the state is hollowed out, no longer viewed as a force for the public good. The inventory of public concerns ignores any notion of the civic imagination and the ideas, values, and institutions that connect it to an ongoing struggle over social, political, and economic rights. There is more at work here than a diminished capacity for democratic resistance, racial change, and the failure of the civic imagination. Yet, this is not meant to underestimate the struggle of emergent movements of resistance to liberate the public imagination from the grip of neoliberal ideology, white nationalism, militarized policing, systemic racism, and right-wing populism. Such movements are alive and offer more than a glimmer of hope for the future. At the same time, it would be reckless politically and morally to underestimate the challenge posed by the ongoing transformation of America into an updated fascist-like state, reproduced, in part, through a plague of manufactured ignorance, repression, and racist motivated violence.[30]

The current historical era is plagued by the abandonment of human rights, democratic institutions, and formations; the latter is aided and abetted by the concentrated power of a corporate-controlled social media dominated by incivility, bigotry, racism, and lies. Under such circumstances, it is crucial to understand how the different threads of oppression and anti-democratic tendencies mutually inform and sustain a totalizing network of state violence. Furthermore, it is essential to comprehend how the diverse elements of oppression are rooted in the language, symbols, and culture of society's everyday habits and social relations.

America's descent into fascist politics demands a rethinking of how education and the shaping of agency, values, and modes of identification have become most important to politics while legitimizing and normalizing systemic violence and the punishing state as defining features of governance, culture, and everyday life. As James Baldwin once noted presciently, 'habits of thought reinforce and sustain the habits of power'.[31] Not only do such 'habits of thought' necessitate analysing the common sense assumptions that shape consciousness, but they also point to the need to change the power relations in which they are produced and legitimated. Education in this formulation is the terrain in which habits of thought are shaped and the possibility of resistance exists. Repressive forms of education reinforce habits of thought that must be identified and interrogated in order to connect ideas to action and challenge habits of power. In order to prevent power from translating into tyranny, critical ideas must be coupled to the struggle over relations of power. In this case, critical thought, historical memory, and moral witnessing are crucial preconditions and a bedrock of resistance in the fight against pedagogies of repression. It is important to stress that critical pedagogy about more than developing crucial insights into how power works, it is also the material of politics that enables the connection between consciousness, understanding, and social change. This suggests as Frederick Douglass once stated

> If there is no struggle, there is no progress. Those who profess to favor freedom, and yet depreciate agitation, are men who want crops without plowing up the ground. They want rain without thunder and lightning. They want the ocean without the awful roar of its many waters. This

struggle may be a moral one; or it may be a physical one; or it may be both moral and physical; but it must be a struggle. Power concedes nothing without a demand. It never did and it never will.[32]

In an age in which all social problems are treated as simply a matter of individual responsibility and unconstrained choices, it has become more difficult to translate private troubles into broader, systemic considerations. The self is now organized around notions of freedom and choice that view matters of the public good, community, and social responsibility as a regressive if not reactionary set of obligations. Translation as a political form has been rendered incoherent under the onslaught of manufactured ignorance and the cult of conformity. The failure to connect the dots among a diverse number of issues and social problems is frequently the result of the depoliticizing logic of neoliberal individualization and privatization. There is also the problem that comes with a left politics that defines itself through a range of siloed differences, however crucial politically. The result is a politics that is fractured and unable theoretically and politically to develop a unified movement capable of mass struggle and collective resistance.

Connecting Capitalism and Racial Hierarchies

In 2014, Eric Garner was arrested and murdered for the crime of selling cigarettes on the streets of Staten Island. Prior to his death, Officer Daniel Pantaleo put Garner in a chokehold while another officer put pressure on his chest. Even though he repeated eleven times that he could not breathe, Garner, who was unarmed, died as a result of this inhumane and vicious treatment.[33] Within a short time, 'I cannot breathe' became a rallying cry and compelling shorthand for a protest movement against racist-inspired police brutality and mass incarceration. George Floyd uttered the same phrase more than twenty times prior to dying because of Officer Derick Chauvin putting his knee on Floyd's neck for over 9 minutes in full view of many people witnessing this act of murderous violence. While these two cases are the most celebrated for launching protests against police brutality across the globe, it has been estimated that over seventy people have used the exact phrase while in police custody.[34]

Building on the work of the Black Lives Movement and other activist groups protesting what Noam Chomsky calls '400 years of hideous crimes and atrocities', George Floyd's assassination prompted one of the largest protest movements in American history.[35] What was different about this movement was that it exposed globally acts of police racism, violence, and brutality in terms of both its history and its existing policies regarding domestic terrorism. What this movement illuminated was the notion that police violence could only be understood within the lengthy reach of a racist history whose roots were in the long legacy of slavery, the genocide waged against Native Americans, the Jim Crow era, and the rise of the carceral or punishing state that emerged in full force since the 1980s.[36] George Floyd's murder, once again, unleashed the brutal cascading violence that comes with decades of institutional racism and the ruthlessness of a carceral state. It exposed and reminded Americans of the racist lies pushed by Trump and his Confederate-loving allies in the corporate and media worlds. The phantoms of history had come out of the shadows, revealing the detritus of dashed hopes, enduring hardships, and racist violence. The United States had not simply lost its way morally and politically, it had slipped into the ugly gorge of fascist politics.

From the 1970s on, neoliberal capitalism nourished, amplified, and intensified fascist passions, and by the time of Trump's election in 2016 to the presidency of the United States, America had entered the storm clouds of an updated version of authoritarianism. The protest movements that emerged in response to the symbolic and real violence unleashed by the cry 'I can't breathe' represent a much-needed form of historical remembrance and the unfreezing of a history of systemic repression and racism. Such movements have also exposed not only the re-emergence of a new wave of white supremacy, police violence, voter suppression, the rise of the punishing state, and the ongoing criminalization of social problems, but also, to a lesser degree, the ascendancy of a savage form of financial capitalism that has created a new political formation that has tipped the alleged American dream into the American nightmare.

As I stress throughout this book, one lesson to be learned regarding the racial roots of fascism in the United States is that it is a 'protracted social process' that can be understood as a historical arc that identifies the lingering extent of a parasitic fascist politics in the United States and its re-emergence in different forms today. Alberto Toscano rightly highlights this point in referencing the rise of the Black Lives Matter movement, which has argued that:

> the threat is not of a 'return of the 1930s' but the ongoing fact of racialized state terror. This is the ever-present danger that animates present-day anti-fascist energies in the United States—and it cannot be boiled down to the necessary but insufficient task of confronting only those who self-identify as fascists.[37]

One of the challenges faced by the emergence of this new era of fascist politics is the need for a new vocabulary capable of analysing how neoliberalism works through a wide range of oppressive practices in various sites to reproduce a totalizing system of violence.[38] The aligning of racial violence and fascism necessitates connecting, as Samir Amin once noted, 'the return of fascism on the political scene to the ongoing crisis of contemporary capitalism'.[39] According to Amin, fascism rejects the most essential elements of democracy, which includes 'theories and practices of modern democracies [based on a] recognition of a diversity of opinions, recourse to electoral procedures to determine a majority, [and] guarantee of the rights of the minority'.[40] Against democratic values and rights, fascism proposes 'the values of submission to the requirements of collective discipline and the authority of the supreme leader and his main agents'.[41]

Connecting racial violence and fascism also suggests a critical historical and contemporary analysis of the rise of the punishing state in a range of institutions, spaces, and social relations that shape daily life. In this logic, capitalism and violence become synonymous.

Robin D. G. Kelley reiterates this point in his insistence that capitalism and racism are not distinct from one another and that racial hierarchies are a governing principle of capitalism.[42] Under such circumstances, it is not possible to 'eliminate capitalism, overthrow it, without the complete destruction of white supremacy, of the racial regime under which it's built'.[43]

David Harvey is right in asking how neoliberalism has managed to cancel out the future, render invisible the main centres of oppression, and extend market-driven values far beyond the economic realm to a range of institutions, spaces, and social actors.[44] Similarly, it is crucial to analyse how neoliberalism has enabled the re-emergence of white supremacy, white nationalism, and systemic racism as the foundation for merging neoliberalism and an updated version of fascist politics.[45] A central question here is how has the reach of violence changed under neoliberalism, and how has the ethical collapse of political horizons, language, and a shared sense of meaning and values furthered the destruction of public spaces, public imagination, and the rise of fascist politics?[46]

In an era of rampant anti-intellectualism, rising Christian nationalism, the elevation of blind faith for critical reason, and the advancement of consumerism to a national ideal, manufactured ignorance reinforces the destruction of those crucial public spheres where the discourse of the common good, public life, and social justice can be taught and learned. Under such circumstances, everyday life is militarized as predominantly white males are considered citizen-soldiers waging war against those viewed as disposable in a society where the public sphere is deemed only available to white people.[47] In this view of the social order only whites have a legitimate claim to citizenship.

The Politics of Disposability

As politics is emptied of its democratic values and its institutions are rendered powerless, human bonds are undermined, and shared meanings collapse, resulting 'in the brutal tearing of social solidarities'.[48] Disposability has become a central feature of both police violence and a broader system of terror with its 'racist grammars of suffering, state violence', malice, hardship, elimination, and death.[49] Racist police practices, acts of viciousness, and violence must be understood within this broader politics of disposability in which people of colour assume the status of unknowable, rootless, undeserving, and open to gratuitous violence. Disposability has become a central discourse of the current movements of white supremacy unleashed as a badge of honour by former President Trump. Disposable lives refer not only to the violence and sometimes killing of people, whether on the border or the streets of America, but also to the stripping away of their dignity, ability to survive, and their humanity. The politics of disposability uses violence to attack those considered most vulnerable and, in doing so, raises the question of who determines and under what circumstances whose lives are unreal and not worthy of being considered 'lives at all'.[50] Moreover, the logic of disposability and systemic racism cannot be abstracted from a neoliberal society in which levels of rising inequality in wealth and power have reached obscene levels.[51]

Neoliberalism radiates violence, which circulates between the state and people of colour in an ongoing tsunami of armed policing, militarized masculinity, and a culture in which people of colour are viewed as dangerous and suspect populations. Racial violence is now integral to national politics and represents a full-fledged attack on civic culture and democracy. This system of civic death represents a new form of biopolitics conditioned by a permanent state of class and racial exception. As Achille Mbembe observes under this form of social death, 'vast populations are subject to conditions of life conferring upon them the status of living dead', largely invisible in the global media, or, when disruptively present, defined as redundant, pathological, and dangerous.[52]

One consequence is that an increasing number of groups, such as Black people and undocumented immigrants, are forcefully deprived of their human rights and are methodically eliminated as speaking and acting human beings. Such actions are normalized through a conservative media that now weaponizes the language of racial exclusion. Patriotic frenzies become the order of the day edged on by conservative media apparatuses that operate in the service of a white supremacist state and a ruling financial elite. Under former President Trump, the call for 'law and order' became an enabling tool for violence against Black people and others deemed excessive, unworthy, or enemies of the state. The demand for law and order in line with previous precedents morphed into a malignant form of lawlessness. While the Biden administration has toned down the racist rhetoric, Republican Party legislators at the state level are enacting new forms of racial cleansing with the proliferation of voter suppression policies along with 'a slew of anti-protest laws pending in Republican-led states, [with some] already passed, such as in Florida'.[53] As of April 2021, '81 anti-protest bills have been introduced in 34 states', all of which aim at criminalizing dissent.[54] Governor DeSantis of Florida has labelled them 'anti-riot' bills.[55]

America has become a permanent racialized and class-specific war culture. Under neoliberalism, violence permeates its institutions, culture, and everyday life, bolstered by a national preoccupation with the accumulation of capital, selfishness, privatization, and unbridled individualism. Critical agency and social justice are undermined in a neoliberal society in which ethics and justice are viewed as a private affair rather than a public good.[56] Massive inequalities in wealth and power fuel an iniquitous race and class-based court structure, a perverse criminal justice system, a punitive welfare order, and a harsh system of mass incarceration.[57] Neoliberalism is a criminogenic machinery of political repression and economic exploitation that accelerates the suffering of the poor and racially marginalized. It produces expansive modes of symbolic and concrete violence legitimated through judicial institutions, workplaces, social services, and courts, all the while normalized through cultural apparatuses such as social media, right-wing cable networks, talk radio, and public and higher education.

At the same time, this form of gangster capitalism thrives on and increases the tactics of the punishing state through varied racist policies and practices. These include the ongoing intensification of the criminalization of social issues such as persistent poverty, unemployment, racism, nativism, classroom misbehaviours, the daily routines of Black people, and peaceful protests against police violence.[58] The criminalization of Black people, in particular, is both capacious and deadly, cutting across a range of institutions from the schools to the courts. Drawing on the work of Khalil Gibran Muhammad, Jill Lepore provides an illustration of these daily and systemic acts of violence. She writes:

> Police patrolled Black neighborhoods and arrested Black people disproportionately; prosecutors indicted Black people disproportionately; juries found Black people guilty disproportionately; judges gave Black people disproportionately long sentences; and then, after all this, social scientists, observing the number of Black people in jail, decided that, as a matter of biology, Black people were disproportionately inclined to criminality.[59]

What Lepore gives credence to is that neoliberalism is now married to white supremacy doctrines, which have emerged in solidarity with each other to dissolve not only the bonds of justice and reciprocity but also the ideals, promises, practices, and institutions of an already weakened democracy.

Visualizing Racial Violence in the Age of the Spectacle

Violence no longer hides in the shadows or repressed history of American life. In the age of mobile phone videos, police abuse has emerged with the force of a hurricane. The violence waged almost daily by the police against Black people is now filmed, photographed, uploaded, and circulated almost instantly around the globe. This spectacularized violence waged by the police against Black people has been on full display since the highly publicized killing of Rodney King, Eric Garner, Michael Brown, Walter Scott, Alton Sterling,

Freddie Gray, Philando Castile, and more recently Breonna Taylor, George Floyd, and Duante Wright. Weapons of mass destruction are now used to kill Black children, often caught on film and relegated to an official version of a spectacularized act of violence. One tragic example was the killing of twelve-year-old Tamir Rice for the crime of carrying a toy gun—a killing that was filmed by a bystander. Police violence is more difficult to suppress, given the rise of an image-based culture.

In an age of mass police violence and white supremacy, Black children, the most vulnerable of populations, are added to the list of those viewed as excess, expendable. In a post-George Floyd era, how else to explain the police killings of seventeen-year-old Laquan McDonald, thirteen-year-old Adam Toledo, sixteen-year-old Ma'Khia Bryant, among others. The violent behaviour of the police disproportionality waged against Black people cannot be separated from what I have called the youth–control–criminal complex.[60] The behaviour of young people, especially poor Black and brown youth, is now being criminalized in multiple spheres that extend from the streets to the schools. This is a system deeply rooted in the legacy of slavery and is designed to make Blacks invisible, relegated to punitive institutions that have become havens of social abandonment.

For instance, zero-tolerance policies in schools bear down in a highly discriminatory way on poor minorities who are subjected to harsh disciplinary practices for trivial offences that often result in them being handcuffed, removed from the school, taken to prison, and shepherded into a punitive criminal justice system. In this instance, schools become a feeding portal for the school-to-prison pipeline.[61] Zero-tolerance policies have morphed into forms of cruel and unusual punishment and are best understood as part of a war waged against young people of colour. Moreover, such laws have become vital to the punishing state, which also uses these punitive policies to attack public services, public goods, welfare recipients, and primary institutions crucial to a functioning democracy.

Domestic Space as a Battlefield

Domestic space, whether in the streets or a grocery store, has become a battlefield with tragic results. Heightened fear and paranoia, intensified by a racist culture, has resulted in Black people being arrested or killed for reasons as trivial as selling untaxed cigarettes, minor traffic offences such as jaywalking, failing to signal a lane change, or alleged passing a fake $20 bill at a grocery store.[62] Duante Wright, a twenty-year-old unarmed Black man, was pulled over for a minor technicality, and in an absurd and tragic turn of events, was killed by a police officer who confused her Taser with her gun. Ahmaud Arbery was out jogging near his home when he was chased and run off the road by three men in two pickup trucks who eventually shot and killed him.

African Americans are far more likely to be killed by the police. From a broader historical perspective steeped in the brutality of slavery and the public lynching of Black men, deadly mistakes of this sort happen predominantly to those individuals who are rendered faceless, symbolizing pathology, evil, criminality, mayhem, and danger.[63] According to Aaron Morrison, Blacks are 'far more likely than whites to die at the hands of the police'. He writes:

> Various studies of criminal justice data show that African Americans are far more likely than whites to be pulled over by police and are as much as three times more likely to be searched. Black people are roughly 13 percent of the population, whereas the white population is about 60 percent. Black men were about 2.5 times more likely than white men to be killed by police between 2013 and 2018, according to an August 2019 study published by the National Academy of Sciences. Black women were 1.4 more times likely than white women to be killed by police, according to the same study.[64]

Police in the United States act with impunity in targeted neighbourhoods, public schools, college campuses, hospitals, and almost every other public sphere. Not only do the police view protesters, Black and Indigenous people, and undocumented immigrants as antagonists to be controlled, they are also armed with military-grade weapons. This police militarization is a process that dates as far back as President Lyndon Johnson when he initiated the 1965 Law Enforcement Assistance Act, which supplied local police forces with weapons used in the Vietnam War. The public is now regarded as dangerous and suspect; moreover, as the police are given more military technologies and weapons of war, a culture of punishment, resentment, and racism intensifies as Black people are viewed as a threat to law and order. Unfortunately, employing militarized responses to routine police practices has become normalized. One consequence is that the federal government has continued to arm the police through the Defence Logistics Agency's 1033 Program, which allows the Defence Department to transfer military equipment free of charge to local enforcement agencies.

The scope of the 1033 Program is alarming given that 'Since its inception, more than 11,500 domestic law enforcement agencies have taken part in the 1033 Program, receiving more than $7.4 billion in military equipment.'[65] There is also the federally run 1122 Program, which allows the police to purchase military equipment at the same discounted rate as the federal government. In addition, there is the Homeland Security Grant Program, which provides funds for local police departments to buy military-grade armaments and weapons. The military-grade weapons provided through these federal programmes include armoured vehicles, assault rifles, flashbang grenades launchers, bomb-detonating robots, and night-vision items. Arming the police with more powerful weapons reinforced a culture that taught police officers to learn, think, and act as if they were soldiers engaged in a war. Moreover, as Ryan Welch and Jack Mewhirter wrote in *The Washington Post*, the more militarized and armed the police are, the greater the increase in civilian deaths. As they point out:

> Even controlling for other possible factors in police violence (such as household income, overall and black population, violent-crime levels and drug use), more-militarized law enforcement agencies were associated with more civilians killed each year by police. When a county goes from receiving no military equipment to $2,539,767 worth (the largest

figure that went to one agency in our data), more than twice as many civilians are likely to die in that county the following year.[66]

This arming and militarizing of the police was intensified after the 9/11 attacks and privileged a police ethos defined by 'the use of violent tactics and non-negotiable force over compromise, mediation, and peaceful conflict resolution'.[67] Police brutality is endemic to American history. As Mariame Kaba argues,

> There is not a single era in United States history in which the police were not a force of violence against black people. Policing in the South emerged from the slave patrols in the 1700 and 1800s that caught and returned runaway slaves. In the North, the first municipal police departments in the mid-1800s helped quash labor strikes and riots against the rich. Everywhere, they have suppressed marginalized populations to protect the status quo.[68]

Police brutality cannot be separated from the toxic nature of white supremacy, and in its recent incarnations was transformed into 'the war on crime'. Under President Nixon and every American president after him, the war on crime continued to expand and intensify into a war on Black communities. The call for 'law and order' repeatedly served as a smokescreen for racist and militarized police practices that equated Black behaviour with criminality and authorized the use of force against them.[69] This is the organizing principle of a war mentality adopted by the police throughout the United States.

As the reach of the culture of punishment expanded, its targets included protesters, immigrants, and those individuals and groups marginalized by class, religion, ethnicity, and colour as the other—an enemy. This is the organizing principle of a war mentality adopted by the police throughout the United States in which the behaviour of Black people and other marginalized communities is criminalized.[70] It comes as no surprise that, as one study reports, 'Police kill, on average, 2.8 men per day.... Police homicide risk is higher than suggested by official data. Black and Latino men are at higher risk for death than are White men, and these disparities vary markedly across place.'[71]

A militarized culture breeds violence. It wastes money on the security industries and policing and drains money from the socially necessary programmes that could prevent violence. Violence is both shocking and part of everyday life, especially for those who are poor, Black, Indigenous, trans, disabled, and/or otherwise disenfranchised. In the last few decades, Francesca Mari writes, 'the US has had the highest homicide rate of any high-income country, and according to preliminary data released in March by the FBI, it rose by 25 percent in 2020, when an estimated 20,000 people were murdered—more than fifty-six a day'.[72]

Police brutality became code for a more violent expression of racism that emerged with the rise of neoliberalism in the 1980s.[73] This was especially obvious under the Trump administration as the racist adoption of both white supremacy and a wave of police brutality against Black peoples and undocumented immigrants was presented to the American public as a badge of honour and an act of civic pride.

As the power of the police expanded, along with their unions, social programmes were defunded. These included job programmes, food stamp programmes, health centres, healthcare programmes, and early childhood education. In many states, more money was spent on prisons than on colleges and universities, as documented by Ruth Gilmore in her book *Golden Gulag: Prisons, Surplus, Crisis, and Opposition in Globalizing California*.[74] Targeted cities inhabited mostly by poor Black and brown people were now under siege as the war on poverty morphed into the war on crime. Instead of 'fighting black youth poverty', the new crop of white supremacist politicians fought what Elizabeth Hinton labelled 'fighting black youth crime'.[75]

As Jim Crow re-emerged in more punitive forms, immigration was criminalized, the war on youth of colour intensified, and the culture of punishment began to shape a range of institutions. This was particularly evident as mass incarceration became a defining organizing institution of the narrow, racially sanctioned policies of criminalization in America and, by default, the prison its most notorious welfare agency. America has been in the midst of an imprisonment binge since the 1960s.[76] As Angela Y. Davis writes in *Abolition Democracy*:

> [I]mprisonment is the punitive solution to a while range of social problems that are not being addressed by those social institutions that might help people lead better, more satisfying lives. This is the logic of what has been called the imprisonment binge: Instead of building housing, throw the homeless in prison. Instead of developing the educational system, throw the illiterate in prison. Throw people in prison who lose jobs as the result of de-industrialization, globalization of capital, and the dismantling of the welfare state. Get rid of all of them. Remove these dispensable populations from society. According to this logic the prison becomes a way of disappearing people in the false hope of disappearing the underlying social problems they represent.[77]

The numbers speak for themselves. Historian Khalil Gibran Muhammad makes this clear in his new preface to *The Condemnation of Blackness: Race, Crime, and the Making of Modern Urban America*. He writes:

> By population, by per capita incarceration rates, and by expenditures, the United States exceeds all other nations in how many of its citizens, asylum seekers, and undocumented immigrants are under some form of criminal justice supervision.... The number of African American and Latinx people in American jails and prisons today exceeds the entire populations of some African, Eastern European, and Caribbean countries.[78]

Punishment Creep and the War on Youth

As the culture of violence and punitiveness expanded through the police, prisons, social services, border control and other agencies of repression, the prison increasingly became the model for other institutions such as public schools and social services, making it easier for American society to criminalize more and more forms of behaviour, especially those behaviours associated with Black and brown youth.[79]

Punishment has a long history as a structuring force in the United States, but it has taken on a particularly savage and cruel turn in the age of Trumpism.

For example, the war on youth reached a new level of punitiveness due to a Supreme Court ruling on April 20, 2021. In *Jones v. Mississippi*, 'the court upheld the life-without-parole sentence a Mississippi court imposed on a 15-year-old who stabbed his grandfather to death in a dispute over the boy's girlfriend'.[80] In doing so, the court enabled the justice system to condemn youth to prison for life without a chance for parole. The racist nature of this decision is obvious given the fact that in a country that is 73 per cent white, '70% of all youth sentenced to life without parole are children of colour'.[81]

Punishment, once again, proliferates in tandem with a culture of immediacy, distraction, and disposability. Only in this case, state violence is being used against young people who have barely grown to maturity and are treated as seasoned and incorrigible criminals. Justice Brett M. Kavanaugh, one of the three conservative justices who wrote the verdict, is the product of a privileged white conservative society and culture that has long supported the racist notion that poor Black and brown youth were super predators, a position that gave legitimacy to the police harassment of Black youth enacted under the 'broken windows' approach to racial profiling, which was both popularized and gained notoriety under New York City police commissioner William Bratton and Mayor Rudy Giuliani.

This verdict is part of a war on youth that has been going on since the 1980s. The culture of punishment travels across a range of institutions and spaces and has accelerated since the 1980s. Anne-Marie Cusac characterizes the acceleration of this form of criminogenic lawlessness as a form of 'punishment creep', which has deep roots in the punitive acts of brutality handed out during slavery and the Jim Crow period of American history.[82] Punishment creep moves with increasing intensity and expansion across time and space and includes, among other actions, schools being modelled after prisons, the return of capital punishment, the recently revealed history of the torture of Black suspects by Chicago police, the rise of zero-tolerance policies that disproportionately punish youth of colour, and the use of massive surveillance techniques by the state to monitor and discipline welfare recipients.[83]

Michelle Brown has argued persuasively in her book *The Culture of Punishment* that the rise of police violence, especially against people of colour, indicates that increases in the scale of punishment cannot be abstracted from a parallel rise in both power and apparatuses of punishment—extending from the law enforcement, military services, private security forces, immigration detention centres to intelligence networks and surveillance apparatuses.[84]

Moreover, the culture of punishment increasingly defines both subjects and social problems through the registers of punishment, pain, and violence. How else to explain the actions of the South Carolina Gov. Henry McMaster, who in 2021 signed legislation giving 'people on death row the grotesque choice between a firing squad and electrocution'.[85] Frank Knaack, the Executive Director of the South Carolina's ACLU, stated that capital punishment and the new law 'evolved from lynchings and racial terror, and it has failed to separate its modern capital punishment system from this racist history'.[86]

Gun Pathology and the Politics of Liberal Reforms

The criminalization of Black behaviour is now matched by the criminalization of social problems, made even more fascistic as the social state is hollowed out and the punishing state expands. One register of the punishing state is America's obsession with guns and the normalization of violence. There are more guns in the United States than the entire population of the United States, and during the first year of the pandemic, gun sales have soared. Paul Street points out that

> More than 7,500 Americans have died from gun violence during the first five months and three weeks of 2021, a 23 percent increase over the previous year. Police shootings did not end with the Biden presidency.[87]

As of June 14, 2021, the US experienced 272 mass shootings. Moreover, 'the total number of mass shootings is about 40% higher than at this point in 2020, and about 65% higher than at this point in 2019'.[88]

According to data compiled by CNN and the Gun Violence Archive, on the weekend of June 11–13, 2021, 'from Friday afternoon to Sunday, at least 10 people were killed, and another 50 were injured in nine mass shootings in six states'.[89]

A society saturated with guns legitimizes easy access to weapons that facilitate an endless occurrence of racially motivated mass shootings. The examples are too numerous to cite, but include shootings in Atlanta, Georgia; El Paso, Texas; Charleston, South Carolina; Orlando, Florida; and Gilroy, California. Within the first few months of 2021 'a total of 371 civilians [have] been fatally shot, 71 of whom were Black'.[90] It gets worse. A report by the 'Raza Database Project and UnidosUS… documented the deaths of 32,542 people who have been killed by police since 2000, 60% of whom constitute people of colour, who make up just 40% of the U.S. population'.[91]

As the culture of violence becomes routine, gun violence has accelerated, and the human costs have been most evident with respect to the violence done to women, and the most vulnerable, children.[92] For instance, in the United States, 'on average, one child is shot every hour; over the past decade, roughly 30,000 children and teenagers have been killed by gunfire—recently eclipsing cancer as their second-leading cause of death'.[93] Martin Luther King, Jr, James Baldwin, and Rabbi Abraham Herschel rightly argued that any society that abandons its children and is unresponsive to such a heinous act is indifferent to its own criminal acts and inhabits the dark side of politics. Violence against women, especially during the pandemic, has been called by global leaders 'the human rights issue of our time'. Cheryl Thomas, the head of the organization Global Rights for Women, stated that 'One hundred-thirty-seven women a day are killed by their intimate partners or their family member'.[94] The COVID-19 pandemic both increased the risk of domestic violence against women and at the same time made it more difficult for them to access help. Weak gun laws in states such as

'Missouri, Texas and Utah, [have made] it difficult to seize guns from abusers—even those legally barred from owning firearms.... [another] factor that raises the risk of domestic homicide, studies have found, is the presence of a gun in the home, and gun sales spiked during the pandemic'.[95]

The Plague of Gun Violence and the Failure of Liberal Reforms

Police aggression, the criminalization of social problems, massive inequality, a proliferating culture of lies, and the rise of white nationalism, power, and the easy availability of guns represent a mosaic of factors contributing to a larger culture of violence. This culture of aggression has not gone unnoticed by a public increasingly disturbed by racist violence. The spread of gun violence, police brutality, and mass shootings have galvanized public attention and produced a widespread debate focused largely on defunding the police and 'legislative initiatives for how to better prevent gun violence [that] may lead to substantial state gun policy changes'.[96] Increasingly, the call for reform has challenged the notion that police violence is the result of the behaviour of a few rogue or bad cops and has little to do with the availability of guns in America.

Liberal reforms aimed at violence have done little to restrict the proliferation of guns in American society. A more sustained and louder call for reform against systemic violence has built upon earlier calls for defunding the police, abolishing the police completely, and eliminating prisons. At best, these various critiques have pushed the criticism of police violence into mainstream conversations and produced a newfound public concern with the institution of policing and issues of safety and protection. What has been ignored or under-theorized in the mainstream concern with police brutality is what Keeanga-Yamahtta Taylor, citing Mariame Kaba, refers to as a larger system of violence and punishment with its 'death-making institutions' organized to produce entire systems of 'harassment, violence, and surveillance' whose function is 'to keep oppressive gender and racial hierarchies in place'.[97] While not without merit, such calls for reform, especially those advocated by liberal politicians and the mainstream media, do not go far enough to understand the reach and power of violence in America, especially regarding a politics and culture that fuels racist forms of police brutality. What is missed in these calls for police reform is a broader interpretation of the culture of violence, especially as it has emerged with the melding of neoliberalism with fascist politics defined through the lens of white supremacy and white nationalism. The problem of police violence is part of a broader crisis and must be addressed within a more comprehensive view of racism and class oppression, produced through a neoliberal politics that merges the market-driven imperatives of a criminal economy with a fascist politics defined increasingly by its advocacy of white supremacy and racial cleansing.

Sociologist Alex Vitale rightly insists that calls for change regarding policing should not be about producing 'better' police through technocratic reforms such as the increased use of body cameras and bias training but rather with a 'larger structure of economic life in America'.[98] In the age of neoliberal austerity, the defunding of the welfare state has given way to a range of social problems, extending from the criminalization of homelessness and the relentless erasure of human rights to the mass proliferation of surveillance and the placing of police in the schools—all of which have contributed to the expansion of police power as a way to control people 'disconnected from meaningful participation in the global economy'.[99]

Turning over every social problem for the police to fix is more than an impossible task; it is a failed, if not diversionary, political decision.[100] This is a strategy divorced not only from a history in which the police have been murdering Black people with impunity, but also from the emergence of neoliberal social order in which economic activity is indifferent to social costs. Under such circumstances, state-sanctioned acts of corruption, a politics of state violence, culture of force, and white supremacy have become normalized and removed from the grammar of social and ethical responsibility. Investing in force as the first strategy of police engagement and a widespread acceptance of lawlessness have accelerated and expanded the power of the police. This perfecta of violence constitutes a first principle of policing and is part of what Cornel West calls 'a failed social experiment'.[101] According to West, this experiment is rooted in a form of capitalism that brutalizes people of colour and is built on staggering levels of inequality, a culture of anti-intellectualism, and concentrated economic power that tramples 'on the rights of poor people and minorities decade after decade'.[102]

Police violence has become what Mark LeVine has called in a different context 'a necropolitics of the oppressed'.[103] This can be understood as a form of systemic terror instituted intentionally by different levels of government against populations at home in order to realize economic gains and achieve political benefits through practices that range from assassination, extortion, incarceration, violence, and intimidation or coercion of a civilian population.[104] Some of the more notorious racist expressions of such terror include the assassination of Black Panther Party leader Fred Hampton by the Chicago Police Department on December 4, 1969; the MOVE bombing by the Philadelphia Police Department in 1985; the existence of COINTELPRO, an illegal counter-intelligence programme designed to harass anti-war and Black resistance fighters in the 1960s and 1970s; the use of extortion by the local police and courts practiced on the largely poor Black residents of Ferguson; and the more publicized killings of Ahmaud Arbery, Breonna Taylor, and George Floyd by the police, to name just a few instances of acute state violence. Domestic terrorism is informed both by the scale of increased militarism, violence at the level of everyday life, and the increase in technologies of surveillance, arrests, convictions, and privatized prisons. In our digitally mediated world, marginalized populations are tracked, reduced to data, and mapped onto different avenues of disposability.

The discourse of criminality and control has produced a slew of law enforcement measures that targeted urban schools, social services, and public housing, all of which became terrains of surveillance and fodder for the expansion of the punishment state.[105] At work here is also a move away from the war on poverty to a war on the poor. As welfare programmes were defunded, a culture of punishment morphed into a war on drugs that became synonymous with a generalized war youth. According to Vitale, police reform must move from talk about police accountability to political accountability to address police violence as part of a broader set of economic and political issues. He writes:

> the decision to turn social problems over to the police is a political decision (as is the creation of the social problems in the first place). Responding to this deeply entrenched form of governance requires a new politics. We just cannot fix policing with a set of superficial, technocratic reforms, because they don't address the way the most basic needs of people have themselves been defunded, creating the 'crime' that must be policed in the first place.... This is not about just getting the police out of the homelessness and mental health business: this is about a radical rethink about how safety is produced.[106]

The liberal call for reforming the police largely fails to address what Zach Beauchamp calls police culture, or the tenets of police ideology, which are shared by police departments throughout the United States. Police ideology is part of the hidden register of police culture, and while it is not taught overtly in police academies, it is often part of a silent rite of passage that is passed down to each generation of police officers and offers 'a deeply disturbing picture of the internal culture of policing', which Beauchamp describes as follows:

> The tenets of police ideology are not codified or written down but are nonetheless widely shared in departments around the country. The ideology holds that the world is a profoundly dangerous place: Officers are conditioned to see themselves as constantly in danger and that the only way to guarantee survival is to dominate the citizens they're supposed to protect. The police believe they're alone in this fight; police ideology holds that officers are under siege by criminals and are not understood or respected by the broader citizenry. These beliefs, combined with widely held racial stereotypes, push officers toward violent and racist behavior during intense and stressful street interactions.[107]

What is often not evident to the public and liberals is that this is an armed culture that trains the police to be an occupying army, views Black communities as a threatening population, and privileges the use of violence as a privileged response to dealing with targeted Black communities.[108] This approach to policing cannot be separated from a broader neoliberal fascist culture in which whiteness becomes both a badge of solidarity and is shaped by larger forces of structural racism. It is no accident that 'the officer corps remains overwhelmingly white, male, and straight [and] that police heavily favor Republicans'.[109] The unabashed transformation of the Republican Party into a party of white supremacists after Trump lost the presidential election to Joe Biden points to a racist system in which the targeting of Black populations has the potential to get worse rather than better in the future.

The legacy of police violence runs deep in American history and is reinforced by a culture of violence that extends far beyond the police. The United States is the major arms dealer in the United States, rings the globe with its 800 military bases, and is the largest nuclear power.[110] Moreover, it has used, trained, and exported its police tactics to numerous right-wing countries across the globe. Not only were the police militarized in the United States, but they also became a model counter-insurgency force whose ideology and methods were exported abroad, and, as Jill Lepore observes, helped to provide:

> assistance to the police in at least fifty-two countries, and training to officers from nearly eighty, for the purpose of counter-insurgency—the suppression of an anticipated revolution, that collection of private nightmares [that] contributed 'the international dimension to the Administration's War on Crime.' Counterinsurgency boomeranged, and came back to the United States, as policing.[111]

Violence Beyond Policing

Policing cannot be understood outside of the history of criminogenic culture and a racist punishing state marked by both staggering inequities in wealth, income, and power, as well as a collective mindset in which those considered non-white are considered less than human, undeserving of human rights, and viewed as disposable.[112] The journalist Robert C. Koehler rightly argues that underlying both the larger culture and the culture of policing is a deeply ingrained white supremacy marked by a system of growing inequalities in which economic rights do not match political and individual rights. Koehler writes:

> it is racism that is the trigger that disproportionately escalates police encounters with people of colour. However, even more sadly, it is systemic racism that normalizes it, or legitimates it, making it largely acceptable to white American eyes and consciences. For it is not only the police who have this problem, but our entire society.[113]

Under gangster capitalism, the market was unprepared to deal with the crisis caused by the virus. As Alfredo Saad-Filho has argued, the failure of neoliberalism in the face of a widespread catastrophe was predictable. He writes 'The pandemic hit after four decades of neoliberalism had depleted state capacities in the name of the "superior efficiency" of the market, fostered deindustrialization through the "globalization" of production, and built fragile financial structures secured only by the state, all in the name of short-term profitability.'[114] The virus made clear that the market's celebration of austerity and financialization failed to either contain the virus or the rising infections and deaths produced by it. Under the collapse of its claim that state had no role to play in enriching the common good, it aligned itself openly with the fascist impulses that had always been part of its project, however hidden.

As I argue throughout this book, inequality is the plague neoliberal capitalism contributes to the world. In the midst of the pandemic, economic conditions have worsened, along with a deepening of the climate crisis while 'pushing tens of millions more people into hunger. Mass unemployment and severely disrupted food production have led to a 40 per cent surge in global food prices—the highest rise in over a decade.'[115] An Oxfam report, *The Hunger Virus Multiplies*, 'says that as many as 11 people are likely dying of hunger and malnutrition each minute. This is more than the current global death rate of COVID-19, which is around seven people per minute'.[116] Oxfam's Executive Director Gabriela Bucher states: 'Today, unrelenting conflict on top of the COVID-19 economic fallout, and a worsening climate crisis, has pushed more than 520,000 people to the brink of starvation.'[117]

As neoliberalism failed to deliver on its promises of upward social and economic mobility, it shifted attention for its broken social experiment to attacks on immigrants, Blacks, and other populations deemed unworthy, inferior, and a threat to white people. In doing so, gangster capitalism has become armed, spiralling into a form of authoritarianism that has merged the savagery of market despotism with the rancid ideology of white supremacy. Cornel West is right in arguing that neoliberal capitalism, with its emphasis on materialism, racism, and harshness 'allows for endemic inequality and a culture of greed and consumerism that [has trampled] on the rights and dignity of poor people and minorities decade after decade'.[118]

The American nightmare that has descended upon the United States points to a crisis of power, agency, equality, community, education, and hope. The effects of the neoliberalism's death-dealing machinery are everywhere, and police abuse is only one thread of this criminogenic social formation. The United States is suffering through many crises—medical, political, economic, and ideological—although it is not enough to suggest its current malaise is merely about political incompetence, hubris, or the failure to learn. Forces much darker now shape American identity. Massive collective resistance to the long legacy of racism in the aftermath of the murder of George Floyd and police violence that has become omnipresent visually has re-energized a backlash by a Republican Party and Trump's supporters who now embrace, even more aggressively, a white nationalist ideology and politics. The calls for social justice and racial equality have given birth once again to state repression, censorship in schools, and voter suppression policies led by politicians who believe that only whites should have the rights that give a democracy any substance.

Rather than fade into the past or disappear beneath the propaganda techniques of right-wing disimagination machines, massive inequalities in wealth and power, inadequate health care, large-scale rootlessness, fear-mongering, social atomization, racially segregated schools, voter suppression, and the politics of disposability are alive and well.[119] As I have stressed repeatedly, the politics of Anglo-Saxon white nationalism and repression are now unabashedly reproduced and defended by a Republican Party that has become the overt symbol of white supremacy, economic ruthlessness, and manufactured ignorance.

Widespread corruption is now matched by a climate of fear and a willingness on the part of Trump's political allies to inflict violence on undesirable members of the public along with anyone voicing criticism or dissent. The scaffold of resistance now faces a malignant fascist politics growing across the globe. Disturbing revelations no longer expand the reach of justice. They now set in motion machineries of repression, falsehoods, and conspiracy theories. Fascist politics in the United States has been accelerated and expanded, most evident during Trump's reign in office and after his defeat, especially with the power of the Republican Party in the Congress and in many state legislatures. If the systemic violence and deformations of the law deny Black communities a claim to human rights, citizenship, and dignity are to be challenged, it is important to understand how neoliberal fascism becomes a machinery of dread, tearing apart the social fabric while cancelling the future. As a regime of ideology, neoliberal fascism wages a political and pedagogical war against the conditions that make thinking, agency, the search for truth, and informed judgement possible.

The heart of American violence does not reside merely in the culture and practice of policing in America, or for that matter in its prison-industrial complex. Its centre of gravity is more comprehensive and is part of a broader crisis that extends from the threat of nuclear war and ecological devastation to the rise of authoritarian states and the human suffering caused by the staggering concentrations of wealth in the hands of a global financial elite. The roots of these multilayered and intersecting crises lie elsewhere in a new political and social formation that constitutes a racialized criminal economy that has embraced greed, violence, disposability, denial, and racial cleansing as governing principles of the entire social order. This is the rule of capital on speed. It is also an extermination machine rooted in a vapid nihilism that fuels the celebration of materialism and social atomization with a belief in unshakable loyalty, purification through violence, and a cult of heroism.

It is crucial to understand how the threads of racial violence in its broader historical context, comprehensive connections, and multidimensional layers shape capitalism in its totality to produce what David Theo Goldberg calls a machinery of proliferating dread.[120] It's no wonder that the same activists who are working to defund the police are also part of a collective movement to bring an end to neoliberal capitalism. Mariame Kaba writes:

> People like me who want to abolish prisons and police, however, have a vision of a different society, built on cooperation instead of individualism, on mutual aid instead of self-preservation. What would the country look like if it had billions of extra dollars to spend on housing, food, and education for all? This change in society wouldn't happen immediately, but the protests show that many people are ready to embrace a different vision of safety and justice.[121]

The challenge that Kaba and other abolitionists are posing does not advocate for liberal reforms. Their call is to advance a radical restructuring of society. Fundamental to their call for social change is that such a task be understood as both political and educational. This necessitates the development of political and pedagogical struggles that take seriously the need to rethink the attack on the public imagination and attack on critical agency, identity, and everyday life. Also at stake is the need to identify and reclaim those institutions, such as schools, that are necessary to produce and connect an educated public to the struggle for a substantive and radical democracy. The current crisis cannot be faced through limited calls for police reforms. It demands a more comprehensive view not only of oppression and the forces through which it is produced, legitimated, and normalized but also of political struggle itself.

Voter Suppression and the Plague of White Supremacy

It is worth remembering that neoliberal fascism has taken a more dangerous turn in the aftermath of Trump's defeat. While neoliberalism has since the 1980s persistently relied on the punishing state and criminalizing of social problems as a response to poverty and inequality, it took a more perilous turn during and in the aftermath of the Trump presidency. Not only did Trump and the Republican Party play the race card with a vengeance, but they have also resurrected and re-energized the language of Jim Crow. In part, this took place by dropping any pretence to democracy in their affirmation of authoritarian politics and the embrace of white supremacy. This was evident in their weaponizing of identity, support for a range of discriminatory policies of exclusion, the construction of a wall that became a resurgent symbol of nativism, and their internment of children separated from their undocumented parents at the southern border. The rush to construct a home-grown form of fascist politics was also clear in the era of Trumpism in the passing of a barrage of voter suppression laws introduced in Republican-controlled state legislatures, all based on baseless claims of voter fraud. Voter suppression has become the new currency of fascist politics and is matched only by the threats by the Republican Party to control how votes are counted and legitimated. Some states such as Georgia, Texas, and Florida have enacted them into law. As of April 1, 2021, 361 bills had been put into play in 47 states. The Georgia and Florida bills either restrict or prohibit mobile drop boxes and with respect to Georgia, the bill:

> eliminates weekend voting days, most notably Sundays, when Black churches hold 'Souls to the Polls' voting drives, restricts the use of ballot drop boxes, prevents counties from accepting nonprofit grants to improve their elections, adds new voter ID requirements for voting by mail, gives local election officials less time to send out mail-in ballots and voters less time to return them, 'and even makes it a crime to distribute food and water to voters waiting in line.[122]

What we are witnessing here is not only a return of another ideological and political register of white supremacy but the use of corporate power and dark money to destroy the last remnants of democracy. For example, *Public Citizen* claims that over $50 million has been spent since 2015 to undermine voting rights; during the 2020 election cycle, $22 million went to legislators/lawmakers who support voter suppression bills. *Public Citizen* also notes that 'Among the Fortune 100, 81 companies have contributed to these lawmakers, giving a combined total of $7.7 million. Among the Fortune 500, 45 percent of companies have contributed to these lawmakers, giving a combined total of $12.8 million.'[123] The companies that have given the most to these white supremacist efforts include: 'AT&T [which] has given $811,000. AT&T is followed by Altria/Philip Morris ($679,000), Comcast ($440,000), UnitedHealth Group ($411,000), Walmart ($377,000), State Farm (315,000) and Pfizer ($308,000). More than 60 corporations have contributed more than $100,000.'[124] Such efforts do more than weaponize the lie that the American presidential election was stolen; they also represent an attempt to impose policies that amount to a form of racial cleansing, both of which echo an earlier legacy of slavery and Jim Crow policies in the United States and the fascist genocidal politics that emerged in Europe in the 1920s and 1930s.

In addition, conservative groups such as the Heritage Foundation, Wallbuilders, and the Koch-backed American Legislative Exchange Council are helping right-wing legislators to craft model voter suppression bills.[125] Voter suppression laws represent both an expression of an updated form of Jim Crow and must be seen as part of a neoliberal fascist project intent on eradicating the foundations of citizenship, expanding the punishing state, waging war on truth, elevating ignorance over reason, and pandering to white supremacists and right-wing extremists, while merging elements of twentieth-century fascism and neoliberal rationality.

The United States has entered a period marked by the production of a neoliberal rationality, which includes normalizing the notion that the market is a template for all social conditions, asserting that democracy and capitalism are synonymous, normalizing ideologies of race/culture supremacy, and legitimating the use of state-sponsored violence to repress dissent and those populations considered disposable. It should be clear that fascism thrives in moments of severe capitalist crisis. Moreover, the main reason for its return in the present moment of plagues and pandemics cannot be removed from the failure of neoliberalism 'to offer any real hope to segments of the population facing increasing inequality and a downward spiral of social and economic mobility'.[126] As the social contract withers, civic culture disappears, and any notion of meaningful and democratic citizenship is eroded, neoliberalism reveals its fascist alignments by tapping into deep-rooted fears, uncertainties, and racialized popular anger.

Neoliberal fascism attempts to legitimate and manufacture a culture of fear, anxiety, and hatred. It is a pedagogy rooted in racism and bigotry and is used to divert public attention away from the various crisis of capitalism marked by needless deaths caused by a health crisis during the pandemic and 'a downward spiral of social and economic inequality'.[127] Senator Raphael Warnock is right in arguing that voter suppression laws are resuscitating a full-fledged assault on voting rights 'unlike anything we've ever seen since the Jim Crow era. This is Jim Crow in new clothes'.[128] This updated version of Jim Crow is waged through the power of political policies and right-wing disimagination machines—it diverts, represses, excludes, and creates the subjective conditions for advancing the cause of a racialized authoritarianism. Jim Crow also hides under the liberal call for unity, and a refusal to translate political responsibility into moral responsibility. How else to explain Democratic Senator of West Virginia Joe Manchin's echoing of Republican Party talking points about voter rights bills and support for the filibuster. Manchin has refused to support the For The People Act, a bill that would protect the nation's voting rights, because it would destroy bipartisan legislation, as if it existed in the current politically hyper-polarized climate.

Manchin enacts a soft version of white supremacy hiding behind the false call for political unity across party lines, despite the current reality of political gridlock. Manchin wants the Democrats and Republicans to come together at a time when the Republican Party only believes in a notion of unity organized around a full-fledged attack on civil rights and democracy itself. A New York Democratic Congressman, Mondaire Jones, was right in stating that Joe Manchin's position on voting rights 'might be titled, "Why I'll vote to preserve Jim Crow"'.[129] Manchin's claim that passing a voting rights bill will only 'destroy the weakening binds of our democracy' does more than ring hollow; it reaffirms the long legacy of Jim Crow and the white nationalists' hatred of Black people.[130] This is an insult to the thousands of Americans who died on the battlefields of the Civil War, fought for freedom in two world wars, and gave their lives to expand civil rights and social justice.

It is one thing to condemn Manchin for his unholy alliance with a party that is resurrecting the legacy of Jim Crow, it is another thing for him to be in alliance with a party that thrives on ignorance, lies, and white supremacy. Manchin appears blind in his support for a party that has a weak connection with reality, apparent in the fact that 63 per cent of Republicans claim the election was stolen from Trump along with '23 percent [who] believe that the world is controlled by Satan-worshipping pedophiles'.[131] Another 25 per cent support the inane and outlandish claims of QAnon, with its 'imaginary global syndicate of Satan-worshipping child traffickers'.[132]

Voter suppression laws breathe new life into white supremacy and fit nicely into the racist argument that whites are under siege by people of colour who are attempting to dethrone and replace them. In this case, such laws, along with an ongoing attack on equality and social justice, are defended as justifiable measures to protect whites from the 'contaminating' influence of immigrants, Black people, and others considered unworthy of occupying and participating in the public sphere and democratic process. Voter suppression laws are defended as legitimate attempts to provide proof of 'real Americans', dog whistle policies for defining people of colour as 'counterfeit citizens'.[133]

Voter suppression laws are an updated version of 'racial capitalism', which as James Baldwin pointed out, are designed to make Black people hate themselves, to enact their disappearance, and to turn democracy into a 'universal obscenity'.[134] In response, Baldwin calls for a new consciousness, one that refuses silence, which is not only 'criminal but suicidal'.[135] C. Wright Mills, a counterpart of Baldwin, reads the crisis of democracy as part of the crisis of agency, one that is never posed as a problem to solve, but is essential in reimagining for bridging the gap between critical thinking and informed action.[136] What both believed was that no structural or ideological change would take place without making education vital to politics.

The collapse of historical agents of change and the lack of a unified mass movement to fight the current era of police violence, neoliberal savagery, persistent racism, and rise white supremacy must be addressed as both a political and education problem. The time has come to build connections among oppressed groups, social movements, youth groups, and labour unions to imagine and make possible a future beyond neoliberalism capitalism. The urgency of the moment demands not only the necessity to question the conditions that have moved America into a fascist politics, but also to embrace the power of consciousness and the possibility of change. Theodor Adorno was right in insisting that 'we must educate people toward the idea that they are more than what simply exists. Otherwise, education is altogether complete nonsense'.[137] Without self-reflection, practice no longer qualifies either the test of truth or as a crucial condition for social change. The time has come to do both.

3

Trumpism and its Afterlife

It was a bright cold day in April, and the clocks were striking thirteen.

—George Orwell

The storming of the US Capitol in Washington, DC by a mob of neo-Nazis, white supremacists, and other right-wing extremists provided yet another example that the United States no longer lives in the shadow of authoritarianism and has tipped over into the abyss. Stoking the crowd's sense of resentment and thirst for destruction, Trump gave an incendiary speech before the insurrection in which he once again falsely claimed that the presidential election was rigged and told the rowdy crowd 'you'll never take back our country with weakness. You have to show strength, and you have to be strong'.[1] He told his supporters, 'We fight like hell and if you don't fight like hell, you're not going to have a country anymore', a refrain that did not directly urge his followers to be violent but was uttered against past comments in which he promoted or encouraged violence among his followers.[2] Trump's language of hate and inciting violence has a long history that extends from his 2015 primary run to the end of his term as president.[3] However, Trump was not alone in creating a pretext for such violence. Prior to the assault on the Capitol, the right-wing media, especially 'Parler, Twitter, TikTok, and the pro-Trump message board The Donald', posted messages incessantly 'calling for violence—including the arrest and execution of politicians'.[4]

His inflammatory rhetoric of lies and call for retaliation was exacerbated further by several Republican politicians who actively promoted conspiracy theories and dangerous propaganda in order to invalidate the Biden election, some of whom appeared at a rally just before the invasion of the Capitol and used inflammatory language to further incite the crowd. For instance, Trump's discredited and debarred lawyer, Rudy Giuliani, told the crowd: 'If we're wrong, we will be made fools of. But if we're right, a lot of them will go to jail. So, let's have trial by combat.'[5] Senator Josh Hawley, in a display of shameful political opportunism, greeted the crowd of neo-Nazis, Confederacy defenders, and racist agitators with a raised fist as they marched on the Capitol. Hawley's gesture of resistance stood as a symbol of what followed the insurrection.

Along with his fellow Republican Party members, Hawley not only refused to investigate the insurrectionist attack, but also supported Trump's version of the 'Stop the Steal' big lie, while leading the charge of anti-democratic forces attempting to resurrect the spirit of the Confederacy with its history of voter suppression laws, public lynchings, robed Klansmen, and Jim Crow laws. Hawley, Ted Cruz, and their band of followers are doing more than protesting the peaceful transfer of power and the consent of the governed; they are also putting in place a white supremacist ideology that represents one of the most destructive pathologies and sicknesses of our times. The United States is at war with itself. This is a war waged by the Republican Party that has adopted the politics and doctrines of white supremacy. The danger it poses to American democracy is as serious as anything the United States has faced since the Civil War.

Under Trump's rule, the purging of truth, the promotion of ignorance, and the thirst for violence took on a more toxic direction. Both during and after Trump's presidency, the power of his zombie ideas seeped into the culture like a deadly virus. The persistence of these ideas does not bode well for the future of American democracy. Since leaving office, he has continued to spread conspiracy theories; he still falsely claimed that he won the 2020 election and has repeatedly insisted that he would be 'reinstated' as POTUS by August 2021.[6] He lied about the seriousness of the coronavirus and has stated that children should not be vaccinated because they are rarely affected by the virus. In short, he is an ignorant, stunted man-child who both undermines democracy and makes a wasteland of the truth. He is also a threat to public health and will continue to be.

Within the last few years, his destructive anti-democratic ideology—popularly known as Trumpism—has encouraged violence waged against immigrants, Black and brown people, and the poor. It also enabled and initiated the violence of a right-wing mob that attacked the police, rampaged through the Capitol, and occupied the House and Senate chambers. Trump not only initiated a call for a demonstration against the Capitol among his supporters, but he also brought to the event a history of encouraging his supporters to express themselves through violence.[7]

What Trump and the mob shared was their hatred of democracy, however fragile, and the discredited belief that the election was stolen. In the aftermath of the mob violence, Trump sent out a series of tweets supporting the actions of the violent mob, only to be later removed by Twitter.[8] At the same time, the acts of domestic terrorism that took place on January 6 were about more than Trump's lies and his use of language in the service of violence.[9] It was also about the emergence of a new political formation called Trumpism, with its mix of white supremacy, voter suppression, market fundamentalism, and unabashed authoritarianism.

Trump's presidency and its aftermath represented a frontal attack on civic literacy, racial justice, and democratic values. Trumpism in its various formations gave Americans, mostly white evangelical Christians, the petit-bourgeois, and affluent groups from the suburbs free rein 'to openly embrace and advance authoritarian and white nationalist values'.[10] Trumpism's anti-communism and incessant attacks on socialism also appealed to a sizeable number of deeply conservative Latinos. Moreover, Trump played on the legitimate resentment of rural voters towards a society in which there are 'huge swaths of the rural U.S. with no hospitals and no grocery stores [and] left many Americans with limited access to essential health care and fresh food'.[11]

Culture, with its underlying power to shape identity, in this instance, was a mechanism for destroying language and the mental and moral bearings that enabled people to relate self-reflectively to themselves, others, and the larger world. Manufactured ignorance became a tool of power and manipulation that produced and legitimated a form of civic illiteracy that both infantilized and depoliticized many of Trump's followers. As a form of wilful ignorance, people found in Trump a reason to embrace their own racism and to gloat over their pride in being politically incorrect. Ignorance turned a racial firestorm into a celebration for the bigoted. Trumpism represents a new form of fascism in which older elements of a fascist past are recycled, modified, and updated. The famed historian of fascism, Robert O. Paxton, has argued that Trump is not an authoritarian in the manner of Berlusconi. Rather, he is closer to a fascist past than most historians and critical intellectuals are willing to admit and deserves the fascist label. He writes:

> I resisted for a long time applying the fascist label to Donald J. Trump. He did indeed display some telltale signs. In 2016, a newsreel clip of Trump's plane taxiing up to a hangar where cheering supporters awaited reminded me eerily of Adolf Hitler's electoral campaign in Germany in July 1932, the first airborne campaign in history, where the arrival of the Führer's plane electrified the crowd. Once the rally began, with Hitler and Mussolini, Trump mastered the art of back-and-forth exchanges with his enraptured listeners. There was the threat of physical violence ('lock her up!'), sometimes leading to the forceful ejection of hecklers. The Proud Boys stood in convincingly for Hitler's Storm Troopers and Mussolini's squadristi. The MAGA hats even provided a bit of uniform. The 'America First' message and the leader's arrogant swagger fit the fascist model. Trump's incitement of the invasion of the Capitol on January 6, 2020, removes my objection to the fascist label.... His open encouragement of civic violence to overturn an election crosses a red line.[12]

Another testimony referencing Trumpism's as a form of fascist politic demonstrated in the systemic lying that was not only at the heart of Hitler's regime but key to Trump's rise to power and the development of his social base, although the latter expressed itself in a different context and through a unique set of cultural apparatuses. The Yale historian, Timothy Snyder, is instructive on this issue.

> Post-truth is pre-fascism, and Trump has been our post-truth president. When we give up on truth, we concede power to those with the wealth and charisma to create spectacle in its place. Without agreement about some basic facts, citizens cannot form the civil society that would allow them to defend themselves. If we lose the institutions that produce facts that are pertinent to us, then we tend to wallow in attractive abstractions and fictions. Truth defends itself particularly poorly when there is not very much of it around, and the era of Trump… is one of the decline of local news. Social media is no substitute: It supercharges the mental habits by which we seek emotional stimulation and comfort, which means losing the distinction between what feels true and what actually is true.[13]

It has become clear that Trumpism will have a long afterlife despite Trump having left the White House. As Samuel Farber observes, Trump may have left the White House, 'But the conditions that gave rise to his brand of noxious politics aren't going away anytime soon.'[14] Trump came to power on the failure of the Washington elite and establishment to address the inequities caused by neoliberalism and systemic racism. Globalization, the stagnation of wages for workers, persistent racism, and the plague of Wall Street give resonance to Trump's economic populism and white nationalist ideology. As John Feffer points out, what was missed by his followers was that Trump's concerns for the grievances of the economic disadvantaged was simply a ploy to advance 'the power of the wealthy elite and of white privilege. In the process, legitimate economic grievance became entangled with anti-immigrant, anti-foreigner, and blatant racist rhetoric.'[15] What was also missed, especially by many commentating on Trump's rise to power was the power of his appeal to racism among many affluent whites, not just an alleged conned working class.

Trading on a politics of racial resentment, and economy of decline, his ability to conceal his ties to big capital, and his alleged image as an outsider, Trumpism emerged as a 'political mood and state of mind, and... movement' with a social base that 'is more likely to endure than Trump himself'.[16] Kenny Stancil, a writer for *Common Dreams*, points out that 'One indication of the blind loyalty of Trump's base can be seen in the fact that "Among Republican voters, 45% approve of the storming of Capitol, 30% think the perpetrators are 'patriots', 52% think Biden is at least partly to blame for it, and 85% think it would be inappropriate to remove Trump from office after this".'[17]

Trump's diverse mob of neo-Nazis, white supremacists, and die-hard white Christian followers had been building for years in the dark recesses of conspiracy theories, white rage, the backlash to the Civil Rights and Black Power movements of the sixties, and a hatred of those critics denounced as un-American or treasonous.[18] President-elect Biden called the January 6 attack an insurrection, making it clear that Trump had poured petrol on a fire through his language of denial and incitement, particularly evident in the speech he gave before the mob stormed the Capitol building. This was Trumpism in full bloom, with all its ignorance, racial hatred, and penchant for lawlessness on full display.

Trump's alignment with extremist groups, ethically comatose far-right lawyers, and his use of executive power to use the Department of Justice as his personal law firm in order to overthrow the election results points to a fascist politics that begins with language, pushes unlawful policies, and ends with violence. The mob violence aimed at shutting down the counting of electoral ballots was reminiscent of the thugs that roamed the streets of Germany in the 1930s attempting to brutalize dissenters and those considered disposable in the deranged Nazi notion of racial and political cleansing. Trump has unleashed his fascist impulses consistently through the language of meanness and divisiveness aided by the right-wing media such as Fox News, Breitbart, and others. Under the Trump administration, ignorance has turned lethal. Moreover, as David Theo Goldberg has pointed out, 'politics today is nothing short of a civil war' marked by divisions and disunity in which life for most of the inhabitants of the United States becomes both unbearable and dangerous.[19]

This is not surprising given Trump's support and display of affection (We love you) and allegiance to an array of neo-fascists and right-wing extremists, many of whom marched on the Capitol building.[20] The acts of domestic terrorism on display in the storming of the Capitol reach far beyond the toxic personal politics, incompetency, and corruption of Trump himself. Such violence has a long history in the US and has been normalized under the aegis of Trumpism as a right-wing populist movement, which Trump brought to the surface of American politics as a badge of honour.

What is necessary to comprehend is that the violence behind the storming of the Capitol did not begin with the march by right-wing fanatics and white supremacists; it erupted more openly with Trump in 2016 when he seized upon and manipulated the fears of anxiety ridden whites and white supremacists who imagined themselves as under siege and oppressed outsiders. For four years, he incited violence and spewed despicable racist sewage as a vehicle to inspire and energize his white supremacists and fascist followers. The endpoint of his inflammatory lies, racist remarks, and conspiracy theories was the attack on the Capitol police and the setting up of a noose attached to a wooden beam across from the Capitol.[21]

Every era produces a language and cultural markers that offer insights into its politics, values, and vision of the past, present, and future. This is especially true regarding the economic, public, and cultural influence of the Trump presidency and mode of governance. Trumpism is not limited to the personal behaviour of Donald Trump. It refers less to a person than to a dangerous movement and social base and operates as a social and political pathology whose endpoint is the destruction of democracy itself. Equating Trump and Trumpism personalizes politics and disconnects the neoliberal fascist ideology Trump has endorsed from the conditions that produced it and the diverse politicians, media apparatuses, and political movements that are reproducing it.

As a new cultural and political construct, Trumpism merges a ruthless capitalist rationality, widening inequality, and a commitment to white supremacy. These forces have deep historical roots in the United States. However, what is distinctive is that they have congealed into a unique political and cultural formation under the Trump regime marked by an emotively charged, spectacularized, and updated form of authoritarianism that echoes elements of a fascist past. In the current historical moment, Trumpism has intensified and quickened the dark forces of hate, racism, ultra-nationalism, and white supremacy. Trump was the last president of the Confederacy, resurrecting the dark, violent history of the past to merge American exceptionalism and white supremacy.[22] As William Barber II, Liz Theoharis, Timothy B. Tyson, and Cornel West have argued, white supremacy has once again turned deadly and has put democracy on trial. They write:

> Even now, the ancient lie of white supremacy remains lethal. It has left millions of African-American children impoverished in resegregated and deindustrialized cities. It embraces high-poverty, racially isolated schools that imperil our children—and our future. It shoots first and dodges questions later. 'Not everything that is faced can be changed,' James Baldwin instructs, 'but nothing can be changed until it is faced.'[23]

Trump merged the mobilizing passions of an updated fascist politics with the financial institutions and regressive values of a cruel and savage capitalism to undermine democratic institutions and values. Trump's presidency had its roots in the long-standing history of economic inequality, racial injustice, nativism, and a war on the social state, while Trumpism as a social movement merged from the shadows of history, revealing fascist elements that moved from the margins to the centres of power.

At the heart of Trumpism is a shocking political and ideological system of repression created by a hateful, heartless, and ethically vacuous president who, as Masha Gessen argues, 'taught Americans that no one will take care of us, our parents, and our children, because our lives are worthless, disposable... that this country is a dangerous place [and that] we are forever on the brink of disaster and that no one will protect us, whether from illness or economic hardship.'[24] Trumpism is a dystopian nightmare on steroids, which has accelerated a culture of fear while using a variety of tools of repression—ranging from mass incarceration, surveillance, and police brutality to a full-fledged attack on those who would bring reality into play and hold power accountable. Trumpism's modus operandi is to enforce a world view in which a flight from social justice and ethical responsibility become the order of the day.

Trumpism is an ongoing historical and political interlude dominated by a language of forgetting, moral irresponsibility, and the spectacle of malice and violence. Relying upon the insights of the Italian Marxist Antonio Gramsci, Trumpism occupies the interregnum between 'the old world [which] is dying, and [a] new world [struggling] to be born'.[25] Trumpism is the third space between the old and the new in which 'a great variety of morbid symptoms appear'. While it is not clear what is being born, it is obvious that the struggle between the forces of authoritarianism and new modes of collective resistance have taken on a new urgency. That we now live in a time of monsters suggests such symptoms are upon us. This was especially true as Trump was about to leave office. He defended the legacy of the Confederacy, spewed lies about the legitimacy of a free and fair presidential election, which he lost, proceeded to pardon a host of war criminals, corrupt politicians, loyalists, and personal friends, and he threatened to use martial law to force a new election.[26]

As journalist Jennifer Evans observes, Trump may have lost the election, 'but Trumpism is alive and well, along with the conditions that propelled him to power in the first place. At best, the post-election future might be one of regrouping and rebuilding; at worst, there will be more challenges to legal norms and truths by the outgoing president and the Republican Party.'[27] As the enemy of democracy, Trumpism is a mix of a capacious authoritarian ideology, a right-wing propaganda machine, and a fascist ethos. At its worse, it is a mix of racial cleansing and an attempt to disempower people of colour by defining them as counterfeit citizens. Its power and influence far exceed Trump's presidency, and it has not come to an end with the election of Biden. In fact, the current Republican Party efforts in numerous red states to pass voter suppression laws, their increasing attacks on critical education, and their refusal to denounce the big steal lie, testify that Trumpism is more powerful than ever. Moreover, Trump's quislings are not mounting a campaign in numerous states to give more power to partisan officials to overturn an election that does not go their way. This is a lie that continues to define the Republican Party in spite of the fact that even Trump's utterly conservative former Attorney General, William Barr, admitted that Trump's claim of election fraud 'was all bullshit'.[28]

In its afterlife, this baseless claim of a stolen election in 2020 will continue to sabotage democracy in the name of minority rule, and its only endpoint is the tyranny of authoritarianism. As an anti-democratic ethos, it has opened a political chasm in which any attempt to unify the nation appears almost impossible. Trump's relentless politics of divisiveness is a toxic platform for inciting violence, affirming a culture of viciousness, and promoting a politics of exclusion and racial cleansing.

Trump's ongoing penchant for violence is obvious in the urging of his right-wing followers to engage in 'wild' protests when they gathered on January 6 in Washington, D, the day Congress was due to certify President-elect Joe Biden's electoral college victory.[29] Trump's extremist supporters, like the Proud Boys, not only needed someone to blame for their seething resentment of immigrants and Black and brown people, but they also valued violence as the only cathartic remedy available to provide their extremists' fantasies any vestige of resolve, emotional relief, and gratification. There was more at work here than a long-standing assault on the truth, reality, and democracy. There was also an embrace of the more dangerous elements of a fascist politics with its regressive authoritarian impulses and its embrace of politics as an extension of war, and violence as the ultimate register of battle in which there are only winners and losers. Trumpism makes evident that the dark forces of barbarism are no longer hiding in the dark; if they are to be resisted, there is a need for a new language, politics, and a sense of collective struggle.

Trumpism is a cancer whose roots have long infected the body politic. In the current age of brutality, it symbolizes governance without empathy or compassion, and dismisses government as a public good. As is largely recognized, Trumpism exhibited a deafening silence to the shocking and unnecessary deaths of hundreds of thousands infected and dying from COVID-19.[30] All the more appalling because the deadly effects of the raging pandemic were largely the result of the bungling leadership of an administration that chose conspiracy theories over science, replaced the authority of public health officials with Fox News incompetents, and lied about the severity of a virus that spread through the population and across the globe like an out-of-control wildfire. As a toxic form of cultural politics, Trumpism further removed the government from any obligation to be socially and politically responsible. National leadership disappeared into a chasm of ignorance and ethical irresponsibility both with respect to controlling the spread of the virus and organizing the vaccination campaign. Instead, apathy, brutality, and moral indifference were elevated to a central mode of governance.

In another example, Trump and his army of sycophants and cult followers remained shockingly silent in the face of the murder of a young woman, Heather Heyer, who was killed protesting in Charlottesville against neo-Nazis. In addition, indifferent to human suffering, Trump and his white supremacist senior speech writer Stephen Miller delighted in enacting unjust travel bans, cruel deportation laws, and the separation and caging of migrant children who have experienced conditions defined as 'horrific' in a detailed report by Americans for Immigrant Justice.[31]

Trump's 2016 election and reign of power made it obvious that authoritarianism was once more on the march and that a new and revised form of fascist politics had emerged in the United States, mimicking a similar pattern abroad. Of course, the seeds for this updated model of authoritarianism had long been in the making under capitalism, especially since the 1970s, with its marriage of money and politics and its willingness to make corruption and inequality an instrument of control. Under Trump, political corruption and cronyism no longer hid in the shadows but became glaringly visible given Trump's claim to holding what appeared to be a call for unchecked executive power and the right to exercise flagrant acts of lawlessness. The latter is all the more evident as more and more information has revealed that 'the Justice Department under former attorneys general William Barr and Jeff Sessions... regularly [put] Trump's personal and political interests ahead of the law'.[32] Sarah Kendzior has argued that Trump not only committed crimes in an often brazen and obvious manner, but that he needs to 'let you know that he got away with it [and that] the thrill is in the flaunting, the in-jokes, the admissions so blunt that, perversely, few take them seriously'.[33]

Under the reign of Trumpism, the merging of power, repression, and corruption was mobilized increasingly in the political and cultural spheres to both shape public consciousness and undermine, if not destroy, any institution that held authority to a measure of accountability. Trumpism redefined corrupt power relations, flagrantly displayed immoral and criminogenic behaviour, and unabashedly brandished the trappings of tyranny. As Masha Gessen writes in describing Trump's presidency:

> In plain view, Trump was flaunting, ignoring, and destroying all institutions of accountability. In plain view, he was degrading political speech. In plain view, he was using his office to enrich himself. In plain view, he was courting dictator after dictator. In plain view, he was promoting xenophobic conspiracy theories, now claiming that millions of immigrants voting illegally had cost him the popular vote; now insisting, repeatedly, that Obama had had him wiretapped. All of this, though plainly visible, was unfathomable, as Trump's election itself had been.[34]

Trumpism enacts a form of turbo-charged, militarized power, intent on not only capturing institutions of the state for personal and political gain, but also to redefine and control language, social media, and popular culture as a way of emptying politics of any substance by turning it into a spectacle. Language now operates in the service of violence, and all forms of criticism are reduced to the category of fake news, unworthy of serious reflection or critical analysis. Trumpism, at its core, is a cultural politics that shreds any viable notion of shared values and national unity, and in doing so, transforms essential human connections into bonds of distrust and fear. It views the space of the social, common good, and democratic values, as a register of weakness and resentment bristling with hatred if not a seething logic of disposability.

The distinctiveness of Trump's reign, however debated, emerged as a new political formation, and came to signify a merging of power, culture, politics, and everyday life that combined the harshest elements of a cutthroat global capitalism with the lingering malignancy of neo-fascist forces that ranged from 'white supremacist, white nationalists, militia, and neo-Nazis and Klans, to the Oath Keepers, the Patriot Movement, Christian fundamentalists, and anti-immigrant vigilante groups'.[35] Moulded in the language of populist, racist, economic nationalism, and authoritarian nationalism, Trumpism gave birth to a tsunami of repressive political, economic, and social policies that moved from the margins of society to the White House and state and local governments around the country.

For instance, anyone who opposed Trump was publicly criticized and often dehumanized, 'law and order' revived the language of Jim Crow, and the police were increasingly urged to enact violent behaviour against Trump's critics. The children of undocumented immigrants were put in cages, walls emerged as a normalizing symbol of nativism, state terrorism defined the role of US Immigration and Customs Enforcement (ICE) and became visible in the use of military forces to attack peaceful demonstrators in cities such as Portland and Washington, DC. As the social state came under severe attack, the punishing state grew with its ongoing militarization of civil society and its increasing criminalization of social problems. War, dehumanization, divisiveness, hate, and the language of racial cleansing and sorting became central governing principles and set the stage for the rebirth of an updated fascist politics.

Trumpism reached into every niche and crack of civil and political society, and in doing so, cross-pollinated politics, culture, and everyday life with a range of right-wing policies, authoritarian impulses, and the emerging presence of right-wing movements. Right-wing militia were now used to patrol the southern border of the United States; authoritarian forms of parliamentary state governments wrapped in the mantle of democratic elections waged wars on people of colour through voter suppression and vote counting laws. In addition, the Republican Part,y mobilized by an unmitigated hatred of democracy and support for a minority government, became the political arm of Trumpism, embracing the dictates of white nationalism, conspiracy theories, and an unapologetic right-wing version of American exceptionalism.

Increasingly, near the end of Trump's term, many members of the party voiced attempts to overthrow an American election based on bogus conspiracy theories and no evidence of fraud, which in some cases appears to come close to committing a criminal act of sedition.[36] That the President and his enablers may have committed a seditious act was all the more resonant in the face of the mob of pro-Nazis and white supremacists storming of the Capitol and their direct and indirect support for such actions—a view that appeared to be supported by President-elect Biden in a speech given in the aftermath of the 'failed insurrection'. Biden stated that such lawless actions 'bordered on sedition'.[37] The violence, racism, bigotry, and criminogenic actions that marked the assault on the Capitol represent the new face of a politics inhabited by 'genuine fanatics and ideologues' who, in their blind loyalty to Trump and their own need for power, prove that 'cowardice is contagious'.[38]

Trumpism, on one level, emerged out of the crisis of transnational neoliberalism, which could no longer lay claim to democratic values while concentrating wealth and power in the hands of the ruling class, all the while further accelerating wars and an unprecedented degree of economic inequality in wealth, income, and power worldwide. While many critics have defined Trumpism in terms of its debasing, toxic language, and cruel policies—all of which are important issues—few have analysed it as a pedagogical practice whose impact on political culture redefined and reshaped the collective consciousness of millions who embraced Trumpism more as a cult than as an ideology fabricated in lies, false promises, and authoritarian populism.[39] Trump's egregious bungling of the COVID-19 crisis, which cost the lives of over 300,000 by the end of 2020, his 'disdain for immigrants, for women, for disabled people for people of colour, for Muslims—for anyone who isn't an ablebodied white straight American born male', and his blunt embrace of ignorance have had poisonous consequences. Yet, his actions did little to undermine his base of support.[40] In mobilizing the support of over 74 million Americans, Trumpism made clear that changing consciousness through his use of social media and right-wing cultural apparatuses were more persuasive politically and ideologically than reverting to state violence.

What this suggests is that politics follows culture. As Stuart Hall observes, 'Cultural change is constitutive of political change and moral awareness of human consciousness.'[41] Culture is the primary vehicle through which people engage and understand the material circumstances and conditions that affect their lives. Culture is the ideological capital that gives meaning to identity, agency, and how one relates to the world. Culture is the machinery of language, affect, images, and materiality of power, conflict, and oppression in which the struggle over the hearts and minds of people appears as the first step in creating the political subject. It spawns new forms of life and hence it compels us to confront those symbolic and material conditions in which politics gains a voice and comes to life. As a repressive pedagogical social formation, it constructs, supports, and normalizes a fascist politics in which justice dies, language loses its moral and critical bearings, and the widespread practice of lying becomes a virtue.

Massive inequality has made the struggle to survive a central component of everyday life for millions. In this instance, what is at risk is not just the ability to fulfil basic needs but the very nature of one's identity, dignity, and sense of agency. Trumpism created a culture that induced a moral and political counter-revolution, legitimated by a sycophantic, Vichy-like Republican Party normalized by a right-wing corporate-controlled mainstream social media. Trumpism is a giant pedagogical disinformation machine whose aim is to colonize culture, public consciousness and undermine any viable form of robust and critical modes of agency, identification, and solidarity.

Trumpism is a political ideology, pedagogical tool, and cultural force designed to reshape the public sphere by emptying it of democratic values along with destroying the institutions that nurture critical thought and civic courage. How else to explain Trump's reactionary call for 'patriotic education', and his disdain for the New York Times '1619' educational project, which attempted to place the history of slavery and the achievements of Black Americans at the centre of history.[42] In addition, there was his concerted effort to destroy public education with the appointment of Betsy DeVos, a publicly acknowledged sworn enemy of public schooling and higher education.[43] Unsurprisingly, the New York Times Editorial Board described DeVos 'as perhaps the most disastrous leader in the Education Department's history'.[44] With the election of Biden she disappeared into a whirlwind of oblivion and the legacy she left behind marks her as the worse Secretary of Education ever appointed to office.

Under Trumpism, the centrality of education to politics and culture to power became obvious with the growing use of twenty-first-century cultural apparatuses such as Twitter, Facebook, Google, along with new media outlets such as Fox News, Newsmax, and Breitbart. These pedagogical apparatuses produced a distinctive cultural space that furthered the marriage of power and manufactured civic illiteracy and worked to eliminate the crucial question of what civic education and literacy should accomplish in a democracy.[45] Favouring instant reactions and a culture of ignorance, the new media and new image-based cultural forms turned chaos, catastrophe, and collapse into a spectacle that called forth instant pleasure, along with a kind of 'digital sublime' in which such platforms are 'mythologized as both convenient and infallible'.[46] Flooding the media ecosphere with lies, misrepresentations, and dangerous, if not deadly, falsehoods, these new cultural–pedagogical apparatuses packaged hate and undermined the critical role of intellectuals, journalists, experts, and other voices working on the side of truth, evidence, and meaningful authority.⁴⁷ Regardless of design, one outcome was to undermine and weaken traditional markers of freedom of expression and democracy. They also made clear that new political and cultural formations had emerged that complicated the traditional concerns about where knowledge was produced and surfaced as well as the institutional conditions that produced and regulated different fields of culture.

Trumpism performs politics as a form of entertainment and digital drama. It does so by transforming the political realm and society into a form of spectacularized theatre, not unlike what Guy Debord once called a *Society of the Spectacle*.⁴⁸ As a right-wing cultural apparatus, spectacle of disintegration, and tribal ethos, Trumpian politics becomes an all-encompassing tool of propaganda and pedagogy of repression, functioning as a form of cultural politics under the control of a corporate elite. As a reactionary cultural and pedagogical conduit, Trumpism undermines critical dialogue, shared values, shared responsibilities, and informed judgements while promoting authoritarian narratives that disdain historical consciousness, critical thinking, and the idea, if not principles, of participatory democracy. Hard boundaries, precarity, a culture of fear, untrampled individualism, an all-encompassing ethos of self-help, and a profound unease constitute the currency of Trumpism. In this instance, economic justice, meaningful solidarities, and the common good are removed from the discourse of politics and citizenship.

In addition, Trumpism enacts, without apology, a form of historical amnesia that proves particularly dangerous in a world wrought with anxiety, uncertainty, and a precarious present enveloped in a deadly surge of pandemics and plagues. Subject to a politics of erasure by government and corporate disinformation machines, historical consciousness loses its sense of critique, contexts, and buried memories of the value of individual and collective resistance in the face of systemic oppression. Historical vision, moral witnessing, and democratic ideals are now buried in a glut of misinformation and the spectacle of political corruption, a plague of consumerism, and a culture of immediacy. Bombarding the culture and public spheres with a blitz and barrage of events that are comparable to bombs exploding daily, Trumpism produces a relentless tsunami of events that obliterate the space and time for contemplating the past while freezing the present in a fragmented display of shocks and spectacles. Trumpism is an updated version of Orwell's doublethink. Truth, language, and history are now inverted, remade under the banner of 'fake news'. Trump's 'Ministry of Truth' now creates 'alternative facts' as a way of life, making Orwell's *1984* feel palpable and terrifyingly prescient.

Under such circumstances, the lessons of history disappear along with similarities between an authoritarian past and an authoritarian present. One consequence is that public consciousness of the space needed for critical reflection withers along with a rendering of the past as a source of critical insight. History, with its dangerous memories, becomes something that cannot happen in the present; that is, it cannot happen in a country that makes a claim to exceptionalism and in doing so argues that Trump's behaviour is more performative than dangerous. In this discourse, the dark shadows of an updated fascist politics disappear in the claim that Trump is merely incompetent and that his politics are inept and bear no resemblance to an incipient dictator.[49] Conservatives who believe that the market is the only template for politics and governance refuse to see Trump's reign as an outgrowth of their own disdain for the welfare state and redistribution of wealth and power. The liberal infatuation with individual freedom and responsibility makes them fearful of recognizing that neoliberal capitalism poses the greatest threat to democracy and creates the conditions for the ongoing threat of fascism.[50] This view provides a breeding ground for liberals who argue that Trumpism is a passing and failed anti-democratic exception to the rule.

For instance, the historical record needs to be revisited regarding the liberal view of Trumpism especially evident in the work of Professor Samuel Moyn, who argued that traditional institutional checks proved successful against Trumpism. He also falsely claimed that Trump provided a 'portal for all comers to search for alternatives beyond [neoliberalism], and never provided a systemic threat to American democracy."[51] Moyn's notion that Trump was anti-militarist and a champion of the working class, at least initially, rings especially false. Not only did Trump give the financial elite a $1.5 trillion tax break at the expense of funding crucial social programmes, he also passed endless policies that promoted what research assistants for Economic Policy at the Center for American Progress Action Fund, Saharra Griffin and Malkie Wall, call corporate wage theft. These included derailing 'an Obama-era plan to extend overtime protections to more Americans and instead lowered the salary threshold.... Workers [were] denied an estimated $1.2 billion in earnings annually due to Trump's overtime protection rollback."[52] Trumpism made it difficult for workers to unionize while making it easier for employers to eliminate unions. This anti-worker campaign also included reducing workplace safety regulations, discriminating against people with disabilities, and the weakening of civil rights protections for workers.

What disappears from this view is that Trumpism is the endpoint of the historical failure of capitalism that has morphed into a nihilistic death drive—a quickened call to ugliness, violence, and dehumanization—reinforced by market values that destroy any vestige of moral and social responsibility.[53] Trumpism is not simply about Trump, the bungling leader, a decrepit Republican Party, or a pseudo-authoritarian as Samuel Moyn, Jeet Heer, Cass Sunstein, Ross Douthat, Dylan Mathews, and others have wrongly argued. What characterizes this view is a politics of denialism and an honest analysis of Trump's undisguised authoritarian impulses.

Also overlooked are the mobilizing elements of a fascist politics that represents an extension of capitalism and whose recent endpoint, once again, emerged with the violent assault on both the Capitol and democracy itself.[54] Trump's administration may not have constituted a fully formed fascist regime, but as Sarah Churchill, Timothy Snyder, Paul Street, Robert O. Paxton (more recently), and Jason Stanley have argued, it consistently embraced the long-standing and malignant traditions of American fascism.[55] The historian Timothy Snyder dismisses the liberal claim, at one time advanced by the historian Richard Evans that the fascist label does not apply to Trump because his ideology and policies do not invite a direct comparison.[56] Snyder writes

> These last four years, scholars have discussed the legitimacy and value of invoking fascism in reference to Trumpian propaganda. One comfortable position has been to label any such effort as a direct comparison and then to treat such comparisons as taboo. More productively, the philosopher Jason Stanley has treated fascism as a phenomenon, as a series of patterns that can be observed not only in interwar Europe but beyond it. My own view is that greater knowledge of the past, fascist or otherwise, allows us to notice and conceptualize elements of the present that we might otherwise disregard and to think more broadly about future possibilities.[57]

Moyn, Sunstein, and others such as Corey Robin engage in a politics of denial, refusing to look honestly at key elements of fascism that Trump mobilized. These included: flooding America with lies and launching a full-fledged attack on the truth and science; enacting racist fear-mongering and a politics of disposability; promoting extreme nationalism and celebrating an alignment with dictators; endorsing a discourse of winners, along with a list of losers and enemies who became the object of contempt, if not violence; he also labelled the American press as an 'enemy of the people'; legitimated a culture of dehumanization, called immigrants vermin and rapists; reinforced the language of misogyny and xenophobia; and used a powerful right-wing propaganda machine to legitimate a culture of autocratic power and political corruption.

What is missed by centrist liberals is that Trumpism is the unapologetic plague of neoliberal capitalism that induces massive inequalities, manufactured ignorance, and horrific degrees of hardship and suffering among diverse groups of people, who are rendered excess. It concentrates wealth and power in the hands of a financial elite, who control not only obscene concentrations of wealth but also undue political power and influence.[58] Trumpism is the logical outcome of a savage gangster capitalism that colonizes subjectivity to turn people into isolated shoppers and atomized individuals, willing to suspend their sense of agency and deem all social bonds untrustworthy. Social bonds are now replaced by market relations, ensuring that all social interactions are valued according to the imprimatur of capital. Ways of imagining society through a collective ethos or as a public good now fall by the wayside.

In this discourse, fate becomes a matter of individual responsibility, irrespective of wider structural forces. Missing here is what the late Tony Judt called 'the thick mesh of mutual obligations and social responsibilities' to be found in any substantive democracy.[59] The logical outcome of this upending of social connections that expand the common good is an individual and collective need for the comfort of strongmen—a default community that offers the swindle of fulfilment.[60] Trumpism is a worldview in which critical thought collapses into what Robert Jay Lifton calls 'ideological totalism'.[61] Under the influence of 'ideological totalism', narratives of certainty are produced through a language frozen in the assumption that there is 'nothing less than absolute truth and equally absolute virtue', all of which provides the conditions for 'sealed off communities'.[62]

Frank Bruni, an opinion writer for the *New York Times*, raised the question of just how rotten must Trump be for his followers to wake up and realize what a threat he is to both democracy and their very lives. In raising this issue, Bruni puts into high relief the cult-like and mind-boggling submission and irrationality that shapes the consciousness of many of Trump's followers. He writes:

> Trump was impeached. A plague struck. Tens of millions of Americans lost their jobs and huge chunks of their savings. Trump responded with tantrums, lies and intensified attacks on democratic traditions. Trump's supporters reinvented or decided to ignore his coronavirus denialism, which made America a world leader in reported infections and recorded deaths and has had catastrophic economic consequences. They disbelieved or forgave all of his cheating: on his taxes, in his philanthropy, when he tried to extort the president of Ukraine, when he grabbed another Supreme Court seat in defiance of the Merrick

Garland precedent. They accepted or outright embraced his racism and nativism. They shrugged off his lying, which is obvious even through the pore-minimizing filters of Fox News and Rush Limbaugh. They endorsed his viciousness and made peace with his tantrums and erratic behavior.[63]

Coco Das goes further and argues that America has a Nazi problem that will not go away on its own and must be addressed. Das observes:

> We have a Nazi problem in this country. Some 73 million people voted for it.... They don't, for the most part, wave swastikas and salute Hitler, but we have a Nazi problem in this country as deeply as the German people had a Nazi problem in the 1930s. Their minds waterlogged with conspiracy theories, they take lies as truth, spread hate and bigotry, wrap themselves in several flags—American, Confederate, Blue Lives Matter—and use the Bible as a weapon of violence and repression. They are a grotesque expression of the worst of this country, of its ugly narcissism, its thuggish militarism, its ignorance... They carry the torch of slavery, genocide, and Jim Crow terror. Gunned up and maskless, they exalt above all the right to kill.[64]

Considering the refusal to view seriously the emergence of an updated fascism under Trumpism, a more comprehensive critical analysis of Trumpism is necessary. Such an approach should offer insights into the blind allegiance of Trump's followers and the legacy of an authoritarian malignancy, such as white supremacy, consolidated corruption, and loss of freedom, among others, that has resurfaced in American political culture. One necessary insight is the recognition that any rendering of Trumpism as a version of authoritarianism carries with it elements of a fascist past that can easily disappear into a discourse in which historical similarities are dismissed. For example, Corey Robin goes so far as to claim that Trump was a weak leader marked by political incompetence and failed in his attempt to change the political culture.[65] This wild misreading of Trumpism goes hand in hand with the charge that those who claim Trump has resurrected the mobilizing passions of fascism represent what David Klion called 'unhinged reactions to the Trump era.'[66]

It is difficult to take such a charge seriously considering a range of policies enacted under the Trump regime that are as cruel as they are oppressive. These range from voter suppression and the unleashing of the military on peaceful protesters to savagely cruel anti-immigration policies and a politics of disposability that mimics what Richard A. Etlin calls the Nazi policy of "'Vernichtung lebensunwerten Lebens', that is, the "destruction" or "extermination" of "lives not worth living".[67] The effect that Trump has had on political culture in the United States is far more significant than the policies he enacted. The real damage and corrosive impact produced by the Trump regime was shockingly visible given its assault on ethics, the rule of law, Blacks, and the blatant disregard for the truth, evidence, and science. Trump legitimated a culture and pedagogy of hate, dehumanization, uncertainty, and authoritarian nationalism. These forces will surely outlast Trump's retreat to Mar-a-Lago, his Palm Beach estate.

There is no acknowledgement by Moyn, Robin, and others of the centrality of cultural politics and neoliberal and authoritarian pedagogies at work under Trumpism and how they 'get people to give up their ideas of freedom and civility [while] giving them a taste for savagery'.[68] Moreover, dismissing left critics who address authoritarian, if not fascist elements in Trumpism as unhinged is an egregious example of bad faith.

The lessons of history wither in the discourse of denial, especially because 'the all too protean origins of totalitarianism are still with us: loneliness as the normal register of social life, the frenzied lawfulness of ideological certitude, mass poverty and mass homelessness, the routine use of terror as a political instrument, and the ever-growing speeds and scales of media, economics, and warfare'.[69] Moreover, the argument ignores the groundwork of forces laid long before Trump came to power and it says little about the enormous ways in which he used Twitter, the Internet, conservative foundations, and the right-wing media to turn the Republican Party into a group of morally and politically vacuous sycophants.[70] More specifically, it both ignores and underestimates the power of Trumpism in creating slightly more than

74 million followers who inhabit right-wing populist spaces where 'reality can be dispensed and controlled'.[71] It also overlooks the power of Trumpism to create cult-like followers who disregard reason and reality for the image of the strongman who demands unmitigated loyalty and ideological purity.[72]

The power of Trumpism in the cultural realm affirms the success of a new cultural/social formation and testifies less to the personalized issue of incompetence than to the success of Trumpism to shape consciousness among large segments of the American public and create regressive modes of identification that further strengthened and integrated into centres of governmental power once marginal elements of a fascist politics. Thoughtlessness and the collapse of civic culture and moral agency echo a dark period in history in which criminality and corruption entered into politics, and as Stephen Spender once argued, 'the future is like a time bomb buried but ticking away at the present'.[73] In the age of Trump, language reinforces the central fascist notion of friend/enemy distinction as an organizing principle of politics. In this instance, language is used to vilify those considered other while normalizing far-right extremist views. In this case, the language of environmental fairmindedness, governmental responsibility, and racial justice disappears.

More shockingly, as I stated previously, Trump infamously used language to imply a moral equivalence between white supremacists and neo-Nazis marching in Charlottesville and peaceful protesters. At the same time, he employs the language of white supremacists to protest against politicians removing Confederate flags and symbols from the American landscape. Referencing the January 6 riot at a Conservative Political Action Conference on February 26, 2021, Trump stated, 'These were peaceful people, these were great people'.[74] Trump conveniently forgot that this was a riot, which he incited, that left five people dead, while 140 police officers were assaulted, beaten, or injured. Over 500 of these 'great people', whom Trump labelled as patriots, have been charged by the FBI with an array of crimes. Since the January 6 violent insurrection, Trump has emboldened a mass fascist movement which has hardened, becoming more consolidated and widespread. Trumpism exerts enormous influence in purging dissenters within the Republican Party of any power and operates powerfully at the state level to undermine abortion, immigration rights, voting rights, equity, and the overall framework of justice. Trumpism is an updated poison of fascist politics working hard to put democracy into the graveyard of history.

Trumpism is a worldview that defines culture as a battleground of losers and winners, a world in which everything is rigged against whites.[75] This is a world in which unity disappears into Trump's right-wing assault on the public good, truth, the common good, as reality itself dissolves into a right-wing propaganda machine in which politics becomes 'a plot to steal from [whites] their natural due as Americans'.[76] Trumpism defines power as immunity from the law, and that the most admirable representatives of power are those who are 'triumphant and innocent in the face of every accusation of incapacity, criminality and unethical conduct'.[77] How else to explain Trump's pardoning of grifters, political cronies, and war criminals?

Far from being the 'almost opposite of fascism', Trumpism paves the way for deeply entrenched legacies of hate to be passed on to his followers and future generations. His goal is to destroy any vestige of democracy as we know it, however flawed, and replace it with a form of neoliberal capital unmoored from any sense of social, political, and ethical commitment. Trumpism will long outlive the language, actions, values, and views that have defined Trump's presidency.

What is crucial to recognize is that any starting point for challenging Trumpism and its fascist politics must begin, as Kali Holloway and Martin Mycielski observe, by

> recognizing the reality of what is happening... how much damage is being done, how much earth was already scorched. The year has somehow flown by yet seemed interminable. It's good to remember the very big, very frightening picture before us, how far we've already come, and to consider what recourse we have with complicit and corrupt forces standing in the way.[78]

Trumpism did not disappear once Trump left office. On the contrary, its afterlife seems assured if its politics is endlessly reproduced through reactionary policies, and the reactionary cultural workstations that generate its lies, regressive notions of agency, hatred, and disdain for the truth. Trumpism represents both a crisis of the civic imagination and an educational crisis.

Until it is understood as a cultural crisis rather than defined simply as an economic and narrowly political crisis, Trumpism will continue to undermine the ability of individuals and institutions to think critically, question themselves, and produce enlightened citizens and aligned social movements that can fight collectively for and sustain a radical democracy. There is no democracy without a knowledgeable and informed citizenry, and no democracy can survive under the banner of Trumpism. This is a political formation that concentrates power in the hands of a ruling elite, produces a glut of ignorance, reduces citizenship to the dictates of consumerism, uses corporate-owned media as a propaganda tool, and aggressively pushes illusions of freedom.[79]

Drawing upon history, Masha Gessen argues that Trump's defeat offers a choice 'between two paths: the path of reckoning and the path of forgetting'.[80] She further argues that the price for forgetting is too high and would leave in place a rationale for giving immunity to terror, lawlessness, and corruption. On the other hand, to avoid becoming complicitous with the crimes of Trumpism, it is necessary for the Biden administration to put in place a national project—which would include investigations, hearings, court trials, public assemblies, journalistic inquiries, and other invented formats—in order to hold accountable those who committed crimes under the Trump regime, including, I would hope, those individuals and politicians who advocated sedition by baselessly claiming voter fraud and attempting to overturn results of the Biden election.[81] Georgetown University professor Neal Katyal goes further and argued that Trump should be indicted for trying to illegally overturn the election in the hope that he would then be barred from holding any political office in the future. He is not alone.

There is no indication that the Biden administration will hold Trump responsible for his crimes and corruption while in office, although he may face criminal charges on a state level for earlier corrupt and possibly illegal business practices. A small gesture of justice could be sent to the twelve Republican Senators and more than half of Congressional Republicans who doused the Constitution with fire through their attempts to create what amounted to a coup by supporting the invalidation of Biden's election while creating the groundwork for undermining free and fair elections in the future, if not democracy itself. Unfortunately, since Trump has left office, a number of newspapers and politicians have condemned Senators Josh Hawley and Ted Cruz for stating the election was rigged. George Will, the celebrated conservative columnist, rightly labelled them as 'repulsive architects' of the Capitol riot who committed sedition and, by implication, should resign. Unfortunately, they have escaped any legal actions, the ranks of their followers seem to be growing, and the entirety of the Republican Party appears to support their obscene authoritarian views.[82]

Impeaching Trump twice was an important step, if only symbolic, in holding him accountable. It would be a serious political blunder to forget that he did not act alone. The broader political and economic forces aligned with his ongoing acts of corruption, discrimination, and violence must be included in any critique of the Trump regime, and should include the crimes of Wall Street, the right-wing extremist media conglomerates who lied about the election, and the financial elite who provided the funds for Trump's political and cultural workstations of denial, diversion, and falsehoods. The violence Trump used to stay in power did not happen in a vacuum. The governing principles of genocide, militarism, and violence have a long history and should also be on trial as a moment of self-reckoning in a time of political and ethical crisis. It is impossible to separate the violent attack on the Capitol and democracy itself from both Trump's language of violence and the systemic violence characteristic of neoliberal governance in the US. As Charles H. Clavey observes, violence is a core principle of Trumpism. He writes:

> At the very heart of Trumpism... stands the threat of violence: the agitator's constant promise that his followers will visit revenge—in the form of physical harm, political persecution, and social sanction—on those who, they believe, demonized, and excluded them. Violence is both the animating principle of Trumpism and one of Trump's most powerful tools. Trump's most fervent followers, from QAnon conspiracists to white nationalists, glory in the conviction that arrests of prominent Democrats, purges of pedophiles, and pitched street battles against the left are just around the corner. From his assertion that there were 'good people on both sides' at Charlottesville to his order that the Proud Boys 'stand back and stand by,' Trump has shown, time and again, that there is no Trumpism without violence. During an October rally in Michigan, Trump casually remarked that there is 'something beautiful' about watching protestors get 'pushed around' by the National Guard. 'You people get it,' he told his loyal followers. 'You probably get it better than I do.'

It is astonishing that in the face of Trump's attempt to overthrow the election, which closely resembles the actions of authoritarian regimes around the world, there is a resounding silence by many academics about America being at the tipping point of becoming a full-fledged authoritarian regime. Fortunately, members of the press recognized clearly and with some urgency the threat of authoritarianism posed by Trump's actions regarding his attempt to overturn an election he decisively lost, even entertaining the use of martial law to do so. Quoting Professor Ruth Ben-Ghiat, *New York Times* journalist Peter Baker writes:

> Mr. Trump's efforts ring familiar to many who have studied authoritarian regimes in countries around the world, like those run by President Vladimir V. Putin in Russia and Prime Minister Viktor Orbán in Hungary. 'Trump's attempt to overturn the election, and his pressure tactics to that end with Brad Raffensperger, the Georgia secretary of state, are an example of how authoritarianism works in the 21st century,' said Ruth Ben-Ghiat, the author of 'Strongmen: From Mussolini to the Present.' 'Today's leaders come in through elections

and then manipulate elections to stay in office—until they get enough power to force the hand of legislative bodies to keep them there indefinitely.'[83]

Amid ongoing assaults on democracy by Trumpism, the Republican Party. and other extremists, it is crucial to develop modes of resistance not only for a project of truth-telling and answerability but also to produce narratives of remembrance in which power can be held accountable, crimes can be revealed, and the stories of the victims heard. Under such circumstances, the historical record can become an object of critical inquiry, culpability, and the rectifying of moral injury. History can be connected to the present, enabling people to refuse to turn away from the threat of fascism and act with resolve and courage to stop it in its tracks. Historical remembrance, critical inquiry, and an understanding of how power works must be the precondition for collective resistance. Such reckoning can also serve as an educational and learning project in which the lessons of the past can create the conditions for connecting critical and empowering forms of education to democratic values, relations, goals, and a redemptive notion of equity and inclusion. Desmond Tutu, in his opening remarks before the convening of South Africa's Truth and Reconciliation Commission in 1996, rightly invoked the power of historical memory and the need to bear witness in the fight against tyranny. He stated: 'We are charged to unearth the truth about our dark past, to lay the ghosts of the past so that they will not return to haunt us.'[84] The power of education, reason, and the search for truth and justice are one mechanism for learning from the past and resisting the ghosts ready to emerge in the present.

The eradication of the public good, the continued growth of neoliberalism's disimagination machines, the individualizing of social problems, a collective indifference to the rise of the punishing state, the repression of historical consciousness, the failure to engage honestly with the full scope of America's racist history, and the crushing role of racial and economic inequality are at their core educational issues. These issues speak powerfully to the task of changing consciousness by dismantling those depoliticizing forces that create apocalyptic visions that render the current social order a world without alternatives. In part, this means intellectuals, artists, and other cultural workers must make the work they produce meaningful to make it critical and transformative. This demands a revolutionary vision and set of values matched by a collective effort to create alternative public spaces that unpack how common sense works to prevent people from recognizing the oppressive nature of the societies in which they find themselves. The ideological tyranny and cultural politics of Trumpism and other elements of a growing fascist politics demand a wholesale revision of how education and democracy mutually inform each other and how they are understood as part of a broader politics in which the oppressed can be heard and a world can be created in which the voices of the suffering find a public space for articulation and resistance.

Any movement for mass resistance needs to become more accessible to working-class people, and there is a crucial need to connect personal and political rights with economic rights. Democracy can only survive as a social state that guarantees rights for everyone. The question of who holds power, and how power is separated from politics, with politics being local and power being global, must be addressed as a condition for international resistance. Neoliberal capitalism has morphed into a form of fascism that produces zones of abandonment where individuals become unknowable, faceless, and lack human rights. Human rights in the age of the pandemic are under attack across the globe.

Under Trumpism, society increasingly reproduces pedagogical 'death zones of humanity' that triumph not only in violence but also in ignorance and irrationality.[85] These are zones that undermine the capacity for people to speak, write, and act from a position of empowerment and be responsible to themselves and others. Against this form of depoliticization, there is the need for modes of civic education and critical literacy that provide the bridging work between thinking critically and the possibility of interpretation as an intervention. Critical pedagogy rejects a neoliberal logic that thrives on the energies of those it dehumanizes while embracing a discourse of denial, existing inequalities, and a willingness to pathologize any viable notion of the common good. In doing so, critical pedagogy embraces a notion of social responsibility and a vision of an alternative society rooted in the ideals of justice, equality, and freedom. As Francis Fox Piven has argued, any viable political vision as a precondition for producing critical social movements is dependent on at least two beliefs. First, people need to believe that the system under which they live is brutally unjust, and in part this means learning from the past; second, they then need 'to believe that they could do something about it'.[86] In addition, there is the need to cultivate the courage to act. One might add that demonstrations are valuable as pedagogical tools in raising awareness, but must be supplemented by long-term strategies, durable organizations, the building of communities of compassion and care, and the overcoming of fractured political identities and movements.[87]

Trumpism evokes the shadow of authoritarianism in the form of a resurgent fascist politics that dehumanizes all of us in the face of a refusal to confront its spectre of racism, mayhem, and brutality. Removing Trump from office was only the beginning of confronting the fascist ghosts of the past, which Trump proved are no longer in the shadows or on the margins of American politics. The influence and legacy of Trumpism will long outlast the aftermath of Trump's presidency, making it all the more urgent to reclaim the redemptive elements of government responsibility, democratic ideals, and the public spheres that make a radical democracy possible. Faced with the rise of fascist politics in the United States and abroad, it is crucial to recognize that capitalism and democracy are not synonymous and that any viable struggle for change must be not only for democracy but against fascism.

Part Two

The Crisis of Pedagogy

4

Fascist Culture and the Challenge to Critical Pedagogy

Those who are against Fascism without being against capitalism, who lament over the barbarism that comes out of barbarism, are like people who wish to eat their veal without slaughtering the calf.

—Bertolt Brecht

America Under Siege

Across the globe, democratic institutions such as the independent media, schools, the legal system, certain financial institutions, and higher education are under siege. The promise, if not ideals, of democracy, however flawed, are receding as the far-right extremists who breathe new life into a fascist past are once again on the move subverting language, values, civil rights, vision, and a critical consciousness. Education has increasingly become a tool of domination as right-wing pedagogical apparatuses controlled by the entrepreneurs of hate to attack workers, the poor, people of colour, refugees, immigrants from the south, and others considered expendable. A Republican Party dominated by right-wing zealots believes education should function as a tool of propaganda, rightly named 'patriotic education'. Dissent is defiled as corrupting American values, and any classroom that addresses racial injustice is viewed as antithetical to 'a Christian and white supremacist world where Black people "know their place"'.[1]

As I mentioned previously, banning instruction on 'critical race theory' has become the new McCarthyism. Noam Chomsky argues that any reference to the history of slavery, systemic racism, or racial injustice now replaces 'Communism and Islamic terror as the plague of the modern age'.[2] Chomsky may not go far enough, because GOP extremists argue that the threat of communism has simply been expanded to include CRT, Black Lives Movement, and other anti-racist protest groups, all connected and viewed as updated forms of Marxism and part of an international communist-global conspiracy. The Red Scare is alive and well in America.[3] The legendary British author John le Carré wrote presciently in a different historical context a few years ago that America had entered a period of historical madness.[4] His words have even more significance today and have come back to haunt the United States.

Amid an era when an older social order is crumbling, and a new one is struggling to define itself, there emerges a time of confusion, danger, and moments of great restlessness. Once again, the present moment is at a historical juncture in which the structures of liberation and authoritarianism are vying for shaping a future that appears to be either an unthinkable nightmare or a realizable aspiration. We have arrived at a moment in which two worlds are colliding and a history of the present is poised at a point when 'possibilities are either realized or rejected but never disappear completely'.[5] First, there are the harsh and crumbling worlds of neoliberal globalization and its mobilizing passions that fuel different strands of fascism across the globe, including the United States.[6] Power is now enamoured of amassing profits and capital and is increasingly addicted to a politics of white nationalism and racial cleansing. Second, there are growing counter-movements, especially among young people, searching for a new politics that can rethink, reclaim, and reinvent a new understanding of democratic socialism, untainted by capitalism.[7]

We now live in a world that resembles a dystopian novel. The COVID-19 crisis created a surrealist nightmare that floods our screens and media with images of fear. We can no longer shake hands, embrace our friends, use public transportation, sit in a coffee shop, or walk down the street without experiencing anxiety and fear. What must be acknowledged is that the pandemic is more than a medical concept.[8] It also refers to ideological and political plagues that emerged because of the irresponsible response of the US and other countries such as Brazil, the United Kingdom, and India to the COVID-19 crisis. Marked by inept leadership rooted in a distrust of science and reason and a blind allegiance to market forces, what emerged over time was unimaginable suffering, massive deaths, and a further legitimation of lies and right-wing violence. The horror of the pandemic often blinds us to the fact that anti-democratic economic and political forces that have prioritized profits over human needs have ground away at the social order for the last fifty years. Since the 1970s, both major political parties in the United States have abandoned the working class by aligning themselves with the corporate elite and the ruling ideology of Wall Street.

The Plague of Gangster Capitalism

Gangster capitalism has waged war on the welfare state, public sphere, and the common good for over fifty years. In its most predatory form, it believes that the market should govern the economy and all aspects of society. It concentrates wealth in the hands of a financial elite and elevates untrammelled self-interest, self-help, deregulation, and privatization as the organizing principles of society. Under neoliberalism, everything is for sale, and the only relations that matter are commercial and subject to the rule of capital. At the same time, gangster capitalism ignores basic human needs such as healthcare, food, decent wages, and quality education. Inequality has become the governing principle of American society, even more, evident given the disproportionate effects of COVID-19 on those marginalized by class, race, and age.[9]

Neoliberalism views government as the enemy of the market, limits society to the realm of the family and individuals, embraces a fixed hedonism, and challenges the very idea of the public good. Under gangster capitalism, poverty, racism, hunger, COVID-related deaths, patriarchy, and climate devastation are accelerated by massive degrees of economic inequality. All of the institutions that are central to neoliberal capitalism must be overturned, and as Michael Yates points out this means we cannot settle for incremental changes and that

> we first must have at least a general idea of the world we want to inhabit, and second, we need to know how to go about bringing such a place into existence. We can start by stating that, if capitalism is the source of the multiple woes facing the working class and its peasant comrades-in-arms, then what we desire is the antithesis of capitalist society.[10]

At the very least, the atrophy of the political imagination caused by neoliberal pedagogy must be challenged on the educational front so as to imagine a future that does not replicate the present. Part of such a struggle would include the fight for an economy that serves the needs of all people and the crucial fight for sustainable environmental policies that reverse 'capitalism's competitive drive for mindless growth that is devouring the environment and roasting the planet'.[11] There is also the need to insist on 'public ownership of all the social institutions that help a society reproduce itself', and a 'radically egalitarian society with equality in all spheres of life—between men and women, among all racial and ethnic groups, among all people irrespective of their gender identity or sexual preference, among and within every country with respect to work, region, and access to all social services and amenities'.[12] There should be no compromise over resisting the neoliberal attacks on health care, public housing, a universal wage, free education, free child care, and the redistribution of wealth and power equitably. What these demands point to is both a call for democratic socialism and a revival of the radical imagination.

We live in a historical moment when economic activity is divorced from social costs, while policies that produce racial cleansing, militarism, and staggering inequality have become defining features of everyday life and established modes of governance. Clearly, there is a need to reclaim a notion of democratic socialism in which matters of justice, equity, and equality become the central features of a substantive democracy. The good news is that the many demonstrations over multiple issues that are taking place both in the United States and across the globe suggest that the spirit of democratic socialism is in the air. Groups such as the Democratic Socialist of America, the Black Lives Matter movement, and various youth groups resisting police violence and embracing socialism, among others, are moving beyond fractured political formations and embracing the struggle for lasting democratic institutions and a unified political movement with durable coalitions. A new generation of Black activists have returned economic inequality, organization building, and class as central elements of collective struggles. They have also reinserted back into the public imagination the notion that 'racism, police violence, and radical prison reform [must occupy] a central place in any viable agenda for the new American left'.[13]

The pandemic continues to reveal in all its ugliness the death-producing mechanisms of systemic inequality, deregulation, a culture of cruelty, and an increasingly dangerous assault on the environment. It has also made visible an anti-intellectual culture that derides any notion of critical thought, that is, any element of culture that equips individuals to think critically, engage in thoughtful dialogue, appropriate the lessons of history, and learn how to govern rather than be governed. At the same time, the claims and promises of neoliberal capitalism have been undermined because of the economic failures and medical horrors let loose by the pandemic.

Thinking the Unthinkable

What was once unthinkable is now said in public by demonstrators across the globe, such as those in the United States protesting police violence and the brutality of economic inequality. Young people are calling for a new narrative to repair the safety net, provide free healthcare, childcare, elder care, and free quality public schools for everyone. There are growing calls against state violence, and the plagues of poverty, homelessness, and the pollution of the planet. Young people, members of the millennial generation, and Gen Z 'are refining the rhythm of resistance and solidarity, aligning their struggles at home with the fights against US empire in the streets of Palestine, Haiti, Colombia, and other countries'.[14]

What these international youth movements have made clear is that they are more than willing to fight against something sinister and horrifying happening to liberal democracies all over the globe. They are well aware that the global thrust towards democratization that emerged after the Second World War is giving way once again to authoritarian tyrannies. Moreover, these tyrannies pose a serious danger not only to economic and political rights but to the planet itself, as the environment which sustains life cannot endure much longer if the assaults and degradation continue. As alarming as the signs may be, the public cannot look away and allow the terrors of the unforeseen to be given free rein. Young people across the globe are increasingly joining social movements that not only support democratic socialism, but also refuse to allow the power of dreams and educated hope to turn into ashes.

The pandemic is a crisis that cannot be allowed to turn into a catastrophe in which all hope is lost. While this pandemic threatens democracy's ability to breathe, it offers the possibility to rethink politics and the habits of critical education, human agency, and elements of social responsibility crucial to any viable notion of what life would be like in a democratic socialist society. And while the worse effects of the pandemic may be receding in the rich countries of the west, its most repressive elements ranging from the inequities in treatment of minorities of colour, its hollowing out of liberal arts programmes in higher education, and its relentless immersion in a culture of lies will continue.

Yet, it is important to remember that power is not entirely about domination and that amid the corpses produced by neoliberal capitalism and COVID-19, there are flashes of hope, a chance to move beyond contemporary resurgences of authoritarianism. Theorists such as Paulo Freire, Ernst Bloch, Hannah Arendt, Angela Y. Davis, James Baldwin, and Howard Zinn, among others, understood that such a politics is rooted in a pedagogy of hope, one that integrated a critical reading of the world with an attempt to put into practice modes of struggle based on the principles of social and economic equality and human freedom.

It is hard to imagine a more urgent moment for taking seriously ongoing attempts to make education a fundamental element of politics. At stake here is the notion that education is a social concept, one rooted in the goal of emancipation for all people. Moreover, this is an education that encourages human agency, one that enables people to be both critical thinkers and committed individuals and social agents. This is a pedagogy that calls us beyond ourselves, and engages the ethical imperative to care for others, dismantle structures of domination, and to become subjects rather than objects of history, politics, and power. If we are going to develop a politics capable of awakening our critical, imaginative, and historical sensibilities, it is crucial for educators and others to remember Freire's ongoing project of radical literacy.

Hope married to power, politics, and agency is a political project in which civic literacy, infused with a language of critique and possibility, addresses the notion that there is no democracy without knowledgeable and civically literate citizens. Such a language is necessary to enable the conditions to forge a collective international resistance among educators, youth, artists, and other cultural workers in defence of public goods. Hope begins with dissent, critique, and the idea of social transformation. Militant hope connects memory and lived experience to a sense of reality infused with a sense of possibility. Hope is more than a wish or empty dream, it is a subversive force, an active presence in opening a space for imagining the impossible, evoking not only different stories but also different futures.

Education, both in its symbolic and institutional forms, has a central role to play in fighting the resurgence of fascist cultures, mythic historical narratives, and the emerging ideologies of white supremacy and white nationalism. Moreover, as fascists across the globe are disseminating toxic racist and ultra-nationalist images of the past, it is essential to reclaim education as a form of historical consciousness and moral witnessing. This is especially true at a time when forms of historical and social amnesia are gaining traction, particularly in the United States, matched only by the masculinization of the public sphere and the increasing normalization of a fascist politics that thrives on ignorance, fear, the suppression of dissent, and hate. As I have noted throughout this book, education as a form of cultural work extends far beyond the classroom and its pedagogical influence, although often imperceptible, is crucial to challenging and resisting the rise of fascist pedagogical formations and their rehabilitation of fascist principles and ideas.[15]

The pedagogical lesson here is that fascism begins with hateful words, the demonization of others considered disposable, and moves to an attack on ideas, the burning of books, the disappearance of intellectuals, and the emergence of the carceral state and the horrors of detention jails and camps. As a form of cultural politics, critical pedagogy provides the promise of a protected space within which to think against the grain of received opinion, a space to question and challenge, to imagine the world from different standpoints and perspectives, to reflect upon ourselves in relation to others and, in so doing, to understand what it means to 'assume a sense of political and social responsibility'.[16]

Zones of Social Abandonment

Cultural politics since the 1980s has turned toxic as ruling elites increasingly gained control of commanding cultural apparatuses, turning them into pedagogical disimagination machines that serve the forces of ethical tranquilization by producing and legitimating endless degrading and humiliating images of the poor, Black people, immigrants, Muslims, and others considered excess, or wasted lives doomed to terminal exclusion. The capitalist dream machine is back with huge profits for the ultra-rich, hedge fund managers, and major players in the financial service industries. In these new landscapes of wealth, fraud, and social atomization, a savage and fanatical capitalism promotes a winner-take-all ethos, normalizes massive inequalities in wealth and power, and aggressively undermines the welfare state while pushing millions into hardship and misery. The geographies of moral and political decadence are expanding and have become the organizing standard of the dream worlds of consumption, privatization, surveillance, and deregulation. Within this increasingly fascist landscape, public spheres are replaced by zones of social abandonment and thrive on the energies of the walking dead and avatars of ruthlessness and misery.

Within the last five decades, education has diminished rapidly in its capacities to educate young people and others to be reflective, critical, and socially involved agents. Under neoliberal regimes, the utopian possibilities formerly associated with public and higher education as a public good capable of promoting social equality and supporting democracy have become too dangerous for the apostles of authoritarianism. Increasingly, public schools are subject to the toxic forces of privatization and mindless standardized curricula while teachers are deskilled and subject to intolerable labour conditions. Higher education now mimics a business culture run by a managerial army of bureaucrats, enamoured of market values, who resemble the high priests of a deadening instrumental rationality. More recently, it is under assault by ideological fanatics who want to ban dissident ideas, books, and critical modes of teaching from the schools. The commanding visions of democracy are in exile at all levels of education.

Critical thought and the imaginings of a better world present a direct threat to neoliberal rationality in which the future must always replicate the present in an endless circle in which capital and the identities that it legitimates merge with each other into what might be called a dead zone of the imagination and pedagogies of repression. This dystopian impulse thrives on producing myriad forms of inequality and violence—encompassing both the symbolic and the structural—as part of a broader attempt to define education in purely instrumental, privatized, and anti-intellectual terms.

What is clear is that neoliberal modes of education attempt to mould students in the market-driven mantras of self-interest, harsh competition, unchecked individualism, and the ethos of consumerism. The assault on the creative possibilities of an inspired imagination are matched by the emptying out of history and the rise of repressive modes of pedagogy. Young people are now told to invest in their careers, pack their résumés, and achieve success at any cost. It is precisely this aggressive dystopian neoliberal project and cultural politics that now characterizes the current assault on public and higher education in various parts of the globe. Under neoliberalism, the mantra of privatization, deregulation, and the destruction of the public good is matched by a toxic merging of inequality, greed, and the nativist language of borders, walls, and camps. Teaching for the test further deadens the imagination and the creative impulse, and functions largely as a disciplinary tool. Politics is now driven by money and is so dangerously sclerotic that it can no longer respond to deeply rooted social and economic problems.

Making the Pedagogical More Political

It is crucial for educators to remember that language is not simply an instrument of fear, violence, and intimidation; it is also a vehicle for critique, civic courage, resistance, and engaged modes of agency. We live at a time when the language of democracy has been pillaged, stripped of its promises and hopes. For instance, under the former Trump regime and other existing authoritarians such as Jair Bolsonaro in Brazil and Viktor Orbán in Hungary, the degradation of language reinforced Umberto Eco's remark that education is an organizing principal feature of fascism. According to Eco, one of the central features of what he called 'Ur-Fascism' was its undermining of civic literacy through 'Fascist schoolbooks [that] made use of an impoverished vocabulary, and an elementary syntax, in order to limit the instruments for complex and critical reasoning.'[17]

If fascism is to be defeated, there is a need to make education an organizing principle of politics and, in part, this can be done with a language that exposes and unravels falsehoods, systems of oppression, and corrupt relations of power while making clear that an alternative future is possible. Hannah Arendt was right in arguing that language is crucial in highlighting the often hidden 'crystalized elements' that make fascism likely.[18] Language is a powerful tool in the search for truth and the condemnation of falsehoods and injustices. Moreover, it is through language that the history of fascism can be remembered and the lessons of the conditions that created the plague of genocide can provide the recognition that fascism does not reside solely in the past and that its traces are always dormant, even in the strongest democracies. Paul Gilroy argues correctly that it is crucial in the current historical moment to re-engage with fascism to address how it has crystallized in different forms and in doing so 'work toward redeeming the term from its trivialization and restoring it to a proper place in discussions of the moral and political limits of what is acceptable'.[19]

Gilroy provides one more reason for educators to make the political more pedagogical and the pedagogical more political. As I stress throughout this book, pedagogy is always a struggle over agency, identities, desires, and values while also acknowledging that it has a crucial role to play in addressing important social issues and in defending public and higher education as democratic public spheres. Making pedagogy essential to politics in this instance suggests producing modes of knowledge and social practices that affirm oppositional cultural work and educational interventions and offer opportunities to mobilize instances of collective outrage coupled with direct mass action against a ruthless casino capitalism and an emerging fascist politics. Such mobilization must oppose the glaring material inequities, structural forces of oppression, and the growing cynical belief that democracy and capitalism are synonymous. At the very least, critical pedagogy proposes that education is a form of political intervention in the world and that it can create the possibilities for individual and social transformation.

A pedagogy of resistance necessitates a number of political interventions and should include a revival of the radical imagination in order to reclaim the democratic and egalitarian impulses crucial to a socialist democracy. There is also the need to develop pedagogical initiatives such as alternative schools, educational spaces in low-income neighbourhoods, and a national media service to counter the mainstream and far-right media. Within public and higher education, the human misery and devastation reaped by neoliberalism, corporate power, and authoritarian policies must be made visible and challenged so students can be given a formidable and critical education capable of addressing such issues. There is also the need to reinvent new visions that offer a sense of possibility, refusing to emulate the present as a natural order while offering a comprehensive politics not limited to single issues. Finally, but far from complete, there is a need to create an international educational movement for the preservation of public goods and the revitalization of democracy itself. This means in part taking seriously the adage of thinking globally and acting locally. Power now works globally and locally and we have to find ways to think politics through its diverse connections and alignments.

The Curse of Manufactured Ignorance

Manufactured ignorance now rules America. Not the simple, if somewhat innocent, ignorance that comes from an absence of knowledge, but a malicious ignorance forged in the arrogance of refusing to think hard about an issue, to engage language in the pursuit of justice. Expressions of such ignorance now rule an entire Republican Party who are climate deniers, believe that Biden stole the 2020 presidential election, and that voter suppression laws are unrelated to an authoritarian politics. James Baldwin was certainly right in issuing a stern warning in *No Name in the Street* that 'Ignorance, allied with power, is the most ferocious enemy justice can have.'[20] Thinking is now viewed as an act of stupidity, and thoughtlessness is considered a virtue. All traces of critical thought appear only at the margins of the culture, as ignorance becomes the primary organizing principle of American society.

As is well known, former President Trump's ignorance is on display daily, though its source is no longer the White House but the gated confines of Mar-A-Logo. Not only is he a sociopathic serial liar, but his ignorance also serves as a tool of power to prevent power from being held accountable. In addition, ignorance is the enemy of critical thinking, committed intellectuals, and emancipatory forms of education. Ignorance is not innocent, especially when it proclaims the space of common sense and labels thinking dangerous while exhibiting a disdain for truth, scientific evidence, and rational judgements. However, there is more at stake here than the production of a toxic form of illiteracy celebrated as common sense, the normalization of fake news, and the shrinking of political horizons. There is also the closing of the horizons of the political coupled with explicit expressions of cruelty and a 'widely sanctioned ruthlessness'.[21] We now live in a new age of brutality in which we are told that the central mark of our agency is to be at war with others, unleash our most ruthless and competitive side, and learn how to survive in the cut-throat, survival-of-the fittest, war-against-all jungle of late capitalism. Millions of people under the banner of Trumpism now collude in hate, revel in their feelings being whipped up in a 'hideous ecstasy of fear and vindictiveness'.[22]

The very conditions that enable people to make informed decisions are under siege as schools are defunded, media becomes more corporatized, oppositional journalists are denigrated or fired, the right to protest is criminalized, and reality TV becomes the model for mass entertainment. Under such circumstances, there is a full-scale attack on thoughtful reasoning, empathy, collective resistance, and the radical imagination. In some ways, the dictatorship of ignorance resembles what the writer John Berger calls 'ethicide', by which he means the mass news media functions as an agent that 'kill[s] ethics and therefore any notion of history and justice.'[23] Words such as love, trust, freedom, responsibility, and choice have been deformed by a market logic that narrows their meaning to either a relationship to a commodity or a reductive notion of self-interest.

Freedom now means removing oneself from any sense of social responsibility so one can retreat unencumbered into privatized orbits of self-indulgence. And so it goes. The new form of illiteracy does not simply constitute an absence of learning, ideas, or knowledge. Nor can it be solely attributed to what has been called the 'smartphone society'.[24] On the contrary, it is a wilful practice and goal used to actively depoliticize people and make them complicit with the forces that impose misery and suffering upon their lives. Under such circumstances, democracy is not weakened or circumvented, it is destroyed. Ignorance allied with the power of capital has put the world on a roadmap to hell.

Beyond Critical Thinking

Given the current crisis of politics, agency, history, and memory, educators need a new political and pedagogical language for addressing the changing contexts and issues facing a world in which capital draws upon an unprecedented convergence of resources—financial, cultural, political, economic, scientific, military, and technological—to exercise powerful and diverse forms of control. If educators and others are to counter global capitalism's increased ability to separate the traditional sphere of politics from the now transnational reach of power, it is important to develop educational approaches that reject a collapse of the distinction between market liberties and civil liberties, a market economy and a market society. Resistance does not begin with reforming capitalism but abolishing it. In this instance, critical pedagogy becomes a political and moral practice in the fight to revive civic literacy, the social contract, and a notion of egalitarian and collective citizenship. Politics loses its emancipatory possibilities if it cannot provide the educational conditions for enabling students and others to think against the grain and realize themselves as informed, critical, and involved citizens. There is no radical politics without a pedagogy capable of awakening consciousness, challenging common sense, and creating modes of analysis in which people discover a moment of recognition that enables them to rethink the conditions that shape their lives. This is the moment of identification and recognition in which, as Ruth Levitas points out, the sense of 'something missing can be read in every trace of how it might be otherwise, how the ever-present sense of lack might be [tempered]'.[25]

As a rule, educators should do more than create the conditions for critical thinking and nourishing a sense of hopefulness for their students. Students also need to learn how to responsibly assume the role of civic educators within broader social contexts and be willing to share their ideas with other educators and the wider public by making use of new media technologies. Communicating to a variety of public audiences suggests using opportunities for writing, public talks, and media interviews offered by the radio, Internet, alternative magazines, and teaching young people and adults in alternative schools to name only a few. Capitalizing on their role as public intellectuals, faculty can speak to more general audiences in a language that is clear, accessible, and rigorous. More importantly, as teachers organize to assert both the importance of their role as citizen-educators and that of education in a democracy, they can forge new alliances and connections to develop social movements that include and expand beyond working with unions.

In the current moment of tyranny, it is even more critical for educators to revive the capacities, knowledge, and skills that enable people to speak, write, and act from a position of agency and empowerment. This is especially true as the landscape of literacy, knowledge production, and cultural apparatuses have both expanded and reshaped the terrain of politics. People should be able to represent themselves in a language that validates their histories, lived experiences, and offers a starting point for them recognize that moment of politics in which they can see how their own sense of critical and social agency has been denied and can be overcome. Educators need to rethink how new modes of literacy have emerged with the rise of an image culture, and its new tools for visual messaging, which point to powerful terrains of learning. Print culture is no longer the dominant terrain for producing knowledge, values, modes of identity, and easily accessible information. Identities, values, and modes of representation have been revolutionized with the rise of an oracular culture. Literacy and its opposite manufactured ignorance now reside and are heavily produced within an image-based culture.

Politics in an Image-based Society

Politics has become image-based and necessitates a rethinking of both the notion of cultural critique and cultural production. In the ubiquitous world of visual imaging and social media, young people and others must be taught not only how to critique new modes of knowledge production but also the knowledge and skills for them to become cultural producers. American politics now inhabit a new world of multiple literacies. As such, young people and others need to learn not only how to read critically visual texts and the cultural apparatuses that support them, but also how to produce them. They should be able to produce different forms of image/aural culture and the public spheres that make them possible. There is a dire need for young people, activists, educators, and researchers to develop new means of communication to fight the right-wing media. This suggests that a critical pedagogy invests heavily in teaching young people and others how to produce films, develop podcasts, and create online magazines to produce alternative and more emancipatory and empowering values, experiences, and social relations in a radical democracy. In part, this suggests that any form of resistance must recognize the symbolic and pedagogical dimensions of struggle and the power of persuasion and beliefs for challenging ideological forms of domination.

As cultural producers, young people can address the racial, economic, social, and political divisions undermining US democracy by addressing those concerns 'through social media, journalism political reform and civic education'—a project that appears more urgent than ever.[26] In doing so, they can enable others to mobilize the tools of an image-based culture, visual politics, and pedagogy in the service of social change. Such a pedagogy would be designed to inform and organize people while also fighting the misinformation that comes from the pervasive hate-filled apparatuses of the right-wing media empire and the dark reaches of the web. One place to learn how such a pedagogy works would be to study the Black Lives Matter movement and other youth movements that have developed in the last decade. These diverse movements are organizing across national boundaries, sharing tactics, connecting issues such as global militarism, neoliberal economics, and militarized policing, while developing new strategies through WhatsApp, Telegram, Instagram, Facebook, and other forms of social media.[27]

Ruth Ben-Ghiat touches on this issue with her insightful commentaries on the waning of liberal democracy in the midst of the image wars, the struggle over visual identities, and the collapse of reason. She points to the need for those struggling over democracy to collectively pivot to those diverse, visual means of communication operating within a range of new cultural apparatuses, in order to rewrite the power of literacy as a mode of resistance and civic courage in a democracy. Civic literacy is crucial to producing the agents who will sustain a democracy and rests on a more capacious apprehension of literacy. Yet, civil literacy is being undermined like never before by the ideological efforts of right-wing social media. This powerful ideological challenge to democracy and to the very nature of reason and literacy necessitate that progressives redefine the relationship between culture, power, and everyday life in a time of emerging fascism. Ben-Ghiat is instructive here and writes:

> With our freedoms threatened, that situation can't stand. We need to renew the image bank of democracy.... As the crisis of democracy deepens in America, visual communication will take on even more importance. We will need to channel the unique power of images to allow us to feel and dream and inspire us to take action as we build a pro-democracy movement for our country.[28]

Education operates as a crucial site of power in the modern world. If teachers are truly concerned about safeguarding education, they will have to take seriously how pedagogy functions on local and global levels. Critical pedagogy plays a vital role in both understanding and challenging how power, knowledge, and values are deployed, affirmed, and resisted within and outside traditional discourses and cultural spheres. In a local context, critical pedagogy becomes an important theoretical tool for understanding the institutional conditions that place constraints on the production of knowledge, learning, academic labour, social relations, and democracy itself. Critical pedagogy also provides a discourse for engaging and challenging the construction of social hierarchies, identities, and ideologies as they traverse local and national borders. In addition, pedagogy as a form of production and critique offers a discourse of possibility—a way of providing students with the opportunity to link understanding to commitment, and social transformation to seeking the greatest possible justice.

One of the most serious challenges facing teachers, artists, journalists, writers, and other cultural workers is the task of developing discourses and pedagogical practices that connect a critical reading of both the word and the world in ways that enhance the creative capacities of young people and provide the conditions for them to become critical agents. In taking up this project, educators and others should attempt to create the conditions that give students the opportunity to acquire the knowledge, values, and civic courage that enables them to struggle to make desolation and cynicism unconvincing and hope practical. The language of possibility in this instance is educational, removed from the fantasy of an idealism that is unaware of the constraints facing the struggle for a democratic socialist society. Thinking beyond the given is not a call to overlook the difficult conditions that shape both schools and the larger social order, nor is it a blueprint removed from specific contexts and struggles. On the contrary, it is the precondition for imagining a future that does not replicate the nightmares of the present, for not making the present the future.

In an age of gangster capitalism and an emerging fascist politics, educators, students, and other concerned citizens face the challenge of providing a language that embraces a militant utopianism while constantly being attentive to those forces that seek to turn such hope into a new slogan or to punish and dismiss those who dare to look beyond the horizon of the given. Fascism breeds cynicism and is the enemy of a militant and social hope. Hope must be tempered by the complex reality of the times and viewed as a project and condition for providing a sense of collective agency, opposition, political imagination, and committed participation. Without hope, even in the direst times, there is no possibility for resistance, dissent, and struggle. Agency is the condition of struggle, and hope is the condition of agency. Hope expands the space of the social and possible;[29] it becomes a way of recognizing and naming the incomplete nature of the present.

Building a better future than the one we now expect to unfold will require nothing less than confronting the flow of everyday experience and the weight of social suffering with the force of individual and collective resistance and the unending project of democratic social transformation. At the same time, for resistance to take on the challenges posed by the rise of a fascist politics, it will have to awaken desire in order to end the collapse of conscience. This form of educated desire is rooted in the dream of a collective consciousness and imagination fuelled by the struggle for new forms of community that affirm the value of the social, economic equality, the social contract, and democratic values and social relations.

The Struggle over Agency, Vision, Identity, and Politics

The current fight against a nascent fascism across the globe is not only a struggle over economic structures or the commanding heights of corporate power. It is also a struggle over visions, ideas, consciousness, and the power to shift the culture itself. It is also, as Arendt points out, a struggle against 'a widespread fear of judging'.[30] Without the ability to judge, it becomes impossible to recover words that have meaning, and create a language that changes how we think about ourselves and our relationship with others. Any struggle for a radical democratic socialist order will not take place if 'the lessons from our dark past [cannot] be learned and transformed into constructive resolutions' and solutions for struggling for and creating a post-capitalist society.[31]

In the end, there is no democracy without knowledgeable citizens and no justice without a critique of injustice. As democracy begins to fail, political life becomes impoverished in the absence of those vital public spheres such as public and higher education in which civic values, public scholarship, and social engagement allow for a more imaginative grasp of a future attentive to the demands of justice, equity, and civic courage. Democracy should be a way of thinking about education, one that thrives on connecting pedagogy to the practice of freedom, learning to ethics, and agency to the imperatives of social responsibility and the public good.[32]

Neoliberal capitalism strips hope of its utopian possibilities and thrives on the notion that we live in an era in which any attempt to think otherwise, or critically, will result in a nightmare. That is, neoliberalism is part of a discourse of erasure, a kind of Machiavellian magic in which social and structural problems rooted in class, racial, gender, and material relations of power disappear, eliminating any sense of injustice or social responsibility. In the age of nascent fascism, it is not enough to connect education with the defence of reason, informed judgement, and critical agency; it must also be aligned with the power and potential of collective resistance. We live in dangerous times. Consequently, there is an urgent need for more individuals, institutions, and social movements to come together in the belief that the current regimes of tyranny can be resisted, that alternative futures are possible, and that acting on these beliefs through collective resistance will make radical change happen.

5

The Scourge of Apartheid Pedagogy

The aim of totalitarian education has never been to instill convictions but to destroy the capacity to form any.

—Hannah Arendt

The toxic thrust of white supremacy runs through American culture like an electric current and has many moving parts. One of its most pernicious is its recurrence as a form of apartheid pedagogy. In the current era of turbo-charged racism, the most prominent version of apartheid pedagogy is present in attempts by Republican Party politicians to rewrite the narrative regarding who counts as an American. This whitening of collective identity is largely reproduced by right-wing attacks on diversity and race sensitivity training, critical race programmes in government, and social justice and racial issues taken up in the schools. These bogus assaults are all too familiar and include widespread and coordinated ideological and pedagogical attacks against historical memory and critical forms of education, especially critical pedagogy. The most aggressive moves by Republican-dominated legislatures are focused on efforts to control how American history, particularly the legacy of slavery and the blight of structural racism, is taught in classrooms. As John Feffer states, this is the educational version of an updated Jim Crow and points to 'a version of white supremacy [that] is being legislated into classrooms in various Republican-controlled states'.[1]

Under the influence of a number of Republican Party governors in Florida, Texas, and other red states, the cult of manufactured ignorance now works through schools and other disimagination machines practicing a politics of falsehoods and erasure. For instance, the Republican governor of Florida, Ron DeSantis, has signed into law a number of bills that require public universities to conduct 'annual surveys of students and faculty to assess their personal viewpoints'.[2] This is a form of ideological surveillance parading as educational reform. It gets worse. He has also put into place the implementation of 'state-mandated curricula that would include "portraits in patriotism" that celebrate the US governing model compared with those of other countries and teach that communism is "evil"'.[3] DeSantis's propagandistic version of a 'pro-American curriculum' is aligned with the historical cleansing and educational approaches used by many dictators. In this infamous alignment, the uncomfortable parts of history are erased and in their place is a view of history absent its complexities, conflicting ideas, and dangerous memories. For example, Vladimir Putin's regressive education law aims to restore a sense of patriotism-code engineered as a pedagogy of repression and conformity; This is similar to Xi Jinping's implementation of 'thought work' in China's schools. James Baldwin was on target in connecting the longue durée of economic and racial injustices to the legitimating power of ideas and education. Baldwin writes: 'It must be remembered—it cannot be overstated—that those centuries of oppression are also a history of a system of thought.'[4]

The fight to censor critical, truth-telling versions of American history and the current persistence of systemic racism is part of a larger conservative project to prevent teachers, students, journalists, and others from speaking openly about crucial social issues that undermine a viable democracy. Such attacks are increasingly waged by conservative foundations, anti-public intellectuals, political operatives, conservative politicians, and right-wing media outlets. These include right-wing think tanks such as Heritage Foundation and Manhattan Institute, scholars such as Thomas Sowell, politicians such as Mitch McConnell, and media outlets such as *City Journal, The Daily Caller, Federalist*, and *Fox News*. The threat of teaching children about the history and systemic nature of racism appears particularly dangerous to *Fox News*, which as of June 5, 2021, posited 'critical race theory' as a threat in over 150 broadcasts.[5]

What is shared by all of these sources is the claim that critical race theory (CRT) and other 'anti-racist' programmes constitute forms of indoctrination that threaten to undermine the alleged foundations of Western civilization, makes white people ashamed of who they are, and defines white people according to their race—all these assumptions about CRT are false. Right-wing attempts to demonize and discredit teaching about racism in public schools echo former President Trump's claim that teaching students about racism is comparable to the claim 'that America is systemically evil and that the hearts of our people are full of hatred and malice [and] is at odds with students receiving a patriotic, pro-American education.'[6]

To this end, Senator Ted Cruz (R-TX) has introduced the 'END CRT Act', based on an utterly false description of CRT. He writes, 'By teaching that certain individuals, by virtue of inherent characteristics, are inherently flawed, critical race theory contradicts the basic principle upon which the United States was founded that all men and women are created equal.'[7] Cruz and other right-wing political operatives have little or no understanding of CRT as a disciplinary field that attempts to understand how law sanctions racial inequality through large and small aspects of structural racism. The underlying message of CRT is to dismantle forms of structural racism in order to create a more fair and just society. This idea of justice and education in the service of an expanded notion of democracy is what Cruz, Steve Bannon, and other right-wing political operatives oppose. History is too dangerous for them, critical pedagogy is a threat, and justice is expendable in order to distort CRT for political purposes. It is hard to make up this display of ignorance and crass opportunism.

The nature of this moral panic is also evident in the fact that anti-CRT bills have become law in eight states, and fifteen state legislatures across the country have introduced bills to prevent or limit teachers from teaching about the history of slavery and racism in American society. In doing so, they are making a claim for what one Texas legislator called 'traditional history', which allegedly should focus on 'ideas that make the country great'.[8] In addition to DeSantis's repressive educational policies, Texas stands out in its efforts to determine what is taught in public schools because it has a huge influence on what textbooks are adopted across the country. As Simon Romero reports in the *New York Times*, Texas along with a 'dozen other Republican-led states seek to ban or limit how the role of slavery and pervasive effects of racism can be taught [amounting] to some of the most aggressive efforts to control the teaching of American history'.[9] He writes that several of the bills proposed by the Republican-led legislature include the following and is worth citing at length:

> One measure that recently passed the Texas House, largely along party lines, would limit teacher-led discussions of current events; prohibit course credit for political activism or lobbying, which could include students who volunteer for civil rights groups; and ban teaching of The 1619 Project, an initiative by *The New York Times* that says it aims to reframe U.S. history by placing the consequences of slavery and the contributions of Black Americans at the center of the national narrative. The bill would also limit how teachers in Texas classrooms can discuss the ways in which racism influenced the legal system in the state, long a segregationist bastion, and the rest of the country. Another bill that sailed through the Texas House would create a committee to 'promote patriotic education' about the state's secession from Mexico in 1836, largely by men who were fighting to expand slavery. And a third bill would block exhibits at San Antonio's Alamo complex from explaining that major figures in the Texas Revolution were slave owners.[10]

Idaho's lieutenant governor, Janice McGeachin, is equally forthright in revealing the underlying ideological craze behind censoring any talk by teachers and students about race in Idaho public schools. She has introduced a task force to protect young people from what she calls, with no pun intended, 'the scourge of critical race theory, socialism, communism, and Marxism'.[11] In this type of ignorance, theoretical and political distinctions evaporate. McGeachin's chilling attack on freedom of expression echoes an earlier period in American history, the McCarthy and Red Scare period of the 1950s, in which heightened paranoia over the threat of communism resulted in a slew of 'laws that banned the teaching of Marxism and communism and required professors to swear loyalty oaths'.[12]

This version of neo-McCarthyism was on full display in Ohio when Republican Representative Fowler Arthur introduced the 'Promoting Education Not Indoctrination Act'. This bill would outlaw the teaching of critical race theory not only in the public schools but also 'in Ohio's large public university system, threatening any institution that allows such teaching with a reduction of one-quarter of its state funding'.[13] The irony here is that there is little evidence that CRT is taught in public schools. Fowler's disdain for democracy, evident in her erasure from state-mandated curriculum guidelines of any notion of the common good, is matched by her distorted views of racism, environmentalism, and critical thinking itself.[14] When Arthur was asked at a press conference to define the substance of the bill, her ignorance of Marxism and support for a ginned up version of neo-McCarthyism was clear in her response, reported by Timothy Messer-Kruse:

> We really focus on defining the Marxist ideology... When asked to define what Marxist ideology was, Representative Fowler Arthur said that 'those are specifically that one nationality, color, ethnicity, race, or sex is inherently superior to another nationality, color, ethnicity, race, or sex... So, the main goal of this definition of divisive concepts is to define the ideology behind some of these Marxist ideals...'.[15]

Such attacks are about more than censorship and racial cleansing. They also ignore any work by prominent Black scholars ranging from Frederick Douglass and W. E. B. DuBois to Angela Y. Davis and Audre Lord. The proponents attacking CRT have nothing to say about its origins and the work of the late Harvard University professor Derrick Bell, who is credited with being the founder of critical race theory as an academic discipline. There is no room for complexity among critics of CRT, just as there is no attempt at either a critique of structural racism or the actual assumptions and complex knowledge that make up its academic body of work. What disappears in the attacks on anti-racist scholarship is any attempt to analyse how its most profound proponents explore and make visible the history and contemporary effects of structural racism on the existing social order.[16] What is missing in conservative accounts of CRT is a complex argument analysing how 'the nation's sordid history of slavery, segregation, and discrimination is embedded in our laws, and continues to play a central role in preventing Black Americans and other marginalized groups from living lives untouched by racism'.[17] Ignored in these reactionary fusillades mounted by the far right is the reality that racism can only exist alongside tyranny and that CRT is not only about racism and an appeal to equality but also about the 'possibility of democracy'.[18]

In this instance, education becomes a site of derision, an object of censorship and repression; it also becomes a way of demonizing schools and teachers who address critical issues of racism and racial inequality. Right-wing politicians now use education and the repressive power of the law as weapons to discredit any critical approach to grappling with the history of racial injustice and white supremacy. In doing so, they attempt to undermine and discredit the critical faculties necessary for students and others to examine history as a resource in order to 'investigate the core conflict between a nation founded on radical notions of liberty, freedom, and equality, and a nation built on slavery, exploitation, and exclusion'.[19] The current attacks on critical race theory, if not critical thinking itself, are but one instance of the rise of apartheid pedagogy.

Apartheid pedagogy uses education in the service of dominant power to normalize racism, class inequities, and economic inequality while safeguarding the interests of those who benefit from such inequities the most. In pursuit of such a project, they impose a pedagogy of oppression, complacency, and mindless discipline. They ignore or downplay matters of injustice and the common good and rarely embrace notions of community as part of a pedagogy that engages pressing social, economic, and civic problems. Instead of an education that enriches the public imagination, Republican Party politicians endorse all the elements of indoctrination essential to formalizing and updating a mode of fascist politics.

The conservative wrath waged against critical race theory is an example of manufactured ignorance parading as a form of 'patriotic pedagogy', which in reality is pivotal to the conservative struggle over concentrated economic and political power, and control in shaping civic culture and the political imagination. Manufactured ignorance is crucial to upholding the poison of white supremacy. Apartheid pedagogy is about denial and disappearance, a manufactured ignorance that attempts to whitewash history and rewrite the narrative of American exceptionalism as it might have been framed in the 1920s and 1930s when members of a resurgent Ku Klux Klan shaped the policies of some school boards. Apartheid pedagogy uses education as a disimagination machine to convince students and others that racism does not exist, that teaching about racial justice is a form of indoctrination, and that understanding history is more an exercise in blind reverence than critical analysis. It is a pedagogy that, at its core, is an attack on critical thinking, critical pedagogy, and an enlargement of the civic imagination. Apartheid pedagogy is also a tool to promote falsehoods about CRT in order, as conservative operative Steve Bannon noted in one of his podcasts, 'to use CRT to elect more Republicans'.[20]

The strategy here is to use CRT as 'a catchall for displaying conservative angst against the recent re-examinations of the role that slavery and segregation have played in American history and the attempts to redress those historical offenses'.[21] It also is relegated to an empty slogan to attack whatever concepts Republicans believe are unpopular with the public as well as to display their anger and opposition over the way race is presented, taught, and comprehended in America. Chris Rufo, another conservative pundit affiliated with the right-leaning Manhattan Institute, was more forthright in stating that CRT was a rallying cry for Republicans to win votes. For Rufo, critical race theory was the new bogeyman, offering a dog whistle scare tactic to be used in the disinformation machines that fed the right-wing culture wars.[22] In one of his tweets, he claimed, 'The goal is to have the public read something crazy in the newspaper and immediately think critical race theory... We have decodified the term and will recodify it to annex the entire range of cultural constructions that are unpopular with Americans.'[23]

Apartheid pedagogy aims to reproduce current systems of racism rather than end them. Conservative institutions such as *No Left Turn in Education* oppose not only teaching about racism in schools, but also comprehensive sex education and teaching children about climate change, which they view as forms of indoctrination. Without irony, they label themselves an organization of 'patriotic Americans who believe that a fair and just society can only be achieved when malleable young minds are free from the indoctrination that suppresses their independent thought'.[24] This is the power of ignorance in the service of civic death and a flight from ethical and social responsibility. Kati Holloway, citing the NYU philosopher Charles W. Mills, succinctly sums up the elements of white ignorance. She writes:

> 'White ignorance,' according to NYU philosopher Charles W. Mills, is an 'inverted epistemology,' a deep dedication to and investment in non-knowing that explains white supremacy's highly curatorial (and often oppositional) approach to memory, history, and the truth. While white ignorance is related to the anti-intellectualism that defines the white Republican brand, it should be regarded as yet more specific. According to Mills, white ignorance demands a purposeful misunderstanding of reality—both present and historical—and then treats that fictitious worldview as the singular, de-politicized, unbiased, 'objective' truth. 'One has to learn to see the world wrongly,' under the terms of white ignorance, Mills writes, 'but with the assurance that this set of mistaken perceptions will be validated by white epistemic authority.'[25]

New York Times columnist Michelle Goldberg reports that right-wing legislators have taken up the cause to ban critical race theory from not only public schools but also higher education. She highlights the case of Boise University, which has banned dozens of classes dealing with diversity. She notes that soon afterward, 'the Idaho State Senate voted to cut $409,000 from the school's budget, an amount meant to reflect what Boise State spends on social justice programs'.[26] Florida Governor Ron DeSantis's educational bills also threatened budget cuts if its public higher education institutions promoted the 'indoctrination of students'.[27] Such attacks are happening across the United States and are meant to curtail teaching about racism, sexism, and other controversial issues in the schools. They are also part of a larger attempt to smear any form of critical thought as a species of communism while instituting a new McCarthyism.[28] Moreover, these bills impose strict restrictions on what non-tenured assistant professors can teach and to what degree they can be pushed to accept being both deskilled and giving up control over their labour conditions. DeSantis, in particular, is waging a full spectrum war on democracy. He signed into law a number of bills designed to criminalize protests, suppress voting rights, and censor the political views of left-leaning educators.

In another egregious example of an attack on free speech and tenure itself, the Board of Trustees at the University of North Carolina initially denied a tenure position to Pulitzer Prize-winning journalist Nikole Hannah-Jones because of her work on *The Times Magazine*'s 1619 project, 'which examined the legacy of slavery in America'.[29] The failure to provide tenure to Hannah-Jones, who is also the recipient of a MacArthur Foundation 'Genius Grant' and an inductee into the North Carolina Media and Journalism Hall of Fame, is a blatant act of racism and violation of academic freedom.

Let's be clear. The North Carolina Board of Trustees first denied Hannah-Jones tenure because she would bring to the university a critical concern with racism that clashes with the strident political conservatism of the board. It is also another example of a racist backlash by conservatives who wish to deny that racism even exists in the United States, never mind that it should be acknowledged in public and higher education classrooms. The decision not to award her tenure created a public uproar and drew a firestorm of criticism among diverse constituencies. Some faculty left for other positions, and Hannah eventually stated through her lawyers that she would not take the job without tenure. The student-body president, Lamar Richards, 'publicly urged Black students and faculty members to go elsewhere'. In the midst of the public outcry and outrage by students, faculty, staff, and alumni, the decision to deny tenure to Hannah-Jones was reversed.[30]

Hannah-Jones declined the offer of tenure at UNC-Chapel Hill journalism school, joining instead the faculty at Howard University, a historically Black university. Her reasons for declining the UNC offer are not hard to fathom, and intimations of her decision are evident in an eloquent statement she issued after accepting the appointment at Howard University. She is worth citing at length because she provides a stinging commentary on the resurgence of Jim Crow in higher education and across the country. Hannah-Jones writes:

> These last few weeks have been very dark. To be treated so shabbily by my alma mater, by a university that has given me so much and which I only sought to give back to, has been deeply painful.... I cannot imagine working at and advancing a school named for a man who lobbied against me, who used his wealth to influence the hires and ideology of the journalism school, who ignored my 20 years of journalism experience, all of my credentials, all of my work, because he believed that a project that centered Black Americans equaled the denigration of white Americans. Nor can I work at an institution whose leadership permitted this conduct and has done nothing to disavow it. How could I believe I'd be able to exert academic freedom with the school's largest donor so willing to disparage me publicly and attempt to pull the strings behind the scenes? Why would I want to teach at a university whose top leadership chose to remain silent, to refuse transparency, to fail to publicly advocate that I be treated like every other Knight Chair before me? Or for a university overseen by a board that would so callously put politics over what is best for the university that we all love? These times demand courage, and those who have held the most power in this situation have exhibited the least of it.[31]

This form of 'patriotic education' is being put in place by a resurgence of those who support Jim Crow power relations. This type of retribution is a part of a long-standing politics of fear, censorship, and academic repression that conservatives have waged since the student revolts of the 1960s.[32] It is also part of the ongoing corporatization of the university in which neoliberal business models now define how the university is governed, faculty are reduced to part-time workers, and students are viewed merely as customers and consumers.[33] Equally important, this case is an updated attack on the ability and power of faculty, rather than Boards of Trustees, to make crucial decisions regarding both faculty hiring and the central decision to decide who gets tenure in a university.[34] Keith E. Whittington and Sean Wilentz are right in stating that the Board's actions to deny Hannah-Jones a tenured professorship are about more than a singular violation of faculty rights, academic freedom, and attack on associated discourses relating to critical race theory. They write:

> For the Board of Trustees to interfere unilaterally on blatantly political grounds is an attack on the integrity of the very institution it oversees. The perception and reality of political intervention in matters of faculty hiring will do lasting damage to the reputation of higher education in North Carolina—and will embolden boards across the country similarly to interfere with academic operations of the universities that they oversee.[35]

Holding critical ideas has become a liability in the contemporary neoliberal university. Also at risk here is the relationship between critical thinking, civic values, and historical remembrance evident in the current attempts to suppress voting rights, dangerous memories, and the developing critiques of racism in the US. The current conservative attack on critical race theory also testifies to the degree to which anti-CRT bills are funded by organizations such as the Koch brothers and the American Legislative Exchange Council, which provide the template for these bills used by many state legislators. Anti-CRT legislation and ideological falsehoods are also funded heavily by the Thomas W. Smith Foundation, the Manhattan Institute, The American Enterprise Institute, and a host of other right-wing institutions and foundations.[36]

What they all share is a contempt for the ideals of racial and economic equality as well as disdain for radical causes that extend from immigrant rights to climate change. David Theo Goldberg has convincingly outlined how the war on CRT and other anti-racist programmes are designed largely to eliminate the legacy and persistent effects of systemic racial injustice and its underlying structural, ideological, and pedagogical fundamentals and components. This is apartheid pedagogy with a vengeance. Goldberg is worth quoting at length:

> First, the coordinated conservative attack on CRT is largely meant to distract from the right's own paucity of ideas. The strategy is to create a straw house to set aflame in order to draw attention away from not just its incapacity but its outright refusal to address issues of cumulative, especially racial, injustice… Second, the conservative attack on CRT tries to rewrite history in its effort to neo liberalize racism: to reduce it to a matter of personal beliefs and interpersonal prejudice…. On this view, the structures of society bear no responsibility, only individuals. Racial inequities today are… not the living legacy of centuries of racialized systems… Third, race has always been an attractive issue for conservatives to mobilize around. They know all too well how to use it to stoke white resentment while distracting from the depredations of conservative policies for all but the wealthy.[37]

Apartheid pedagogy in the form of attacks on CRT also has a chilling effect on freedom of expression, suggesting that even thinking about racism and the legacy of racial injustice is unacceptable pedagogically in the nation's schools. Vincent Wong, a research associate at African American Policy Forum, states that 'it is difficult to separate the conservative critique of CRT from the rise of the Black Lives Matter movement [and] the backlash to constrain, censor, restrict the ability to talk about racial justice both in terms of contemporary inequality but also the history of it'.[38] The attack on CRT is aimed at repressing any attempt to address both the legacy and continued presence of racial injustice and inequality in America. Critics of CRT reject any attempt to interrogate the power of White America with its racial hierarchies and do so by pathologizing such discourses as anti-American. Once again, such attacks represent an updated form of McCarthyism designed to raise the spectre of communism, socialism, and Marxism in order to tarnish any critic who takes issue with America's legacy of slavery, racial injustice, and state violence.

Disinformed to Death in the Age of the Spectacle

The war to destroy the public imagination is now waged on many fronts, particularly through those corporate-controlled media giants and cultural apparatuses that mould our views of the world, 'shape politics, and even the outcome of elections'.[39] The power to dominate the public is done not only through military force but also through a corporate-controlled media empire that includes right-wing talk radio, social media, right-wing cable programmes, and mainstream platforms. All these cultural apparatuses shape knowledge, dominate ideas, mobilize hostile emotions, and filter the public discussion of major social issues.[40] Right-wing media empires increasingly provide a culture, language, psychological space, and melting pot of conspiracy ideas, cultivating a fertile soil for fascist politics.

It is worth noting that the spread and resurgence of white supremacy and right-wing populist movements through right-wing alternative media—Internet, talk radio, print, and television journalism—by hosts such as the late Rush Limbaugh, Glenn Beck, Michael Savage, Alex Jones, Tucker Carlson, Laura Ingraham, and Sean Hannity signal the increased power of right-wing media and culture to promote the symbolic and pedagogical building blocks necessary for an ongoing attack on truth, rational discourse, and enlightenment values. Matters of persuasion and misinformation are two sides of the same coin of toxic propaganda.

Rather than be dismissed as a source of entertainment or the rantings of fringe elements on the right, these Trump-aligned media commentators provide confirmation of both the reconfiguration of the racial state and the need for progressives to understand how issues of common sense, culture, communication, and social media work to reproduce an upgraded form of spectacularized fascist politics. As Amelia Mertha points out, 'spectacle is a necessary condition for white supremacy. When it does not manifest in covert forms, white supremacy is the most emphatic and twisted stage show of all'.[41] The consumption and spectacle of Black pain and suffering have a long history in the United States; only now it does not draw large crowds to public lynchings but to media platforms such as right-wing talk shows and the Internet.

Fox News, Breitbart, Newsmax, One America News, Infowars, and other toxic cultural apparatuses represent a new front in the war to use social media to both depoliticize individuals and discredit critics that would oppose white supremacy and authoritarian nationalism. This media sphere of right-wing cultural apparatuses is not just news-oriented, nor can they be dismissed as clownish propaganda outlets. They are very sophisticated in the way in which they use music, online games, cartoons, and videos not only as ideological props to recruit young people but also as part of an appeal to community and a shared culture with its own language and sense of solidarity, with its false promise of solidarity through appeals to hatred, bigotry, anti-Semitism, misogyny, and racism.[42] This is an example of the neoliberal dream machine where war, violence, and politics have taken on a new disturbing form of urgency within image-based cultures. Violence is not merely reported; it is replayed, stoked for entertainment value, and its new currency is white supremacy ramped up in the service of a fascist politics led by the former president of the United States and his merry band of lackeys. Carlson, along with *Fox News*, relies on the rhetoric of war with its implication for exercising violence against alleged enemies. In this instance, politics becomes an extension of war. Texas A&M communications professor Jennifer Mercieca offers examples of what she calls war rhetoric. She writes:

> War rhetoric typically combines ad baculum (threats of force), reification (treating people as inhuman objects), and ad hominem (personal attacks, name-calling), scapegoating (placing the blame for

problems on the dehumanized other) and victimage (we are innocent, but under threat). The combination of these features is thought to prepare a nation or people to hate, fear and despise an enemy so that it will be motivated to war.[43]

Fascist politics works best amid the merging and constant repetition of ignorance, resentment, and hatred. It destroys the truth, then the institutions that produce it, and it denigrates, or even worse, anyone who cultivates and expresses critical ideas. Right-wing media represents a new tool in the rise of right-wing pedagogy and extremism. The pernicious influence of right-wing media is particularly evident in the ubiquitous presence of Tucker Carlson. In part, this is because his programme, *Tucker Carlson on Fox News* with over three million viewers, is one of the highest-rated and most-watched cable news programmes in the United States. Carlson saturates media space with racist, antigovernment, and Trump-based lies. Carlson's presence in US politics is crucial to understand because he is one of the most prominent media personalities engaging in a successful politics of depoliticization by encouraging his audience to suspend their critical faculties. He hides the truth in the shadows of a poisonous spectacle, and his political commentaries are about more than an assault on facts, evidence, and truth. In sync with Trump's Republican Party, militia groups, QAnon followers, online hate-filled communities, and conspiracy theorists, Carlson's public flirtation with right-wing violence trades not only in the language of the spectacle but endorses the prospect of authoritarian rule at almost any cost.

Carlson floods the media with lies, promotes fear of people of colour, and produces a constant barrage of misrepresentations, such as his claim that immigrants are making America 'poorer and dirtier'.[44] He has defended the actions of seventeen-year-old Kyle Rittenhouse, an American vigilante, who killed two protesters participating in a Black Lives Matter protest in Kenosha, Wisconsin.[45] He has railed against the idea of diversity and pushed racist immigration narratives that make him a favourite on neo-Nazi websites such as *The Daily Stormer*.

Carlson openly touts 'white replacement theory, which argues that "western" identity is under siege by massive waves of immigration from non-European/non-white countries, resulting in a replacement of white European individuals via demographics'.[46] The thread that holds different versions of replacement theory together is the 'common belief… that dominant groups—white people, men, Christians, Americans—face an existential threat from an increasingly diverse society'.[47] More extreme versions argue that Democratic politicians, big tech, and the news media are hatching plans to put white people and those who stormed the Capitol on January 6 in re-education camps.[48] This is ignorance as a form of paranoid politics.

Replacement theory is more than a signpost of right-wing ignorance. It is also a calling card for an alleged civil war to be waged by far-right extremists against a left whom they believe are arguing for the systemic oppression of whites. Kimo Gandall, a former president of the College Republicans at the University of California at Irvine, echoes this sentiment in a podcast made in July 2020. He states, '[t]he leftist narrative now wants you to actually kill each other because you're of a different race… A lot of the leftist, BLM rhetoric—Black Lives Matter—founded itself on wanting racial division, right, when you have whites bow down to Blacks.'[49]

Carlson also calls white supremacy a hoax and shamelessly defends replacement theory knowing full well that it was used as a rallying cry for a Unite the Right rally in Charlottesville in 2017.[50] The march was organized by a motley crew of racist, anti-Semitic, heavily armed white nationalists and white supremacist groups, including neo-Nazis and the Ku Klux Klan. Repeating slogans evoking 'similar marches of Hitler Youth', the marchers yelled, 'Blood and soil!' 'You will not replace us!' 'Jews will not replace us!'[51]

Carlson also denies the Trump-inspired and sanctioned source of violence that took place against the Capitol on January 6. Instead, as Astead W. Herndon writes, Carlson retreats 'to the ranks of misinformation, claiming it was Black Lives Matter protesters and far-left groups like Antifa who stormed the Capitol—in spite of the pro-Trump flags and QAnon symbology in the crowd'.[52] Carlson's lies function largely as permission to legitimate his white nationalist and racist inflammatory rhetoric. Moreover, his embrace of far-right violence is used in the service of authoritarianism and lawlessness while functioning to encourage distrust, if not hatred, of justice, equality, social responsibility, and democracy itself.

Carlson's lies, misinformation, and dangerous rantings prompted the conservative columnist Max Boot to claim that Carlson 'is inciting violence and abetting terrorism. He hits a new low every time he takes to the airwaves'.[53] Like many of his conservative media cohorts, Carlson embraces the unfounded and disproven lie that the presidential election was stolen from Trump. The spreading of such falsehoods in the name of cult-like loyalty to Trump may not be the 'moral equivalent of fascist propaganda. But it serves the same political function'.[54] As Michael Gerson pointedly observes, 'A founding lie is intended to remove followers from the messy world of rationality, facts, and evidence. It is designed to replace critical judgment with personal loyalty. It is supposed to encourage distrust of every source of social authority opposed to the leader's shifting will.'[55]

Furthermore, the spreading of the big lie in the age of Trumpism recalls the belief stated by the Nazi propagandist, Joseph Goebbels, that the bigger the lie, the easier it was to spread than a small one, and that if spread widely enough, the more likely it would be believed. Not only is the most effective propaganda produced through the repetition and saturation of the 'Stop the Steal' campaign—whose success is evident in the millions who believe the 2020 presidential election was stolen—the big lie is also the driving organizing principle in spreading manufactured ignorance, empowering racist haters, and legitimating white supremacist doctrines and a range of dangerous conspiracy theories. The false claim by Republican Party politicians and pundits that the election was stolen works to both legitimate the violent attack on the Capitol on January 6th, and build momentum for passing laws to invalidate elections in the future.

Trump and his acolytes do more than represent a break from reality; they undermine the formative cultures, civic institutions, and modes of empowering education necessary to equip people with the critical skills they need in order to recognize and resist authoritarian models of power. This is part of what Michael I. Niman calls 'a fascist war on empirical reality'.[56] It is also a retreat from any vestige of ethical and social responsibility. This fog of manufactured ignorance reproduced through a 'high-volume diffusion of falsehoods, partial truths, and conspiracy theories' weakens the individual and society's ability to resist the pernicious effects of such propaganda.[57] Drawing upon Jason Stanley's work on propaganda, Carlson, Michael Savage, Glenn Beck, and other right-wing pundits promote a 'flawed ideology' that legitimates the dehumanization of other groups while functioning as 'barriers to rational thought and empathy that propaganda exploits'.[58] More specifically, they operate in the production of fascist agitation, and their aim is to unmoor language from critical reason while turning politics into theatre. Carlson and his right-wing cronies are the new face of fascist agitprop, ensuring that the media transform violence and abuse into a cheap spectacle. Carlson, in particular, has become the symbol of shock-inducing, tabloid politics emptied of moral conscience and filled with thunderous idiocy.

Carlson's racist babble testifies to the inflated relevance in the media eco-spheres of a political theatricality and performance that merges the politics of hate with the razzle dazzle associated with the tawdry underside of the entertainment industry. His bigoted and nativist rhetoric spreads fascist myths about racial purity and cleansing while urging the masses to buy into a 'boiling primordial soup from which more developed and more dangerous forms of fascism might emerge'.[59] Trading in the politics of disposability, Carlson uses the media to promote what Etienne Balibar calls 'production for elimination… of populations that… are already superfluous'.[60] In this instance, an ideology forged in racist contempt, dehumanization, and threat of death now functions 'as a form of political and economic currency'.[61]

The public imagination is now in crisis. Radical uncertainty has turned lethal. In the current historical moment, tyranny, fear, threats, and hatred have become defining modes of governance and education. Right-wing politicians bolstered by the power of corporate-controlled media relentlessly construct ways of thinking and feeling that prey on the anxieties of the isolated, disenfranchised, and powerless. This form of apartheid pedagogy is designed to substitute disillusionment and incoherence for a sense of comforting ignorance, the thrill of hypermasculinity, and the security that comes with the militarized unity of the accommodating masses waging war on democracy. The public imagination is formed through habits of daily life, but only for the better when such experiences are filtered through the ideals and promises of a democracy. This is no longer true. The concentration of power in the hands of a ruling elite has ensured that any notion of change regarding equality and justice is now tainted, if not destroyed, because of what Theodor Adorno called a retreat into apocalyptic bombast marked by 'an organized flight of ideas'.[62]

The Spectacle of Violence

Violence in the United States has become a form of domestic terrorism—that is, it is home-grown and targets people in the US; it is omnipresent and works through complex systems of symbolic and institutional control. It extends from the prison and school to the normalizing efforts of cultural apparatus that saturate an image-based culture. Violence registers itself in repressive policies, police brutality, and ongoing processes of exclusion and disposability; it is also present in the weaponization ideas and the institutions that produce them through forms of apartheid pedagogy. It is not too far-fetched to argue that the refusal on the part of Republican Party legislators to develop policies that in the face of the delta virus protect the lives of their citizens, and actually do the opposite, constitutes a state-sponsored form of domestic terrorism. Just as one could argue that anti-abortion laws endangering the lives of millions of women represent another version of domestic terrorism. In both cases, these actions fit the description of terrorist activities carried out by American citizens that are dangerous to human life and are intended to do harm to a civilian population.

Fear now comes in the form of both armed police and repressive modes of education. As the famed artist Isaac Cordal observes, 'We live in societies... that use fear to make people submissive... Fear bends us [and makes us] vulnerable to its desires... Our societies have been built on violence, and that heritage, that colonial hangover which is capitalism today still remains.'[63] In the current age of fascist politics, the poverty of the civic and political imagination is taking its last breath. Under gangster capitalism's reign of power, fear and distrust breed state violence often wrapped in the mantle of criminality. Governing through crime now defines 'a notion of citizenship framed less in terms of a social contract founded on liberty and the good life than with reference to the imperatives of safety, security, and righteous self-enrichment... imperiled from all sides by the uncouth, the undocumented, and the underserving.'[64]

Authoritarian societies do more than censor and subvert the truth; they also shape collective consciousness and punish those who engage in dangerous thinking.[65] For instance, the current plague of white supremacy fuelling neoliberal fascism is rooted not only in structural and economic forms of domination but also intellectual and pedagogical forces, making clear that education is vital to politics. It also points to the urgency of understanding that white supremacy is first and foremost a struggle over agency, assigned meanings, and identity—over whose lives count and whose don't.

This is a politics that often leaves no traces. In the age of Google, disappearance resurfaces as a mode of politics. Under the reign of digital media and an image-based culture with its culture of immediacy and manufactured ignorance, the public is bombarded in the post-Trump era with an endless barrage of images of spectacularized violence that fill screen culture with mass shootings, police violence, and racist attacks on Blacks and Asian Americans. Disconnected and decontextualized, such images vanish in an image-based culture of shock, entertainment, and organized forgetting. In an age when both politicians and media pundits openly defend white supremacy, there is a price to be paid when power is held accountable. When critical ideas come to the surface, right-wing politicians and pundits attack dissidents as un-American and the oppositional press as purveyors of 'fake news'. Right-wing propaganda parading under the totalitarian notion of 'patriotic education' is now used to attack public and higher education and censor academics who criticize systemic abuses.[66] Former President Trump waged a relentless attack on the media, and in ways too similar to ignore, echoed written and spoken sentiments that Hitler used in his rise to power.[67] In this instance, culture, increasingly shaped by an apartheid pedagogy, has turned oppressive and must be addressed as a site of struggle while working in tandem to develop an ongoing massive resistance movement.

The connection between the rise of state-sponsored racist police violence, the suppression of voting rights, and the call for racial cleansing defined increasingly by an attack on anti-racist pedagogies is important because it signals the unapologetic resurgence of white racism at the centres of power in the United States. This suggests the need for a more comprehensive understanding of politics and the power of the educational force of the culture. Such connections necessitate closer attention be given to the pedagogical and cultural power of a neoliberal corporate elite, who use their mainstream and social media platforms to shape pedagogically the collective consciousness of a nation in the discourse and relations of hate, bigotry, ignorance, and conformity.

Recasting the Social Imagination

We live in an era in which the distinction between the truth and misinformation is under attack. Ignorance has become a virtue, and education has become a tool of repression that elevates self-interest and privatization to a central organizing principle of both economics and politics. The socio-historical conditions that enable racism, systemic inequality, anti-intellectualism, mass incarceration, poverty, state violence, and the war on youth must be remembered in the fight against that which now parades as ideologically normal. Historical memory and the demands of moral witnessing must become part of a deep grammar of political and pedagogical resistance in the fight against neoliberal capitalism and other forms of authoritarianism.

At stake here is the struggle for a new world based on the notion that capitalism and democracy are not the same and that we need to understand the world, how we think about it and how it functions, in order to change it. In the spirit of Martin Luther King Jr's call for a more comprehensive view of oppression and political struggle, it is crucial to address his call to radically interrelate and restructure consciousness, values, and society itself. In this instance, King and other theorists such as Saskia Sassen call for a language that ideologically ruptures and changes the nature of the debate. This suggests more than simply a rhetorical challenge to the economic conditions that fuel neoliberal capitalism. There is also the need to move beyond abstract notions of structural violence and identify and connect the visceral elements of violence that bear down on and 'constrain agency through the hard surfaces of [everyday] life'.[68]

Fundamental to any viable notion of pedagogical resistance is the courage to think and take on the challenge of what kind of world we want—what kind of future do we want to build for our children? These are questions that can only be considered when addressing politics and capitalism as part of a general crisis of democracy. This challenge demands the willingness to develop an anti-capitalist consciousness as the basis for a call to action, one willing to dismantle the present structure of neoliberal capitalism. Chantal Mouffe is on target in stating that 'before being able to radicalize democracy, it is first necessary to recover it', which means first rejecting the common sense assumptions that capitalism and democracy are synonymous.[69]

Clearly, such a project cannot combat poverty, militarism, the threat of nuclear war, ecological devastation, economic inequality, and racism by leaving capitalism's system of power in place. Nor can resistance be successful if it limits itself to the terrain of critique, criticism, and the undoing of separate oppressive systems of representation. Pedagogies of resistance can teach people to say no, become civically literate, and create the conditions for individuals to develop a critical political consciousness. The challenge here is to make the political more pedagogical. This suggests analysing how the forces of gangster capitalism impact consciousness, shape agency, and normalize the internalization of oppression.

At a time when civic culture, public goods, and the social contract are under siege, it is all the more crucial to produce a language along with a massive resistance movement capable of challenging and toppling the forces of structural racism, militarism, and economic inequality. There is a need to overcome the fragmentation and politicized sectarianism all too characteristic of left politics in order to embrace a Gramscian notion of 'solidarity in a wider sense'.[70] There is ample evidence of such solidarity in the policies advocated by the progressive Black Lives Matter protest, the call for green socialism, movements for health as a global right, growing resistance against police violence, emerging ecological movements such as the youth-based Sunrise Movement, the Poor People's Campaign, the massive ongoing strikes waged by students and teachers against the defunding and corporatizing of public education, and the call for resistance from women across the globe fighting for reproductive rights. All of these movements for social change are held together by the recognition that fascist politics at its core is a cultural force, an educational movement 'built on the pillars of persuasion and misinformation'.[71]

What must be resisted at all costs is a fractionalized politics, rooted in the notion that a particular mode of oppression, and those who bear its weight, offer political guarantees. Identifying different modes of oppression is important, but it is only the first step in moving from addressing the history and existing mechanisms that produce such trauma to developing and embracing a politics that unites different identities, individuals, and social movements under the larger banner of democratic socialism. What is needed is a social movement in which differences are respected but not isolated from each other; at the same time, left politics needs to speak to people through narratives that touch their lives while developing policies that appeal to and unite a broad coalition of interests. This is a politics that refuses the easy appeals of narrow ideological messages, which 'limits access to the world of ideas and contracts the range of tools available to would-be activists'.[72]

A pedagogy of resistance necessitates a language that connects the problems of systemic racism, poverty, militarism, mass incarceration, and other injustices as part of a totalizing structural, pedagogical, and ideological set of conditions endemic to capitalism in its updated merging of neoliberalism and fascist politics. Audre Lorde was right in her insistence that 'There is no such thing as a single-issue struggle because we do not live single-issue lives.'[73]

We don't need master narratives, but we do need a recognition that politics can only be grasped as part of a broader social totality. We need a politics in which diverse struggles are connected by calls for equality, social justice, and overlapping differences that bleed into each other. We need relational narratives that bring together different struggles for emancipation and social equality. The drama and narratives of everyday life have to join with a politics and seat of appeals that can bring together a broad coalition of educators, progressives, unions, social movements, and young people.

The only language provided by neoliberalism is the all-encompassing discourse of the market and the false rhetoric of unencumbered individualism, making it difficult for individuals to translate private issues into broader systemic considerations. Mark Fisher was right in claiming that capitalist realism not only attempts to normalize the notion that there is not only no alternative to capitalism, but also makes it 'impossible even to imagine a coherent alternative to it'.[74] This is a formula for losing hope because it insists that the world cannot change. It also has the hollow ring of slow death.

Given the current threats to democracy in the US, the time has come to reclaim the great utopian ideals unleashed by a long history of civil rights struggles, the insights and radical struggles produced by the Poor People's Campaign, the Sunrise Movement, the Black Lives Matter movement, and ongoing youth struggles against the rise of fascism across the globe. There is a need to rethink and relearn the trajectory of history by considering the role that critical education and notions of civic literacy have played in producing a collective anticapitalist consciousness. At stake here is the crucial project of once again creating the critical agents and social movements that refuse to equate capitalism and democracy and uphold the conviction that the problems of ecological destruction, mass poverty, militarism, systemic racism, and a host of other social problems cannot be solved by leaving capitalism in place. Only then can mass movements arise in which the future can be written in the language of justice, compassion, and the fundamental narratives of freedom and equality.

The urgency of the historical moment demands new visions of social change, an inspired and energized sense of social hope, and the necessity for diverse social movements to unite under the collective struggle for democratic socialism. The debilitating political pessimism of neoliberal gangster capitalism must be challenged as a starting point for believing that rather than being exhausted, the future, along with history, is open, and now is the time to act. It is time to make possible what has for too long been declared as impossible. Resistance is no longer an option; it has become the lifeline for democracy to be able to breathe again.

Part Three

From Hope to Resistance in the Age of Plagues

6

Rethinking Paulo Freire's *Pedagogy of Hope* in Dark Times

We must believe in the Principle of Hope.
A Marxist does not have the right to be a pessimist

—Ernst Bloch

Paulo Freire is one of the few writers whose body of work transcends the historical moment in which his contributions first appeared. While his *Pedagogy of the Oppressed* is his most celebrated book, I want to focus on *Pedagogy of Hope*. I believe it is one of those rare books that reaches beyond its time and translates with even more power and relevance for addressing the future. *Pedagogy of Hope* is prophetic and invaluable for navigating a dark time in history, especially at a time in history filled with the growing threat of authoritarianism around the globe; yet history is open and the dire moment in which we live makes all the clearer the need for critical thinking, collective resistance, and a notion of hope that inspires and energizes opportunities and to rethink the connection between education and social change, and to deepen our understanding of politics as part of a broader attempt to redefine and struggle for a future that does not repeat the present.

The mix of hope and despair is everywhere. The intersecting crises of economics, health, climate change, politics, racism, and democracy appear overpowering at times. In the current era, the rise of right-wing extremism, dictatorship, and authoritarianism has ushered in a new urgency to fight the fascist indifference to the distinction between good and evil and attempts to make 'the means of politics into the ends of politics'.[1] The rot of fascist politics has merged in the age of the COVID-19 pandemic with an expansive presence of fear, anxiety, repression, and a politics of despair. A crisis of politics and democracy has turned into an impending catastrophe.

Death and sickness have haunted our existence as the pandemic spread unevenly through those establishments, spaces, and materials that impact the most intimate aspects of our daily lives. Images of fear, if not apocalyptic nightmares, have flooded the news as people either get sick or die from the COVID-19 virus. As the pandemic intensifies and mutates enough body bags cannot be produced to keep pace with the death count. People continue to be told to sterilize just about everything they touched. Long-term stretches of self-isolation for the privileged feel like a form of imprisonment. For the poor, disadvantaged and elderly there are no safe spaces—only the daily risk of contamination, sickness, or worse. All of these registers of misery and suffering have been made worse with the proliferation of conspiracy theories, misinformation, and state-sponsored lies. They both sow confusion in the public mind and undermine the advice of public health experts. With the initial economic collapse, jobs disappeared by the thousands in days while small businesses went bust; the plague of inequality manifested itself in the disproportionate effects the virus had on the poor and others marginalized by class, race, and age.

What role might Paulo Freire's pedagogy and politics of hope have at a time when in the midst of a global pandemic it has become increasingly difficult 'not to feel that something—perhaps the world—is ending, as we struggle to comprehend unprecedented disruptions to our social orders and personal lives'?[2] For Freire, hope is not an antidote to what may be called the new age of pandemics; it is a warning and call to arms in order to understand and mobilize the resources of the imagination and the tools of critical analysis to address how the crises we faced then and today are the results of political, economic, and pedagogical forces that are tied to the mechanisms of predatory global capitalism. These crises are not strictly the product of the forces of nature, but the outcome of destructive ideologies, institutions, and relations of power produced by human beings, forces that can be both challenged and overcome.

For Freire, pessimism is the underside of apocalyptic thinking and functions largely to depoliticize people. He encourages us not to look away in the face of such crisis or to surrender to such events as inescapable acts of fate, but to seize upon them as offering up new challenges and opportunities to make politics, hope, and education pivotal to the challenge of rethinking politics and the possibilities of collective agency and resistance. Freire is not trying to locate redemption in the ruins that plague humankind as much as he believes that the impulses of hope can prevent us from becoming accomplices to the terror imposed by the pandemic and its mounting catastrophes. In the manner of Walter Benjamin, Freire wants to brush history against the grain while affirming his allegiance to the oppressed. In doing so, he reiterates Benjamin's notion that 'Only for the sake of the hopeless ones have we been given hope.'[3]

Freire's work teaches us that crises of this contemporary magnitude offer an opportunity to usher in great changes. As the old order is crumbling and as a new one emerges, there is a moment in which established traditions are questioned, new social formations are produced, and the spirit of resistance comes alive. For instance, in the current age of widespread anxiety, radical uncertainty, and growing precarity, the pandemic has revealed with marked clarity the predatory workings of capitalism, the inability of the market to deal with a public health crisis, and its shocking lack of social and political responsibility. Critical ideas once again have power as millions filled the streets following the murder of George Floyd, demonstrating against police brutality and institutional racism. Young people once again inserted themselves into the script of democracy, fighting for their place in shaping both the present and future through the registers of social, racial, and economic justice. Needless to say, young people alone cannot bear the burden of resisting a myriad of injustices. People of all ages are increasingly involved in a range of political activities to save democracy in the United States. The importance of these intergenerational struggles cannot be emphasized enough.

Radical change once more seems possible as there is talk of embracing collective struggles and exercising power in order to build the institutions, networks, sites, and pedagogical spaces necessary to challenge neoliberal globalization, fascist politics, and its exploitative and racist policies. The mix of despair and hope speaks to a transitional moment in history, ripe with both the promise of radical democracy and the emergence of the dark threat of authoritarianism. It is precisely at this historical interregnum that Paulo Freire's *Pedagogy of Hope* should be read as an invaluable resource both to understand and critically engage the present moment. His work is crucial for educators and other cultural workers who recognize that pedagogy is always political and, in part, is crucial as a form of organized resistance in creating the conditions for individuals to become social agents, responsible for their actions as critical citizens.

Freire was a scholar and public intellectual who built upon his previous work while opening new doors of inquiry. He was a socially committed educator who addressed issues far beyond the confines of academia, and he did so by speaking with courage and conviction to broad audiences. The echoes of suffering and the need to struggle to eliminate such hardships, particularly among the oppressed, never left his work or heart. His interventions were political engagements that crossed boundaries far removed from the academy and its often-sheltered fields of study. He took stances, upheld a humanistic concern with ethics, social responsibility, and justice, while engaging with broader issues of societal significance well beyond the realms of specialized expertise. He recognized with great clarity and insight that under neoliberalism, the chief function of education was repression both in schools and the larger culture. He was highly sensitive to the fact that struggle mattered and recognized Fredrick Douglass's apt insight that 'without struggle there is no progress'. Struggle for Freire took many forms that ranged from individual dissent to the right not to conform and to fight collectively against systems of domination. Ideas mattered for Freire because the struggle over consciousness was the precondition for waging an individual and collective battle over material relations of power. This was not only a fight to produce new ideas and knowledge, but also a struggle over the production, circulation, and uses of meanings, values, pleasure, and how to imagine the future.

Freire regarded capitalism as an evil and repeatedly exposed it as a system of domination that participated in psychological, political, and cultural oppression while ruthlessly exploiting the labour of those considered disposable. He considered capitalism not only as an economic system but also as a cultural and pedagogical system that stripped people of their agency, condemning them to an ideology in which they internalized their own oppression. Freire's emphasis is on a critical pedagogy that promotes critical dialogue among teachers and students so that both can come to understand how the power of the oppressor is internalized and what it means to self-reflectively overcome what Erich Fromm once called the fear of freedom. Freire detested neoliberalism, particularly its regressive notion of freedom, stripped of any sense of the common good, and disdainful of any viable social bonds. For Freire, freedom placed the individual in interconnecting webs of social interactions and was defined within those social conditions and institutions that connected the flourishing of individual agency to larger systems of support, values that sustained solidarity over self-interest, and made justice a social rather than an individual consideration.

Moreover, rejecting a class-only understanding of domination, Freire understood the oppressed to include a wide variety of groups extending from the homeless, Black people, and poor people to undocumented immigrants, refugees, and Indigenous groups. For Freire, inequalities and inequities had to be grasped as part of a series of intersections that made up the totality of the society. Critical pedagogy for Freire was also an intersectional pedagogy in that the forces of oppression and agency were determined by many factors such as race, class, and gender – all of which worked together in informing and shaping each other.[4] He believed that popular sovereignty, social justice, and equality were central elements of the society he wished to bring about. Like the great sociologist C. Wright Mills, Freire insisted that education for critical consciousness was a foundational element of empowerment rooted in the intersection of the individuals' everyday lives, their histories, and existing social structures. Freire keenly understood through his work on literacy as an essential step towards agency, self-reflection, and the ability to read the world critically that culture was at the heart of the struggle over meaning and identity.

His work was passionate, self-reflective, and global in its analysis of the relationship between education and politics. Not only did he view education as crucial to politics, but he also viewed systems of oppression as deeply pedagogical endeavours—hegemonic formations rooted in reactionary common sense assumptions and a regressive notion of agency—a theme vital to his classic books, *Pedagogy of the Oppressed* and *Pedagogy of Freedom*. In opposition to pedagogies of repression, Freire articulated a critical vision of education as an ongoing process of empowerment whose objective was the creation of critically informed and committed agents. Essential to this project was his concern with understanding how matters of identification, desire, values, and agency provided the basis for both a critical consciousness and a deep sense of individual and social responsibility. Most important to Freire's project was a view of civic literacy that rejected the notion that expanding one's knowledge, skills, and understanding of the world could be separated from the task of changing it.

For Freire, pedagogy is always political because it is connected to the acquisition of agency and illuminates how knowledge, identities, and authority are constructed within particular relations of material and symbolic power. Moreover, he viewed pedagogy as a deliberative intervention into how knowledge is selected, shaped, and interpreted as part of a broader ethos in search of political, social, and economic justice. For Freire, teaching and learning had to be connected to developing the critical capacities for informed modes of individual and social agency. At the same time, Freire was insistent that learning took place in a multiplicity of settings. In addition, he strongly argued that critical thinking was not enough. Freire wanted to educate students to be critical and knowledgeable actors capable of intervening in the world. Education was about more than either educating people for the labour force or getting them to think critically about questions of meaning and identity. This meant educating students to both master and use their critical capacities as individual and social agents so as to enable them to intervene in the world. At the same time, Freire urged educators to provide the conditions to teach students to learn how to govern, understand how power worked within different levels of everyday life, and embrace democracy as an unfinished process that demanded constant vigilance, learning, and struggle. He wanted students and others to master the knowledge and skills that would enable them to intercede in the spaces where social identities are shaped, values are distributed, and peoples' lives are shaped by power. Such practices had to take place not only in the schools but also in a range of institutional sites marked by diverse material practices and relations of power.

In spite of what some readers of Freire's work claim, his approach to critical pedagogy does not reduce educational practice to the mastery of methodologies. Freire stressed instead the importance of understanding what actually happens in classrooms and other educational settings by raising questions regarding the following: What is the relationship between learning and social change? What knowledge is of most worth? What does it mean to know something? And in what direction should one desire? What are the obligations of education, particularly the university, in a time of tyranny? Of course, for Freire, the language of critical pedagogy had to be expansive and deeply political without being politicizing. Pedagogy is simultaneously about the knowledge and practices teachers and students might engage in together and the values, social relations, and visions such practices legitimate.

Freire embraced the quest for a sufficient theory of subjectivity and took up the pedagogical task of addressing the conditions that enable people to think critically, make knowledge meaningful, articulate democratic values, and create pedagogical practices that contribute to producing critical agents: all of these concerns were crucial to his notion of a pedagogy of hope. Freire's work was dialectical in that it critiqued those modes of pedagogy that uphold relations of subordination and oppression while enabling pedagogical practices that teach people to engage in problem-solving, connect seemingly disparate events, learn how to hold power accountable, and take risks in doing so. Freire was insistent that educators had to expose themselves to the language, histories, and public cultures of those marginalized groups who inhabited the spaces of a 'bare pedagogy', particularly those who operated in a high threshold of disappearance and were often relegated to zones of social abandonment.

It is important to stress that Freire's theoretical interventions on developing a pedagogy of hope were more than a celebration of the culture of the students or a limited emphasis on enabling students to narrate themselves and refuse their learned sense of voicelessness. Freire's work is also about the necessity of recognizing that all pedagogy has to address matters of context, language, and the everyday conditions that shape students. Pedagogy for him was contextual and personal in that he believed that one entered into knowledge through an understanding of the experiences that individuals brought to the learning process. Yet, he never abstracted the close-up individual engagements and experiences he encountered with students from larger economic, political, social, and ethical considerations. Abstractions for Freire could be a form of violence. Hence, contexts and the histories and experiences that students and others brought to the learning process were crucial to engage and make subject to interpretation and exchange as part of the pedagogical process.

A critical pedagogical practice speaks to the need to affirm the voices and experiences of students in order both to problematize them and to introduce them to historical traditions, intellectual modes of understanding, and diverse knowledge outside of the immediacy of their limited experiences. Freire believed that 'everyday life had a politics and that politics matters' at the level of the ordinary, mundane, and in the workings of popular culture.[5] Moreover, Freire's notion of hope is attentive to the need to develop a language that is historical and relational, one that interrogates everyday experience and foregrounds possibilities that transcend the immediacy of the discourse of everyday life and experience. As Stanley Aronowitz has observed, Freire believes that 'learning begins with taking the self as the first but not the last object of knowledge'.[6] Education does not end with the instances of immediacy or personal experience but expands into the entire world and promotes the notion that education is the basis for students to be informed, capacious thinkers capable of intervening in the world. Education forces us to think about the reality of cultural politics, how it inscribes identities, and how culture shapes and is shaped by power dynamics.

Freire believed that pedagogy was more than a theoretical project; it was part of an emancipatory politics that acknowledged that democracy could not exist without the formative cultures that made it possible. In this instance, pedagogy embraced the experiences of the marginalized, establishing the conditions that enabled them to narrate themselves while subjecting such experiences and voices to the rigour of critical and theoretical analysis. Crucial to such a task was Freire's notion of civic literacy whose aim was to enable students and others to understand how everyday troubles connected to wider systemic considerations.

Crucial here was a pedagogical practice in which individuals could identify with a pedagogical narrative in which they could recognize themselves, and in a moment of recognition be able to identify with the conditions that have relevance for their lives. Without that moment of identification and recognition, pedagogy became an empty abstraction, removed from the daily experiences that shape people's lives. At the same time, Freire insisted that critical consciousness was not enough and must lead to critical interventions in the world. Pedagogy and education were not neutral but defined as a moral and political project.

Freire's notion of pedagogy connected ideas to power and knowledge to informed notions of agency, and in doing so, offered students the conditions for self-reflection and the possibilities for critically examining the forces that shaped their lives. Critical pedagogy revealed how power worked in all of its complexities but using the power of ideas to make diverse forms of oppression visible meant one had to use those ideas to address and resist the material conditions that imposed economic hardships on people.

At work here was an intricate dialectic of affirmation and expansion, an understanding of the immediate forces that shaped students along with the crucial task of broadening those horizons. Education has a history of being enmeshed in political struggles, and its process and outcomes are inextricably related to diverse ideological struggles and struggles over relations of power. Freire was an extensive thinker and rejected one-dimensional accounts of education regardless of whether they came from the right, centre, or left. For instance, he was highly critical of the mechanical economism of a vulgar Marxism, the instrumental rationality and culture of positivism preached by neoliberals, and the conceit of neutrality that defined reactionary liberal and conservative forms of education.

As *Pedagogy of Hope* makes clear through its revisiting of banking education and the necessity for problem-posing education, Freire strongly insisted that education was not a neutral practice. On the contrary, it was unabashedly directive in that it embraced authority as an object of critique and a resource, viewed human beings as unfinished, and consistently promoted self-development as a moral and political practice. According to Freire, pedagogy is, by definition, directive, but that does not mean it is merely a form of indoctrination. On the contrary, as Freire argues, education as a practice for freedom must attempt to expand the capacities necessary for human agency and hence the possibilities for democracy itself. Like the late sociologist Zygmunt Bauman, Freire argued that educators should nourish those pedagogical practices that promote 'a concern with keeping the forever unexhausted and unfulfilled human potential open, fighting back all attempts to foreclose and pre-empt the further unravelling of human possibilities, prodding human society to go on questioning itself and preventing that questioning from ever stalling or being declared finished'.[7] When education was viewed as a neutral enterprise, authority disappeared from the language of pedagogy because it was not problematized. As such, the articulation of education as neutral worked to promote forms of social, political, and cultural reproduction unproblematically. In doing, so it normalized existing relations of power, regressive definitions of agency, schooling, the future, and existing economic and social arrangements.

Under such circumstances, it was impossible to view education and schooling as part of a broader field of power or to recognize it as a crucial element of democratic citizenship. Authority in this pedagogical context was dialectical, many-sided, and inextricably connected to providing the conditions for creating learned citizens and a robust democracy. In addition, pedagogy as a critical practice connected theory with the lived experiences of students as part of a way to not only make pedagogy meaningful to be critical and transformative but also to shift power away from the teacher to the student in a more balanced way so that the latter could learn how to narrate both their individual transformation and the larger issue of social change.

On the other hand, authority in the service of a critical pedagogy of possibility viewed the task of educators to encourage critical thinking, dialogue, and human agency. Freire argued that the distinction between authority and authoritarianism had to be interrogated and viewed dialectically and politically if education was not to dissolve into a form of methodological reification, oppression, or mindless entertainment. As a fundamental element of critical pedagogy, authority for Freire is crucial to understand, analyse and use as part of a sustained attempt to influence how and what knowledge and subjectivities are produced within a particular set of social relations. Moreover, it is a crucial concept for addressing what it means to understand the relationship between how students learn and how they act as individuals and social agents learning to come to grips with a sense of individual and social responsibility. How we deal with authority is crucial for either failing or successfully connecting critical pedagogy with its democratic possibilities.

As an ethical ideal, Freire rejected any form of education that produced forms of indoctrination, embraced a mechanical obsession with methods, and separated education from matters of individual and social change. The quest for knowledge, the truth, and economic justice was not a script that could be imposed in the name of political purity, nor was pedagogy an a priori method that could be imposed in a standardized fashion. For Freire, education takes us beyond ourselves, embraces the unfinished nature of human beings, and insists that human life is conditioned not determined—which involves the permanent act of searching, being creative, and the endless quest to become the subject and maker of history rather than a disconnected, passive object in the world. Fundamental to Freire's pedagogy is the long-standing belief that if students are conscious of their conditioning at the level of everyday life, they can intervene in and re-create the forces that shape their daily relations and visions of the future.

What *Pedagogy of Hope* emphasizes, written twenty-five years after the landmark *Pedagogy of the Oppressed*, is that education is a constructed set of relations that enables individuals to relate critically to themselves, others, and the larger world. Making power visible and challenging its oppressive effects is central to Freire's notion of fostering modes of individual and social change mediated through dialogue, critical exchange, and informed judgements. At the same time, power is not defined exclusively through the forces of domination, but also through pedagogical practices rooted in forms of radical hope. Freire is firm in his insistence that the grotesqueness and brutality of the present does not reside in a set of natural laws in the service of the dark modalities of irrationality and common sense assumptions. On the contrary, it conjures up notions of a present subject to the creative forces of critique and a language of hope capable of imagining a future that is neither trapped by the present nor willing to reproduce it. This is a pedagogy that links knowledge, social responsibility, and collective struggle understood as a form of moral and political practice.

It is worth repeating that Freire is insistent that making the pedagogical conducive to critical thinking and social change was not an activity that only took place in the classroom; on the contrary, it was also inscribed and fundamental to the workings of a variety of sites that extended from the school to cultural apparatuses as diverse as the media and religious institutions. In this sense, Freire expanded the sites of education, the scope of pedagogical practice, and the spaces of struggle and collective resistance. Freire viewed education in the broadest sense as the practice of empowerment and praxis as a central outcome of critical consciousness—none of which were free from struggle or reduced exclusively to the neoliberal forces of consumption, instrumental rationality, privatization, and oppression.

With respect to language, Freire rejected reified notions of theory that traded in jargon and created linguistic firewalls that made it difficult to understand the issues they were addressing. He also criticized academics who removed themselves and their work from the social problems and human suffering that existed outside of the walls of the academy. Similarly, he rejected the anti-intellectualism behind calls to action and practice that rejected theory and rigorous forms of analysis. According to Freire, a pedagogy of hope, theory, and practice mutually informed each other and could not be abstracted or pitted against each other.

Pedagogy of Hope revisits Freire's long-standing argument that teachers should be public intellectuals. He denounced and endlessly criticized the conservative view in which teachers were reduced either to the role of a technician or viewed as functionaries engaged in formalistic rituals, while being indifferent to the political and ethical consequences of one's pedagogical practices and research undertakings. In opposition to this model, with its claims to and conceit of political neutrality, Freire insists that teachers and academics combine the mutually interdependent roles of critical citizen and committed educator. In doing so, they should promote pedagogical practices that teach students and others how to make power visible, write in an accessible language, and address fundamental social issues. According to Freire, this requires finding ways to connect the practice of classroom teaching with the operations of power in the larger society and to provide the conditions for students to view themselves as critical agents capable of making those who exercise authority and power answerable for their actions. Throughout his life, Freire insisted that the role of a critical education is not to train students solely for jobs, but also to educate them to question critically the institutions, policies, and values that shape their lives, relationships to others, and a myriad connection to the larger world.

In an age when solidarity is vanishing, and social atomization, isolation, and loneliness are being normalized, Freire rejected the false neoliberal narratives that defined responsibility solely as an individual undertaking. As part of his discourse of critique and hope, denunciation, and annunciation, he fiercely criticized the notion that one is only responsible to oneself, and all problems should be reduced to the logic of self-responsibility. He was a fierce critic of how the neoliberal emphasis on privatization and competitive individualism eroded communal life, making fragile those public spheres that embraced the social contract, welfare state, the common good and democratic forms of social solidarities. Freire was insistent that the ideology of individual interest, unbridled personal responsibility, and the collapse of the public into the private erased broader systemic forces at work in the mechanisms of oppression. He also insisted that the narcissistic, consumerist, and privatizing logic of neoliberalism served mostly to depoliticize people and displace the idea of the public good and the governing principles of economic equality and social justice.

This neoliberal pedagogy of atomizing individualism distorted peoples' vision of themselves, suggesting they were alone, and that personal responsibility was the only category for addressing every social issue they faced. All failures were now translated into individual failings. Pedagogy, in this instance, collapses the public into the private, individualizes all social problems, and makes it difficult for students to connect private issues to broader public concerns. This is a pedagogy that kills the spirit, promotes conformity, and is more suited to an authoritarian society than a democracy. In opposition to the individualizing of all social problems, Freire embraced the radical nature of how human beings are connected historically, constituted relationally, intertwined, and capable of translating private troubles into larger social deliberations.

At the same time, his work expanded to move beyond focusing on the working class as the only agents of change. Freire increasingly included in his analysis of pedagogies of oppression the varied discourses of misogyny, racism, and climate change. He was always attentive to the plight of refugees and a host of other groups considered disposable within the confines of the empire. In *Pedagogy of Hope*, he revisits many of the shortcomings at work in *Pedagogy of the Oppressed* as well as engaging in a dialectical analysis of many of the substantial and unwarranted criticisms of the latter work. He makes clear that he never viewed class as the sole definition of oppression while at the same time thanking profoundly those feminists who alerted him to his use of sexist language in *Pedagogy of the Oppressed*. In addition, in *Pedagogy of Hope* he updated many of his theoretical assumptions in order to deal with new economic and social formations produced under neoliberalism since the *Pedagogy of Oppression* was published in 1970.

As a scholar and transformative intellectual, Freire's work is accessible and rigorous. Freire's creative power is visible in its ability to develop new insights; everything he examined was filled with new understandings and charged with a radioactive sense of urgency. There is a consistent practice of self-reflection in Freire's work, the promise of lost truths, and the power of educated hope as a form of radical inquiry and practice. As the *Pedagogy of Hope* suggests in its title, hope 'was an adventure in unveiling', a pedagogical practice committed to educating, energizing, and inspiring individuals to struggle for and build a substantive democracy for everyone. Freire believed that in dark times one had to merge the necessity to be critical with an optimism of both the will and the intellect. Freire believed that hope was an ontological category crucial to preventing individuals from falling into despair, cynicism, and passivity. Far from being a hopeless abstraction, Freire argued that hope had to be approached as a political project and an ethical ideal. That is, it had to be rooted in both a historical consciousness and the concrete realities of the time. As Stanley Aronowitz points out,

> Freire aligns himself with those who still dream and keep alive hope for a world without exploitation, inequality, and cultural enslavement. But, unlike neoliberals and some leftists, his conviction is not borne out by some 'scientific' assessment of the current situation. Instead, Freire's belief in the emancipation of men and women is rooted in an

'existential' commitment to an ethical ideal rather than to historical inevitability.[8]

Hope in this instance not only provided the conditions for individuals to think imaginatively and otherwise, but also to act otherwise. This meant making hope and the ability to think outside of the bounds of the existing social and economic realities the precondition for developing the 'kind of practice that is explicitly attentive to questions of power and interests at individual, interpersonal, organizational, structural, and cultural levels'.[9]

Freire's emphasis on the notion of educated hope is particularly relevant at a period in history marked by the emergence of right-wing populist movements and a global fascist politics that echoes the horrors of an authoritarian past. Freire wants to resurrect a hope that matters, makes a difference, and gives theoretical and political support to John Dewey's claim nearly a century ago that 'democracy has to be born anew every generation, and education is its midwife'.[10] In this instance, hope is fundamental to any viable notion of individual and social agency; moreover, agency without hope makes despair inevitable. Hope is crucial for both reimagining and struggling for racial equality, economic justice, and democracy itself. According to Freire, hope is not only mediated by a recognition of the forces that work against it but must also be connected to a radical restructuring of values and forms of collective struggle appropriate to the age in which we live.

Hope in this instance is a social disposition wedded to the notion of collective action; it is based on a vision of how change can be addressed, realized, and how it can motivate people to analyse existing power dynamics that challenge dominant common sense assumptions and develop collective communities of resistance. Against neoliberal privatized notions of hope, Freire argues that hope is both a project and a condition for providing a sense of engaged participation that must be viewed as a form of collective struggle and not simply as an individual task. It is also a crucial condition for overcoming the debilitating political pessimism and endemic toxic public pedagogy essential to what Mark Fisher called capitalist realism.

Fisher was not far from the truth when he described capitalist realism as 'a monstrous, infinitely plastic entity, capable of metabolizing and absorbing anything with which it comes into contact'.[11] Freire turned to educated hope and its emphasis on civic literacy and critical pedagogy as tools to interrogate and challenge what Fisher called capitalism's 'horizons of the thinkable', which banished from critical thought notions of the unthinkable.[12] Hope with its realistic sense of its limits is crucial for illuminating the space of the possible, a space that 'is larger than the one assigned—that something else is possible, but not that everything is possible'.[13] For Freire, hope, in the words of Ernst Bloch, 'contains the spark that reaches out beyond the surrounding emptiness', and the boundaries of the given, the established borders, walls, and intellectual frameworks that normalize domination and pedagogies of oppression.[14]

Freire argues that hope must tap into our most profound experiences and, in doing so, provide the impetus for individuals to see through the causes of their suffering and revitalize their political capacities for individual responsibility, social agency, political imagination, and collective resistance. Hope is a crucial element of political struggle, especially at a time in which the conditions in which we find ourselves are becoming more authoritarian, morally intolerable, and politically dangerous. Without the urge to transcend limits, talk back, and exhibit irreverence towards authority, civic culture wanes and the democratic impulses that sustain a democracy wither.

Freire makes an invaluable contribution theoretically and politically with his insistence that education in its multiple forms and sites is the essential space to create pedagogical conditions that enable young people and others to envision alternatives to the existing society and redraw the map of possible associations, institutional power, and social values. Freire's embrace of a pedagogy of possibility was far removed from an idealist or vulgar utopianism abstracted from the realities of power. He not only connected hope to a rigorous analysis of the material conditions and relations of power that stood in the way of social and economic change, but also insisted that education and diverse cultural institutions were crucial public spheres for identifying and creating the agents, agencies, and practices that would enable radical change.

According to Freire, hope was also linked to the struggle for human rights, dignity, and those memories and histories that provided a legacy of struggle and resistance. His work not only makes visible the power of the possible in forms of self-reflection, self-examination, and a historical rendering of the world, but also displays the courage that comes with refusing to give up the dream of a just and equitable society, one in which matters of literacy, education and pedagogy informed each other in the fight for justice, economic equality, and democracy itself. Progressives need a vision that is expansive and life-giving. It must take the side of the oppressed and provides a sense of hope tempered with courage, and an emphasis on actions that speak strongly to the importance of collective struggles and the need for broad-based social movements. The damage done to democracy in the last decade, especially under the plague, may not be easy to repair. This will be the task of future generations who will struggle to reclaim a sense of resistance, embrace democratic notions of the social, recognize how fragile democracy is, and do everything possible to eliminate the hatred, racism, and economic inequality that has fostered the rise of right-wing extremism and its accompanying demagogues.

Reading the corpus of Freire's work reminds us of its contemporary relevance and the need to reclaim his attentiveness to an empowering vision in an age that seems to lack one. In doing so, it urges educators and others to develop a sense of responsibility in the face of the unspeakable, and to do so with dignity, a deep sense of commitment, and the courage to act in the face of injustice. This is especially crucial at a time when liberal democracy is on the defensive against right-wing authoritarians and lacks a clear sense of vision and resistance in order to fight this dangerous threat. Freire teaches us not only how to learn from the past and commit oneself to a more just future, but also what it means to work in the shadow of a life committed to justice, equity, joy, and civic courage.

7

Towards a Pedagogy of Resistance

If there is no struggle, there is no progress.... Power concedes nothing without a demand. It never did and it never will.

—Frederick Douglass

Dystopian Madness and the Hope of Resistance

The US's slide into a fascist politics demands a revitalized understanding of the historical moment in which we find ourselves, along with a systemic critical analysis of the new political formations that mark this period. Part of this challenge is to create a new language and mass social movement to address and construct empowering terrains of education, politics, justice, culture, and power that challenge existing systems of racist violence and economic oppression. This intersectional strategy can be found in the Black Lives Matter movement and its alignment with other movements fighting against both authoritarianism and struggling to free themselves from a racist history. As Lacino Hamilton argues, what is unique about these movements is that they teach us 'that eradicating racial oppression ultimately requires struggle against oppression in all of its forms [especially] restructuring America's economic system'.[1]

It can also be seen in the growing struggles of Indigenous people to recast their struggles in more militant, less isolated, and global terms, especially in light of growing revelations about the 1800 unmarked graves of Indigenous children who attended residential schools in Canada. In this instance, the government's attempts to erase the culture of entire generations of Indigenous children led to genocidal acts of state violence.[2] Connecting these diverse struggles is especially important as those marginalized by class, race, ethnicity, and religion have become aware of how much in this new era of fascist politics they have lost control over the economic, political, pedagogical, and social conditions that bear down on their lives. Visions have become dystopian, devolving into a sense of being left out, abandoned, and subject to increasing systems of terror and violence. These issues can no longer be viewed as individual or isolated problems but as manifestations of a broader failure of politics, if not the public imagination. Moreover, what is needed is not a series of stopgap reforms limited to particular institutions or groups but a radical restructuring of the entirety of US society as a start toward more global acts of resistance.

The call for a socialist democracy demands the creation of visions, ideals, institutions, social relations, and pedagogies of resistance that enable the public to imagine a life beyond a social order in which racial-, class-, and-gender-based violence produce endless assaults on the environment, and enable systemic police violence, a culture of ignorance and cruelty. Such a challenge must address an assault by neoliberalism on the public and civic imagination, mediated through the elevation of war, militarization, violent masculinity, and the politics of disposability to the highest levels of power. Neoliberal capitalism is a death-driven machinery that infantilizes, exploits, and devalues human life and the planet itself.

Understood properly, neoliberal capitalism is a form of necropolitics, or more specifically, a type of gangster capitalism that is utterly criminogenic. Gangster capitalism thrives on the silence of the oppressed and the complicity of those seduced by its power. As an educational project, it trades in manufactured ignorance. One consequence is that as market mentalities and moralities tighten their grip on all aspects of society, democratic institutions and public spheres are being downsized, if not altogether disappearing, along with the educated citizens without which there is no democracy.

Education and the Recasting of the Radical Imagination

Any viable pedagogy of resistance needs to create the educational and pedagogical tools to produce a radical shift in consciousness, capable of both recognizing the scorched earth policies of gangster capitalism and the twisted ideologies that support it. This shift in consciousness cannot occur without pedagogical interventions that speak to people in ways in which they can recognize themselves, identify with the issues being addressed, and place the privatization of their troubles in a broader systemic context.[3] Niko Block gets it right in arguing for a 'radical recasting of the leftist imagination', in which the concrete needs of people are addressed and elevated to the forefront of public discussion in order to address and get ahead of the crises of our times. He writes:

> This process involves building bridges between the real and the imaginary, so that the path to achieving political goals is plain to see. Accordingly, the articulation of leftist goals must resonate with people in concrete ways, so that it becomes obvious how the achievement of those goals would improve their day-to-day lives. The left, in this sense, must appeal to people's existing identities and not condescend the general public as victims of 'false consciousness.' All this means building movements of continual improvement and refusing to ask already-vulnerable people for short-term losses on the abstract promise of long-term gains. This project also demands that we understand precisely why right-wing ideology retains a popular appeal in so many spaces.[4]

Nico gestures towards but does not mention the plague of manufactured ignorance emerging from both the political arena and the powerful right-wing media. Nor is he clear enough about the merging of political education and cultural politics as a powerful tool for both domination and emancipation. It is precisely this plague of misinformation, civic illiteracy, and ignorance that offers a challenge to appealing 'people's existing identities'. As C. Wright Mills has made clear, in an age when the social disappears and everything is privatized and commodified, it is difficult for individuals to translate private into public issues and see themselves as part of a larger collective capable of mutual support.[5] The erosion of public discourse and the onslaught of a culture of manufactured ignorance 'allows the intrusion of criminality into politics'.[6] As I have argued throughout this book, America has a Nazi problem that has emerged with renewed vigour, and one lesson to be learned from the current assault on democracy regards the question of what role education should play in a democracy. As theorists as diverse as John Dewey, Paulo Freire, and Maxine Greene have observed, democracy cannot exist without an educated citizenry. Wendy Brown states rightly that democracy 'may not demand universal political participation, but it cannot survive the people's wholesale ignorance of the forces shaping their lives and limning their future'.[7]

Education has always been the substance of politics, but it is rarely understood as a site of struggle over agency, identities, values, and the future itself. Unlike schooling, education permeates a range of corporate-controlled apparatuses that extend from the digital airways to print culture. These are the updated sites of apartheid pedagogy. What is different about education today is not only the variety of sites in which it takes place, but also the degree to which it has become an element of organized irresponsibility, modelled on a flight from critical thinking, self-reflection, and meaningful forms of solidarity. Education now functions as part of the neoliberal machinery of depoliticization that represents an attack on the power of the civic imagination, political will, and a substantive democracy. It is also functions as a politics that undermines any understanding of education as a public good and pedagogy as an empowering practice that gets people to think critically about their own sense of agency in relation to knowledge and their ability to engage in critical and collective struggle.

Under Trumpism, education is increasingly defined as an animating principle of violence, revenge, resentment, and victimhood as a privileged form of identity. Right-wingers such as Sen. Tom Cotton are weaponizing education by calling for the firing of faculty who simply refer to critical race theory in their classes.[8] Right-wing legislators want to monitor the views of teachers, pedagogies of repression are modelled after calls to teach for the tests, and schools are threatened with being defunded if they include critical areas of study such a sexism and racism. Courses that deal with inequity are dropped from the curricula and in Tennessee a teacher was fired for teaching Ta-Nehisi Coates's essay 'The First White President'. In this scenario, we are reminded of James Baldwin's claim in *No Name in the Street* that when ignorance merged with power, 'education is a synonym for indoctrination, if you are white, and subjugation, if you are black'.[9] What this suggests is that political illiteracy, too often in the service of racism, has moved from the margins to the centre of power and is now a crucial project that the Republican Party wants to impose on the wider public. As the philosopher Peter Uwe Hohendahl has noted, the real danger of authoritarianism today 'lay in the traces of the fascist mentality within the democratic political system'.[10]

This suggests reintroducing how the cultural realm and pedagogies of closure operate as an educational and political force—enacting new forms of cultural and political power. We must therefore raise questions about not only what individuals learn in a given society but what they have to unlearn, and what institutions provide the conditions to do so. Against such an apartheid pedagogy of repression and conformity— rooted in censorship, racism, and the killing of the imagination—there is the need for a critical pedagogical practice that values a culture of questioning, views critical agency as a condition of public life, and rejects voyeurism in favour of the search for justice within a democratic, global public sphere.

A critical pedagogy rejects the dystopian, anti-intellectual, and racist vision at work under Trumpism and its underlying nativist pathologies, a thrill for authoritarian violence, and its grotesque contempt for democracy. Against gangster capitalism and the Trumpian worldview, there is the need for educators and other cultural workers to provide a language of both criticism and possibility as a condition for rethinking the possibilities of the future and the promise of global democracy itself. Critical educators must struggle against the concentration of power in the hands of the few who now use the instruments of cultural politics to function as oppressive ideological and pedagogical tools.

Beyond the Language of Neoliberal Capitalism

This is a crucial pedagogical challenge in order for individuals to become critical and autonomous citizens capable of interrogating the lies and falsehoods spread by politicians, right-wing pundits, anti-public intellectuals, and social media while being able to struggle for a more democratic and just future. The will to refuse the seductions of false prophets, neo-fascist mentalities, and the lure of demagogues preaching the swindle of fulfilment cannot be separated from learning how to be self-reflective, self-determining, and self-autonomous. But there is more at work here than learning how to be self-reflective; there is also learning how to turn memory and critique into a form of collective resistance. Learning from history is crucial in order to fight the ghosts of the past as they emerge in new forms. Vincent Brown captures this insight in his observation:

> I'm interested in looking to the past to understand the ongoing processes that have shaped our world. The predicaments in which we find ourselves derive in part from the history of colonial conquest, slavery, imperial warfare, and the inequalities that resulted. Our struggles for freedom and dignity emerge from that history. By understanding it, we might discern the scope, force, direction, and likelihood of the changes ahead—and be guided in our decisions by the example of our ancestors. Many people have the idea that the past is over because its events and its actors may be long gone. But processes of transformation—their motivating forces and legacies—are continuous; they connect the past, present, and future.[11]

Theorists and activists as different as Keeanga-Yamahtta Taylor and Andrew Bacevich argue that racism, militarism, white nationalism, materialism, and sexism, among other social problems, can no longer be explained away through the language of neoliberal capitalism, which has become synonymous with massive inequality, staggering poverty, and the looting and destruction of the public sphere and social state. Both agree that the current historical conjuncture is in the midst of a legitimation crisis that demands a new language and support for the unfolding revolts that have spread across the United States in the wake of racialized state violence. Yet rage and massive demonstrations do not fully explain the challenge of addressing the crisis, if not collapse, of consciousness that has produced the mass following that defines Trumpism—a euphemism for an upgraded neo-fascist politics.

The urgency of such calls to acknowledge and support such uprisings say too little about the need to develop forms of popular education that speak to people's needs and promote an anti-capitalist consciousness that allows them to see the interconnections among racism, economic inequality, militarism, patriarchy, and ecological destruction. Any viable form of resistance needs to expand the public's understanding of the social contract so that political and personal rights are joined with economic rights. A massive pedagogical campaign is also needed to deconstruct the regressive notions of freedom and self-interest at the heart of neoliberal ideology. The poisonous refuge of racism and economic inequality has to be confronted in multipole sites as a deeply interwoven political and educational struggle.

The overarching crisis facing the United States is a crisis of the public and civic imagination, and this is a crisis that, at its core, is educational. Such a crisis suggests closing the gap between educational/cultural institutions and the public by creating the ideas, narratives, and pedagogical relations necessary for connecting the shaping of individual and collective consciousness to the conditions necessary for individuals to say no, understand the causes of systemic violence, and free themselves from the social relations put in place by neoliberal capitalism.

At issue here is the urgent need to acknowledge and think through the connections among politics and education, on the one hand, and power and agency on the other. Essential to such a task is developing the intellectual and ethical capacities to address the question of what modes of address, interventions, and institutions are necessary to get people to think, debate, and share power while being able to conceive of a future free of injustice. Key to such a challenge is the need to produce an inspiring and visionary public imagination that enables people to define themselves beyond the regressive neoliberal notions of raw self-interest, regressive notions of individualism, and commodified conceptions of personal happiness. This suggests reclaiming a democratic notion of the social by analysing and legitimating the political, social, and economic connections and supports that provide the conditions for enacting a sense of meaningful solidarity, community, dignity, and justice.

Politics Follows Culture

As I have argued throughout this book, culture is the landscape and bedrock for creating the habits, sensibilities, dispositions, and values crucial to democracy's survival. Democracy needs a formative culture to sustain it. Theorists such as Antonio Gramsci, John Dewey, Raymond Williams, Paulo Freire, C. Wright Mills, Angela Y. Davis, Ellen Willis, and others have argued that democratic conditions do not automatically sustain themselves and that democracy's fate largely rests in the domain of culture—a domain in which people have to be educated critically in order to fight for securing freedom, equality, social justice, equal protection, and human dignity.[12] Institutions, however democratic and just, cannot exist without a critical, informed, and engaged public willing to defend them. Democracy is always unfinished and the formative culture that sustains it must be aggressively nurtured in schooling systems and the broader educational culture.

Education should be the protective site where individuals can learn to fight for the values of justice, reason, and freedom while also learning how to connect personal worries with public issues. Education is always about a struggle over agency, identity, power, and our hopes for the future. Critical pedagogy, in particular, should not only shift the 'way people think about the moment, but potentially to energize them to do something differently in that moment, and how to link [their own education] to... an active engagement of one's critical imagination, and political activism, not in terms of electoral politics but as active engagement within the public sphere'.[13]

If the civic fabric and the democratic political culture that sustains democracy are to survive, education, once again, must be linked to matters of social justice, equity, human rights, history, and the public good. Education in this sense must free itself from the technocratic obsessions with a deadening instrumental rationality, a regressive emphasis on standardization, training for the workplace, and the memorizing of facts. It must also educate students and others to fight the closing down of public and higher education as critical sites of teaching and learning. To make the political more pedagogical, education must affirm in its vision and practices the interdependence of humanity and embrace hope against a paralysing indifference.

Education is not just a struggle over knowledge, but also a struggle about how education is related to the power of self-definition and the acquisition of individual and social forms of agency. More specifically, education is a moral and political practice, not merely an instrumentalized practice for the production of pre-specified skills. The task of education is to encourage human agency, refresh the idea of justice in individuals, and recognize that the world might be different from how it is portrayed within established relations of power. The late Roger Simon adds to this vision of critical pedagogy. He writes that the goal of teaching and learning must be linked to educating individuals 'to take risks, to struggle with ongoing relations of power, to critically appropriate form of knowledge that exist outside of their immediate experiences and to envisage vision of a world which is "not-yet"—in order to be able to alter the grounds upon which live is lived'.[14]

Matters of education are crucial to developing a democratic socialist vision that examines not only how neoliberal capitalism robs us of any viable sense of agency, but also what it means to think critically, exercise civic courage, and define our lives outside of the pernicious parameters imposed by the veneration of greed, profits, competition, and capitalist exchange values. Education is a place where individuals should be able to imagine themselves as critical and politically engaged agents. In a time of oppression, education becomes fundamental to politics. Educators, public intellectuals, artists, and other cultural workers need to make education essential to social change and, in doing so, reclaim the role that education has historically played in developing political literacies and civic capacities, both of which are essential prerequisites for democracy.

The Role of Critical Education in a Democracy

Crucial to such a task is the issue of what is the role of education in a democracy? How might it function as a form of provocation and challenge, rooted in a vision and pedagogical practice that takes individuals beyond the common sense world that they inhabit and refuse the identifications imposed by others? How might critical pedagogy be used to alter the ways in which individuals relate to themselves, others, and the larger world? How might the stories and narratives educators and cultural workers use to shape their cultural work speak to people in a language in which they can recognize and realize themselves as informed and responsible individuals and citizens?

Without a pedagogy of identification and recognition, pedagogy too easily becomes both alienating and a form of symbolic and intellectual violence. As João Biehl has argued, 'subjectivity is the material of politics' and gives credence to the question of what kind of subjectivity is possible when one's voice is unrecognized and 'no objective conditions exist for that to happen?'[15] Without making education meaningful in order to make it critical and empowering, cultural workers run the risk of creating educational spaces where individuals have no voice and are relegated to zones of precarity and social abandonment in which they face oppressive conditions in which their own voices cannot be translated into action.

There is more at work here than affirming the critical function of critical pedagogy that enables an individual to break the power of common sense, there is also the crucial issue of opening up the space of translation, developing modes of meaningful identification, and building bridges of understanding and relevance into the pedagogical practices used in the service of social change. Matters of identity, place, and worth are crucial to developing the formative cultures necessary to challenging the threats waged by authoritarian movements against the ideas of justice and democracy and the institutions that make them possible. Any pedagogy of resistance must conceptualize and enable the conditions in which people can learn the capacities, knowledge, and skills that enable them to speak, write, and act from a position of agency and empowerment.

Stuart Hall has rightly argued that politics must be educative; that is, it must be capable of 'changing the way people see things'.[16] Education as empowerment must be able to take on the task of shifting consciousness in order to enable individuals to narrate themselves, prevent their own erasure, address the economic, social, and political conditions that shape their lives, and learn that culture is an instrument of power. For this to happen, people have to recognize something of themselves and their condition in the modes of education in which they are addressed. This is both a matter of awakening a sense of identification and a moment of recognition. Any viable notion of critical pedagogy has to be on the side of understanding, clarity, persuasion, and belief. Education, in this instance, is a defining political fact of life because it is crucial to the struggle over critical agency, informed citizenship, and a collective sense of resistance and struggle.[17] As a political project, it must press the claims for economic and social justice and strengthen the call for civic literacy and positive collective action.

Rethinking the Future

Rethinking the future suggests making critical education central to politics, functioning as a transformative force that enables people to address important social problems and the modes of resistance needed to defeat them. Such a future is impossible without a politics committed to the understanding that a substantive democracy cannot exist without an informed and active public. As James Baldwin observed at the end of his essay 'Stranger in the Village', 'People who shut their eyes to reality simply invite their own destruction and anyone who insists on remaining in a state of innocence long after that innocence is dead turns himself into a monster.'[18]

At the heart of Baldwin's message is that the state of a country's morality and politics can be judged by the degree to which education becomes a central force in producing a political culture and public imagination that expands the notion of freedom, social justice, and economic equality as part of the long march towards a democratic socialist future. At a time when the fascist ghosts of the past have once again emerged and the monsters are no longer lurking in the shadows, we must reclaim the public imagination and develop the mass educational and political movements that make such a future possible. The forces of resistance and radical collective movements are once again on the march, and it is crucial to remember that education opens up the space of translation, breaks open the boundaries of common sense, and provides the bridging work between schools and the wider society, the self and others, and the public and the private.

Against the dictatorship of ignorance and the destruction of the public imagination is the need for a politics of education that interrogates the claims of democracy, fights the failures of conscience, prevents justice from going dead in ourselves, and imagines the unimaginable.

This is an educational politics that not only connects agency to the possibility of interpretation as intervention, but also illuminates the forces that make people unknowable, make visible how social agency is denied, and where in time and place it is least acknowledged. There is also a need for developing a more comprehensive view of oppression, political struggle, and ongoing efforts to align progressive movements. The peripheral demands of single-issue movements have done a great theoretical service in revealing the wide arch of oppressions under capitalism. But these often siloed movements must translate into wider expectations for social change.

In the face of capitalist oppression, there should be no contradiction between single-issue struggles such as those proposing climate change and women's rights and struggles over economic equality and racial justice. In fact, for instance, the struggle over racial justice cannot be separated from struggles for economic justice, anti-poverty initiatives, universal health care, and climate change. Moreover, single-issue movements should work in tandem with movements fighting for institutional change and not simply a change in consciousness or the public imagination. In this case, ideas, once again, need to be married not only to power, but to unified mass movements. The key here is not only to dream big but comprehensively by connecting the dots in the name of a politics that connects the totality of problems defining neoliberal capitalism. Once the rubble of gangster capitalism as a form of fascist politics is understood and recognized as a criminalized project of tyranny, it becomes easier to destroy it rather than simply ameliorate its worse dimensions. Of course, the call for greater unity must not confuse such a project with reforming the Democratic Party. The left needs a democratic socialist party unburdened by the imperatives of Wall Street peopled by an expansive coalition of activists, social movements, and supporters intent on reaching its long-term goals.

Such movements must be willing to embrace an alternative vision for change that includes the destruction of the neoliberalism capitalism's ideological and structural foundations. At stake here is not only the recognition that capitalism and democracy are at odds with each other, but also that neoliberal capitalism has morphed into an updated form of fascist politics. In this instance, any viable notion of resistance must address specific crises ranging from mass poverty and staggering inequality to the destruction of the environment and systemic racism as not only specific crisis but also strands of a general crisis threatening society as a whole.

Nina Turner is right in arguing that 'good ideas are not enough— we need to marry our ideas to power'.[19] Radicalizing the public imagination suggests viewing democracy as part of a project that can be both recovered and radicalized through the combined struggles for emancipation, social justice, economic equality, and minority rights. Essential to such a challenge would be adopting a common agenda dedicated to developing a vast educational movement in defence of public goods. Any struggle against the dictatorship of ignorance will not only have to take matters of education seriously in the effort to address the current crisis of consciousness, but it will also have to bring diverse movements together in order to build a common agenda under the rubric of creating a critically engaged populace willing to fight for a democratic socialist society.

For any progressive movement to succeed, it has to overcome its differences and be unified. Put differently, it suggests that under the banner of democratic socialism such a movement has to connect a range of issues extending from free health care, free education, and a living minimum wage to cancelling student debt, protecting workers' rights, and supporting the Green New Deal. All of these issues should be struggled over within a broader concern for political, personal, and economic rights, which suggests defunding the military–industrial complex and increasing provisions of the welfare state. All of these struggles must be connected to the larger fight for racial and economic justice, social equality, and radically improving 'the material conditions of working people'.[20] Any mass movement for resistance has to organize diverse groups of people in a variety of spheres and places in ways that speak to their needs, fears, and hopes. This suggests bringing together people from a variety of organizing bases and neighbourhoods. This includes working people, trade union people, and people who are concerned about housing, adequate food, health care, public schools, and decent and meaningful jobs.[21]

Organizing is about more than tackling and connecting issues relevant to people's lives. It is also about using education to change consciousness, attack apparatuses of hopelessness, and inspire people to think beyond the common sense assumptions that shape their lives. As Hannah Arendt has suggested, it means encouraging people to be able to think in the place of others, and to engage in 'thinking without a banister'.[22] It is also about portraying those considered disposable not as victims, but as agents of resistance and a powerful force for social change. Robin D. G. Kelley is right in stating that progressives must be cautious in adopting the language of victimhood and trauma when dealing with oppressed groups. He writes: 'Trauma can be an entrance into activism, it is not in itself a destination and may even trick activists into adopting the language of the neoliberal institutions they are at pains to reject.'[23]

Beyond Manufactured Ignorance-Education and Social Change

Making education a key element of social change is fundamental for any mass movement of resistance to succeed. If popular consciousness is to be shifted, people need to learn from the trajectory of history, develop an anti-capitalist consciousness through diverse modes of institutional and popular education, and rethink the politics of fundamental change. This means recognizing and convincing a larger public that only democratic socialism can provide secure jobs, protect lives, affirm the common good, and establish the life-giving institutions and functions that serve basic needs and provide the conditions that ensure dignity, freedom, and security for everyone.

Ignorance has become wilful in that it is now a right-wing political project in the service of a fascist politics, manufactured and conscious in its pursuit of creating new forms of mass illiteracy. As such, it is no longer merely about the absence of knowledge, but about a depoliticizing project aimed at eliminating the critical faculties and modes of agency crucial to a democracy. James Baldwin captures this process when he writes. 'The will of the people, in America, has always been at the mercy of an ignorance not merely phenomenal, but sacred, and sacredly cultivated: the better to be used by a carnivorous economy which democratically slaughters and victimizes whites and blacks alike.'[24]

As such, ignorance has lost its innocence and has become lethal. In doing so, it has produced a cultural apparatus that denies reason, truth, and social responsibility. We need to recover and reframe the discourse and purpose of education as an empowering political project. Malcolm X was right when he said, 'Education is a passport to the future', but he added to this insight and made the notion of education political when he wrote, 'Power in defense of freedom is greater than power on behalf of tyranny and oppression, because power, real power, comes from our conviction which produces action, uncompromising action.' The language of critique, compassion, and hope must be collective, embracing our connections as human beings, and respecting our deeply interrelated relationship to the planet.

A democratic socialist politics and movement need a language of connections. Any affirmation of the social must ensure that public services and social provisions bind us together in our humanity as human beings. Capitalism has proven that it cannot respond to either society's most basic needs or address its most serious social problems. The pandemic has exposed neoliberal capitalism's criminality, immorality, and inhumanity and its alignment with an emerging fascist politics.[25] There is a need both to reclaim the histories of insubordination and resistance and to update and enact them accordingly in the current historical moment. It has become clear in the age of the plagues and monsters that any successful movement for resistance must be not only for democracy and anti-capitalist; rather, it must also be anti-fascist. We owe such a challenge to ourselves, to future generations, and to the promise of a global socialist democracy waiting to be born.

Notes

Introduction

1. Peter Fleming, *Dark Academic: How Universities Die* (London: Pluto Press, 2021).
2. Henry A. Giroux, *Neoliberalism's War on Higher Education*, 2nd edition (Chicago: Haymarket Press, 2020); Benjamin Ginsberg, *The Fall of the Faculty: The Rise of the All-Administrative University and Why it Matters* (New York: Oxford University Press, 2011).
3. Christopher Newfield, *The Great Mistake: How We Wrecked Public Universities and How We Can Fix them* (Baltimore: Johns Hopkins University Press, 2016).
4. John Feffer, 'Twilight of the Pandemic?' *TomDispatch.com* (June 8, 2021). Online: https://mail.google.com/mail/u/0/#inbox/ WhctKKWxTCSQgWdpVxVWGPdFMmpfqmjrfDRfTWShJBlNCfVnT gkshMnSfMlkHFCKRqcLkhl.
5. Ishaan Tharoor, 'The "Free World" Keeps Shrinking', *The Washington Post* (March 3, 2021). Online: www.washingtonpost.com/world/2021/03/03/ democracy-declining-freedom-house-report/; Arundhati Roy, '"We Are Witnessing a Crime against Humanity": Arundhati Roy on India's Covid catastrophe', *Guardian* (April 28, 2021). Online: www.theguardian. com/news/2021/apr/28/crime-against-humanity-arundhati-roy-india-covid-catastrophe#top; Gunther Günter Frankenberg, 'The Pandemic of Authoritarianism', *Comparative Law Review* 10:1 (2019). Online: www.comparativelawreview.unipg.it/index.php/comparative/article/ viewFile/167/136.
6. Laura Meckler and Hannah Natanson, 'As Schools Expand Racial Equity Work, Conservatives See a New Threat in Critical Race Theory', *The Washington Post* (May 3, 2021). Online: www.washingtonpost.com/ education/2021/05/03/critical-race-theory-backlash/.
7. David Glenn, 'Public Higher Education Is "Eroding from All Sides", Warn Political Scientists', *The Chronicle of Higher Education* (September 2, 2010). Online: http://chronicle.com/article/Public-Higher-Education-Is/124292.

8 Khalid Lyamlahy, 'The Professional Stranger: On Abdelkebir Khatibi's "Plural Maghreb"', *Los Angeles Review of Books* (December 3, 2019). Online: https://lareviewofbooks.org/article/the-professional-stranger-on-abdelkebir-khatibis-plural-maghreb/.
9 Giroux, *Neoliberalism's War on Higher Education*.
10 Gayatri Chakravorty Spivak, 'Changing Reflexes: Interview with Gayatri Chakravorty Spivak', *Works and Days* 28:55/56 (2010), p. 8.
11 Toni Morrison, 'The War on Error', in *The Source of Self-Regard* (New York: Knopf, 2019), p. 30.
12 Jeffrey Edward Green, *The Eye of the People* (London: Oxford University Press, 2011).
13 Jean Seaton, 'Why Orwell's *1984* Could Be About Now', *BBC.Com* (May 7, 2018). Online: www.bbc.com/culture/article/20180507-why-orwells-1984-could-be-about-now.
14 Ibid.
15 Ibid.
16 Charles H. Clavey, 'Donald Trump, Our Prophet of Deceit', *Boston Review* (October 14, 2020). Online: http://bostonreview.net/politics-philosophy-religion/charles-h-clavey-donald-trump-our-prophet-deceit.
17 Roger Berkowitz, 'Thoughts Amidst the Storm', *HAC Bard Amor Mundi*, May 11, 2020. Online: https://hac.bard.edu/amor-mundi/thoughts-amidst-the-storm-2020-11-05.
18 Ben Fountain, 'What Has Minimalist Democracy Gotten Us?' *The New York Review* (November 19, 2020). Online: www.nybooks.com/articles/2020/11/19/election-what-has-minimalist-democracy-gotten-us/.
19 Leon Wieseltier, 'Among the Disrupted', *International New York Times*, January 7, 2015. Online: www.nytimes.com/2015/01/18/books/review/among-the-disrupted.html?_r=0.
20 Ariel Dorfman, 'Defying Fear in Traumatic Times', *CounterPunch* (November 11, 2020). Online: www.counterpunch.org/2020/11/11/defying-fear-in-traumatic-times/.
21 Pierre Bourdieu and Gunter Grass, 'The "Progressive" Restoration: A Franco-German Dialogue', *New Left Review* 14 (March–April 2002), p. 2.
22 Primo Levi, In The Black Hole of Auschwitz, translated by Sharon Wood, 31–34. (Cambridge: Polity Press. 1974, 2005), p. 34.
23 Jean Seaton, 'Why Orwell's *1984* Could Be About Now'.
24 Arundhati Roy, *Power Politics* (Cambridge, MA: South End Press, 2001), p. 3.

Chapter 1

1. See, for instance, Ibram X. Kendi and Keisha N. Blain, eds, *Four Hundred Souls* (New York: One World, 2021) and Eddie S. Glaude, Jr. *Democracy in Black: How Race Still Enslaves the American Soul* (New York: Crown, 2016).
2. George Packer, 'We Are Living in a Failed State', *The Atlantic* ((June 2020). Online: www.theatlantic.com/magazine/archive/2020/06/underlying-conditions/610261/. See also The Economist Intelligence Unit, '*Report: Democracy Index 2020 in Sickness and in Health?*' (London: The Economist, 2021). Online: https://pages.eiu.com/rs/753-RIQ-438/images/democracy-index-2020.pdf?mkt_tok=NzUzLVJJUS00MzgAAAF7rWqgP6DlYFVEAK7Czco7ydAIGm68OjQuI82PV8isAJpp4nLgxDL6DbrcVyHBcm_TZ0o8kJF3cxcOmObEtvxqJW11EnoTS3bBWCDy918Jr0C1Lw.
3. On the American origins of fascism, also see Michael Joseph Roberto, *The Coming of the American Behemoth: The Origins of Fascism in the United States, 1920–1940* (New York: Monthly Review Press, 2018); Henry A. Giroux, *American Nightmare: Facing the Challenge of Fascism* (San Francisco: City Lights Books, 2018).
4. Rick Perlstein, 'The Long Authoritarian History of the Capitol Riot', *Intelligencer* (June 30, 2021). Online: https://nymag.com/intelligencer/2021/06/long-authoritarian-history-january-6-insurrection.html.
5. Ibid.
6. See, for instance, Susan Jacoby, *The Age of American Unreason* (New York: Pantheon, 2008).
7. Max Boot, 'How Can 42 Percent of Americans Still Support the Worst President in our History?' *The Washington Post* (October 13, 2020). Online: www.washingtonpost.com/opinions/2020/10/13/how-can-42-percent-americans-still-support-worst-president-our-history/.
8. Leo Lowenthal, 'Atomization of Man', *False Prophets: Studies in Authoritarianism* (New Brunswick, NJ: Transaction Books, 1987), pp. 181–9; Zygmunt Bauman, *The Individualized Society* (London: Polity, 2001). More recently, see John Douglas Macready, 'The Problem of Loneliness', *Arendt Studies* (June 8, 2021), pp. 1–9. Online: www.academia.edu/49182638/The_Problem_of_Loneliness.

9   Dmitri N. Shalin, 'Identity Politics and Civic Imagination', *Tikkun* (April 5, 2021). Online: www.tikkun.org/identity-politics-and-civic-imagination/?fbclid=IwAR192vcukJz_RfPnqfEGsETpGqdUwYenrLv8WagZ9vjwH8lA8OtOFYdRUyc.
10 Macready, 'The Problem of Loneliness'.
11 Jennifer Gaffney, *Political Loneliness: Modern Liberal Subjects in Hiding* (Lanham: Rowman & Littlefield, 2020); David Chandler and Julian Reid, *The Neoliberal Subject* (Lanham: Rowman & Littlefield, 2016).
12 Erich Fromm, *On Disobedience: Why Freedom Means Saying 'No' to Power* (New York: Harper Perennial Modern Thought Press, 2010), pp. 53–4
13 Adam Weinstein, 'This is Fascism', *The New Republic* (June 2, 2020). Online: https://newrepublic.com/article/157949/fascism-america-trump-anti-police-george-floyd-protests.
14 Douglas Rushkoff, *Team Human* (New York: Norton, 2019); Christian Fuchs, *Digital Demagogue: Authoritarian Capitalism in the Age of Trump and Twitter* (London: Pluto Press, 2018); Robert W. McChesney, *Digital Disconnect: How Capitalism is Turning the Internet Against Democracy* (New York: The New Press, 2013).
15 Eli Zaretsky, 'The Big Lie', *London Review of Books* (February 15, 2021). Online: www.lrb.co.uk/blog/2021/february/the-big-lie.
16 Robert Lipsyte, 'Rush, Roger, Rupert, and The Donald May Ride Forever as Do Pestilence, Famine, War, and Death', *TomDispatch* (March 7, 2020). Online: https://mailchi.mp/typemediacenter/robert-lipsyte-will-the-four-horsemen-of-the-media-continue-to-trample-us?e=5101a5c41c.
17 Klaus Marre, 'The Conservative Outrage–Industrial Complex Goes for Gold', *Who What Why* (July 11, 2021). Online: https://whowhatwhy.org/cartoon/the-conservative-outrage-industrial-complex-goes-for-gold/.
18 Jana Anderson and Lee Rainie, 'The Future of Truth and Misinformation Online', *Pew Research Center* (October 19, 2017). Online: www.pewresearch.org/internet/2017/10/19/the-future-of-truth-and-misinformation-online/.
19 Anthony DiMaggio, 'The Case Against Social Media: Mass Misinformation in the Covid-19 Era', *CounterPunch* (October 9, 2021). Online: www.counterpunch.org/2020/10/09/the-case-against-social-media-mass-misinformation-in-the-covid-19-era/. See also Terry Gross, 'How Internet Trolls and Online Extremists are "Hijacking"

American Politics', *NPR* (November 12, 2019). Online: www.npr.org/2019/11/12/778502116/how-internet-trolls-and-online-extremists-are-hijacking-american-politics. See also Andrew Marantz, *Antisocial: Online Extremists, Techno-Utopians, and the Hijacking of the American Conversation* (New York: Viking, 2019).

20 Victor Klemperer, *The Language of the Third Reich* (London: Bloomsbury, 2006), p. 167.

21 Richard Rodriquez, 'Sign of the Times', *New York Times Style Magazine* (October 19, 2014), p. 58.

22 Thomas Klikauer and Nadine Campbell, 'Capitalism Profits from the Promulgation of Disinformation', *BuzzFlash* (February 19, 2021). Online: https://buzzflash.com/articles/thomas-klikauer-and-nadine-campbell-for-buzzflash-capitalism-profits-from-the-promulgation-of-disinformation.

23 Cited in Raoul Peck, 'James Baldwin Was Right All Along', *The Atlantic* (July 3, 2020).

24 On the issue of violence, one of the best sources can be found in the writings of Brad Evans; see especially his various publications, interviews, and projects on his history of violence site. He is an indispensable source on contemporary violence: www.historiesofviolence.com/.

25 John Dewey, *The Public and Its Problems: An Essay in Political Inquiry* (Athens: Ohio University Press, 2012).

26 Drucilla Cornell and Stephen D. Seely, 'What Has Happened to the Public Imagination, and Why?' *Global-e* 10:19 (March 21, 2017). Online: www.21global.ucsb.edu/global-e/march-2017/what-has-happened-public-imagination-and-why.

27 Ibid.

28 Rob Hopkins, 'Drucilla Cornell on the Power of the Public Imagination', *Resilience* (February 10, 2021). Online: www.resilience.org/stories/2021-02-10/drucilla-cornell-on-the-power-of-the-public-imagination/.

29 The literature on neoliberalism is huge. I particularly like Wendy Brown, *Undoing the Demos: Neoliberalism's Stealth Revolution* (New York: Zone Books, 2015), Simon Dawes and Marc Len Ormand, eds, *Neoliberalism in Context* (New York: Palgrave, 2020).

30 Adam Serwer, *The Cruelty is the Point: The Past, Present, and Future of Trump's America* (New York: One World, 2021).

31. Bess Levin, '"Have a Good Life": Trump Pardons nearly 150 of his Favorite Criminals on the Way out the Door', *Vanity Fair* (January 20, 2021). Online: www.vanityfair.com/news/2021/01/donald-trump-final-pardons.
32. Zygmunt Bauman and Leonidas Donskis, *Liquid Evil* (London: Polity, 2016), p. 93.
33. The Editorial Board, 'Opinion: Greg Abbott is Endangering the Health of Texas and Beyond', *The Washington Post* (March 2, 2021). Online: www.washingtonpost.com/opinions/greg-abbott-is-endangering-the-health-of-texas-and-beyond/2021/03/02/55105860-7ba6-11eb-a976-c028a4215c78_story.html.
34. Dr Kavita Patel, 'Greg Abbott has Left Texans to Fight Covid Alone', *MSNBC* (March 3, 2021). Online: www.msnbc.com/opinion/greg-abbott-has-left-texans-fight-covid-alone-n1259515.
35. Brendan O'Connor, 'Trump's Useful Thugs: How the Republican Party Offered a Home to the Proud Boys', *Guardian* (January 21, 2021). Online: www.theguardian.com/news/2021/jan/21/donald-trump-useful-thugs-proud-boys-far-right-republican-party.
36. Salman Rushdie, 'What's Irretrievable after a Pandemic Year', *The Washington Post* (May 24, 2021). Online: www.washingtonpost.com/opinions/2021/05/24/salman-rushdie-pandemic-losses/.
37. Amy Goodman, 'A New Form of Jim Crow: Ari Berman on the COP's Anti-Democratic Assault on Voting Rights', *Democracy Now* (March 2, 2021). Online: www.democracynow.org/2021/3/2/georgia_republicans_voting_restrictions_ari_berman.
38. Igor Derysh, 'Republicans Roll Out "tidal wave of voter suppression": 253 Restrictive Bills in 43 States', *Salon* (February 27, 2021). Online: www.salon.com/2021/02/27/republicans-roll-out-tidal-wave-of-voter-suppression-253-restrictive-bills-in-43-states/.
39. Robin D. G. Kelley, 'After Trump', *Boston Review* (November 15, 2016). Online: http://bostonreview.net/forum/after-trump/robin-d-g-kelley-trump-says-go-back-we-say-fight-back.
40. Asiah Williams, 'Of Course Republicans Want to Suppress the Youth Vote', *The Nation* (September 20, 2020). Online: www.thenation.com/article/politics/youth-vote-suppression/.
41. David Daley, 'Inside the Republican Plot for Permanent Minority Rule', *The New Republic* (October 15, 2020). Online: https://newrepublic.com/article/159755/republican-voter-suppression-2020-election.

42 Paul Krugman, 'The Deadly Triumph of the Paranoid Style', *New York Times Direct* (July 13, 2021).
43 Alberto Toscano, 'The Long Shadow of Racial Fascism', *Boston Review* (October 27, 2020). Online: http://bostonreview.net/race-politics/alberto-toscano-long-shadow-racial-fascism; Robin D. G. Kelley, 'Birth of a Nation', *Boston Review* (March 6, 2017). Online: http://bostonreview.net/race-politics/robin-d-g-kelley-births-nation.
44 Simon Clark, 'How White Supremacy Returned to Mainstream Politics', *Center for American Progress* (July 1, 2020). Online: www.americanprogress.org/issues/security/reports/2020/07/01/482414/white-supremacy-returned-mainstream-politics/.
45 Brad Evans interviews Vincent Brown, 'Histories of Violence: Violence, Power, and Privilege', *Los Angeles Review of Books* (March 1, 2021). Online: https://lareviewofbooks.org/article/histories-of-violence-violence-power-privilege/.
46 Ruth Ben-Ghiat, 'Culture of Threat: Monitoring the GOP's Normalization of Violence', *Lucid* (June 29, 2021). Online: https://lucid.substack.com/p/culture-of-threat-monitoring-the.
47 Ibid.
48 Ibid.
49 Vasyl Cherepanyn, '"Demand the Impossible": What the Left Should Learn from 1968', *Open Democracy* (December 12, 2018). Online: www.opendemocracy.net/vasyl-cherepanyn/demand-impossible-what-left-should-learn-from-1968.
50 John Gray, 'Forgetfulness: The Dangers of a Modern Culture that Wages War on its Own Past', *New Statesman* (October 16, 2017). Online: www.newstatesman.com/culture/books/2017/10/forgetfulness-dangers-modern-culture-wages-war-its-own-past.
51 Paul Street, 'The Anatomy of Fascism Denial: 26 Flavors of Anti-Antifascism, Part 1', *CounterPunch* (February 7, 2021). Online: www.counterpunch.org/2021/02/07/the-anatomy-of-fascism-denial/; Sarah Churchwell, 'American Fascism: It Has Happened Again', *The New York Review of Books* (May 26, 2020). Online: www.nybooks.com/daily/2020/06/22/american-fascism-it-has-happened-here/; Masha Gessen, *Surviving Autocracy* (New York: Riverhead Books, 2020); Henry A. Giroux, *Race, Politics, and Pandemic Pedagogy: Education in a Time*

of Crisis (London: Bloomsbury, 2012); Henry A. Giroux, *American Nightmare: Facing the Challenge of Fascism* (San Francisco: City Lights Bookstore, 2018); Jason Stanley, *How Fascism Works* (New York: Random House, 2018); Carl Boggs, *Fascism Old and New* (New York: Routledge, 2018); Timothy Snyder, *On Tyranny: Twenty Lessons from the Twentieth Century* (New York: Crown, 2017).

52 Theodor W. Adorno, 'The Meaning of Working Through the Past', *Guilt and Defense*, trans. Henry W. Pickford (Cambridge, MA: Harvard University Press, 2010), p. 215.

53 Harriet Sherwood, 'Nearly Two-Thirds of US Young Adults Unaware 6m Jews Killed in the Holocaust', *Guardian* (September 16, 2020). Online: www.theguardian.com/world/2020/sep/16/holocaust-us-adults-study.

54 Ibid.

55 Michael Moline and Danielle J. Brown, 'Gov. DeSantis Has Found a New Culture-war Enemy: "Critical Race Theory"', *Florida Phoenix* (March 17, 2021). Online: www.floridaphoenix.com/2021/03/17/gov-desantis-has-found-a-new-culture-war-enemy-critical-race-theory/.

56 Coco Das, 'What Are You Going To Do about the Nazi Problem?' *refusefascism.org* (November 24, 2020). Online: https://revcom.us/a/675/refuse-fascism-what-are-you-going-to-do-about-the-nazi-problem-en.html.

57 Shannon E. Reid and Matthew Valasik, 'The Proud Boys are a Far-right Gang. Trump Boosted Them on National TV', *Guardian* (October 3, 2020). Online: www.theguardian.com/commentisfree/2020/oct/03/the-proud-boys-are-a-far-right-gang-trump-boosted-them-on-national-tv.

58 Maggie Haberman and Jonathan Martin, 'After the Speech: What Trump Did as the Capitol Was Attacked', *New York Times* (February 12, 2021). Online: www.nytimes.com/2021/02/13/us/politics/trump-capitol-riot.html.

59 Matin Pengelly, 'Trump Told Chief of Staff Hitler "did a lot of good things", Book says', *Guardian* (July 7, 2021). Online: www.theguardian.com/us-news/2021/jul/06/donald-trump-hitler-michael-bender-book.

60 John Haltiwanger, 'Top US General said Trump Spread "gospel of the Führer" and Threatened US Democracy with 2020 Election Lies: New Book', *Business Insider* (July 15, 2021). Online: www.businessinsider.in/politics/world/news/top-us-general-said-trump-spread-gospel-of-the-

fhrer-and-threatened-us-democracy-with-2020-election-lies-new-book/articleshow/84425362.cms.

61 Martin Pengelly, 'Top US General Warned of "Reichstag moment" in Trump's Turbulent Last Days', *Guardian* (July 14, 2021). Online: www.theguardian.com/us-news/2021/jul/14/donald-trump-reichstag-moment-general-mark-milley-book.

62 Ben-Ghiat, 'Culture of Threat: Monitoring the GOP's Normalization of Violence'.

63 Juan Cole, 'Tucker Carlson Touts "Replacement" Conspiracy Theory; But His Own Ancestor could have been Lynched', *Informed Comment* (March 10, 2021). Online: www.juancole.com/2021/04/replacement-conspiracy-ancestor.html.

64 Tim Elfrink, 'Tucker Carlson Says Protests Intimidated Derek Chauvin Jury into Guilty Verdict: "Please don't hurt us"', *The Washington Post* (August 21, 2021). Online: www.washingtonpost.com/nation/2021/04/21/tucker-carlson-chauvin-floyd-guilty-jury/.

65 Cited in Thom Hartman, 'Was April 7, 2020, the Day that Sealed the Fate of America?' *CommonDreams* (October 29, 2020). Online: www.commondreams.org/views/2020/10/29/was-april-7-2020-day-sealed-fate-america.

66 Media Matters Staff, 'Tucker Carlson: Coronavirus Crisis "may have passed. We'll see but it looks like it may have"', *Media Matters* (March 7, 2020). Online: www.mediamatters.org/coronavirus-covid-19/tucker-carlson-coronavirus-crisis-may-have-passed-well-see-it-looks-it-may.

67 Joe Concha, 'Trump Dings CNN, "Morning Joe" Ratings as Tucker Carlson Sets Record', *The Hill* (July 1, 2020). Online: https://thehill.com/homenews/media/505386-trump-dings-cnn-morning-joe-ratings-as-tucker-carlson-sets-record.

68 Alex Thompson, 'Why the Right-wing Has a Massive Advantage on Facebook', *Politico* (September 26, 2020). Online: www.politico.com/news/2020/09/26/facebook-conservatives-2020-421146.

69 Paige Williams, 'Kyle Rittenhouse, American Vigilante', *The New Yorker* (June 28, 2021). Online: www.newyorker.com/magazine/2021/07/05/kyle-rittenhouse-american-vigilante.

70 William Rivers Pitt, 'Tucker Carlson, Marjorie Taylor Greene, Matt Gaetz Suggest FBI Attacked Capitol', *Truthout* (June 17, 2021). Online: https://

truthout.org/articles/tucker-carlson-marjorie-taylor-greene-matt-gaetz-suggest-fbi-attacked-capitol/.
71 Katie Benner, 'Meadows Pressed Justice Dept. to Investigate Election Fraud Claims', *New York Times* (June 5, 2021). Online: www.nytimes.com/2021/06/05/us/politics/mark-meadows-justice-department-election.html?referringSource=articleShare.
72 Catie Edmondson, 'Far-Right Extremist Finds an Ally in an Arizona Congressman', *New York Times* (July 5, 2021). Online: www.nytimes.com/2021/07/05/us/politics/paul-gosar-republicans-congress-extremism.html?referringSource=articleShare.
73 Ibid.
74 Theodor W. Adorno, *Aspects of the New Right-Wing Extremism* (London: Polity, 2020), p. 13.
75 Cited in Sally Young, 'The Secret History of News Corp: A Media Empire Built on Spreading Propaganda', *The Conversation*' (May 15, 2019). Online: https://theconversation.com/the-secret-history-of-news-corp-a-media-empire-built-on-spreading-propaganda-116992.
76 I take this issue up in detail in Henry A. Giroux, *Racism, Politics and Pandemic Politics: Education in a Time of Crisis* (London: Bloomsbury, 2021).
77 Joshua Sperling cited in Lisa Appignanesi, 'Berger's Way of Being', *The New York Review of Books* (May 9, 2019). Online: www.nybooks.com/articles/2019/05/09/john-berger-ways-of-being/.
78 Angela Y. Davis, *Freedom Is a Constant Struggle: Ferguson, Palestine, and the Foundations of a Movement*, ed. Frank Barat (Chicago, IL: Haymarket Books, 2016), pp. 81–2.
79 Alberto Toscano, 'The Long Shadow of Racial Fascism', *Boston Review* (October 27, 2020). Online: http://bostonreview.net/race-politics/alberto-toscano-long-shadow-racial-fascism.
80 Anthony DiMaggio, 'Limbaugh's Legacy: Normalizing Hate for Profit', *CounterPunch* (February 19, 2021). Online: www.counterpunch.org/2021/02/19/limbaughs-legacy-normalizing-hate-for-profit/.
81 Ibid.
82 Marc Auge, *Oblivion*, trans. Jarjlijn de Jager (Minnesota: University of Minnesota Press, 2004).
83 Richard Evans, 'Why Trump Isn't a Fascist', *New Statesman* (January 13, 2021). Online: www.newstatesman.com/world/2021/01/why-trump-

isnt-fascist. Anthony DiMaggio demolishes this argument in stating 'Historians, despite their valuable contributions to this discussion, are not experts on American politics, political communication, rhetoric, or public opinion. So, by cutting out the views of people outside of history departments, discussions of fascism have often cut out people with the relevant empirical skill sets to study American political structures, political rhetoric, media content, and public opinion, as they relate to the theme of rising fascism. As a result, our discussion of fascism is dismissive, unnecessarily narrow, and truncated, with a predetermined answer that denies the fascist threat without really engaging in the relevant contemporary evidence.' Anthony DiMaggio, 'A (Not-So-New) Profile of the American Right: On the Authoritarian-Fascist Crisis', *CounterPunch* (January 15, 2021). Online: www.counterpunch.org/2021/01/15/a-not-so-new-profile-of-the-american-right-on-the-authoritarian-fascist-crisis/.

84 Anthony DiMaggio, 'Limbaugh's Legacy: Normalizing Hate for Profit', *CounterPunch* (February 19, 2021). Online: www.counterpunch.org/2021/02/19/limbaughs-legacy-normalizing-hate-for-profit/.

85 Ronald Brownstein, 'How the GOP Surrendered to Extremism', *The Atlantic* (February 4, 2021). Online: www.theatlantic.com/politics/archive/2021/02/republican-extremism-and-john-birch-society/617922/.

86 Robert Chnomas, 'Republican Theocracy or the End of Neoliberalism?' *Socialist Project: The Bullet* (March 10, 2021). Online: https://socialistproject.ca/2021/03/republican-theocracy-or-the-end-of-neoliberalism/#more.

87 Richard D. Wolff, 'Why the Neoliberal Drive to Privatize Everything Is Running Out of Gas', *CounterPunch* (June 21, 2021). Online: www.counterpunch.org/2021/06/21/why-the-neoliberal-drive-to-privatize-everything-is-running-out-of-gas/.

88 Franklin Frederick, 'Cuba's Contributions in the Fight Against the COVID-19 Pandemic', *Socialist Project: The Bullet* (March 11, 2021). Online: https://socialistproject.ca/2021/03/cuba-contribution-fight-against-covid19/.

89 Andrea Pitzer, *One Long Night: A Global History of Concentration Camps* (New York: Back Bay Books, 2017).

90 Leon Wieseltier, 'How Voters' Personal Suffering Overtook Reason—And Brought us Donald Trump', *The Washington Post* (June 22, 2016). Online: www.washingtonpost.com/posteverything/wp/2016/06/22/how-voters-personal-suffering-overtook-reason-and-brought-us-donald-trump/.

91 Achille Mbembe, 'Necropolitics', *Public Culture* 15:1 (Winter 2003), p. 18.

92 Konstantin Kilibarda and Daria Roithmayr, 'The Myth of the Rust Belt Revolt', *Salon* (December 1, 2016). Online: https://slate.com/news-and-politics/2016/12/the-myth-of-the-rust-belt-revolt.html.

93 Peter E. Gordon, 'The Utopian Promise of Adorno's "Open Thinking," Fifty Years On', *The New York Review of Books* (August 5, 2019). Online: www.nybooks.com/daily/2019/08/05/the-utopian-promise-of-adornos-open-thinking-fifty-years-on/.

94 Pierre Bourdieu and Gunter Grass, 'A Literature from Below', *The Nation* (July 3, 2000), pp. 25–8. Online: www.thenation.com/article/archive/literature-below/.

95 See, for instance, Stanley Aronowitz and Peter Bratsis, 'Situations Manifesto', *Situations* 1:1 (April 2005), pp. 7–14. Online: http://usir.salford.ac.uk/id/eprint/2329/1/Situations.pdf.

96 Charles H. Clavey, 'Donald Trump, Our Prophet of Deceit', *Boston Review* (October 14, 2021). Online: http://bostonreview.net/politics-philosophy-religion/charles-h-clavey-donald-trump-our-prophet-deceit.

97 I have addressed this issue before in Henry A. Giroux, 'The Scorched-Earth Politics of America's Four Fundamentalisms', *Truthout* (March 6, 2012). Online: https://truthout.org/articles/the-scorchedearth-politics-of-americas-four-fundamentalisms/.

98 Salman Rushdie, 'What's Irretrievable after a Pandemic Year', *The Washington Post* (May 24, 2021). Online: www.washingtonpost.com/opinions/2021/05/24/salman-rushdie-pandemic-losses/.

99 Naomi Klein, *No Is Not Enough: Resisting the New Shock Politics and Winning the World We Need* (Chicago: Haymarket Books, 2017), pp. 89–90.

100 Wendy Brown, 'Apocalyptic Populism', *Eurozine* (September 5, 2017). Online: www.eurozine.com/apocalyptic-populism/.

101 Elizabeth Dias and Ruth Graham, 'How White Evangelical Christians Fused with Trump Extremism', *New York Times* (January 11, 2021). Online: www.nytimes.com/2021/01/11/us/how-white-evangelical-christians-fused-with-trump-extremism.html.

102 Emma Rindlisbacher, 'Boot Camps for Crushing Democracy', *The Daily Poster* (March 25, 2021). Online: www.facebook.com/OurRevolutionSD/posts/4219066951450791.
103 Chris Hedges, *American Fascists: The Christian Right and the War on America* (New York: Free Press, 2006).
104 Zack Stanton, 'It's Time to Talk about Violent Christian Extremism', *Politico* (February 4, 2021). Online: www.politico.com/news/magazine/2021/02/04/qanon-christian-extremism-nationalism-violence-466034.
105 Report, 'White Evangelicals See Trump as Fighting for Their Beliefs, though Many Have Mixed Feelings about His Personal Conduct', *Pew Research Center* (March 12, 2020). Online: www.pewforum.org/2020/03/12/white-evangelicals-see-trump-as-fighting-for-their-beliefs-though-many-have-mixed-feelings-about-his-personal-conduct/.
106 Chris Hedges, *American Fascists*, p. 31.
107 Karen J. Greenberg, 'Down the Memory Hole: Trump's Strategic Assault on Democracy, Word by Word', *TomDispatch* (May 17, 2018). Online: www.tomdispatch.com/blog/176424/.
108 James Baldwin, 'An Open Letter to My Sister, Miss Angela Davis', *The New York Review of Books* (January 7, 1971). Online: www.nybooks.com/articles/archives/1971/jan/07/an-open-letter-to-my-sister-miss-angela-davis/?pagination=false.
109 Zygmunt Bauman and LeonidasDonskis, *Liquid Evil* (London: Polity, 2016), p. 84.
110 Alex Thompson, 'Why the Right-wing Has a Massive Advantage on Facebook', *Politico* (September 26, 2020). Online: www.politico.com/news/2020/09/26/facebook-conservatives-2020-421146.
111 Vishwas Satgar, 'Trump May Be Gone, But Neofascism Remains', *Socialist Project* (February 7, 2021). Online: https://socialistproject.ca/2021/02/trump-gone-neofascism-remains/.
112 Charles H. Clavey, 'Donald Trump, Our Prophet of Deceit', *Boston Review* (October 14, 2021). Online: http://bostonreview.net/politics-philosophy-religion/charles-h-clavey-donald-trump-our-prophet-deceit.
113 Bertolt Brecht, 'Fascism Is the True Face of Capitalism', *Off-Guardian* (December 1, 2018, org. 1935). Online: https://off-guardian.org/2018/12/01/fascism-is-the-true-face-of-capitalism/.

Chapter 2

1. Sarah Repucci and Amy Slipowitz, 'Freedom in the World 2021: Democracy under Siege', *Freedom House* (April 2021). Online: https://freedomhouse.org/report/freedom-world/2021/democracy-under-siege.
2. Concise summaries and elaborations of the Freedom House report can be found in Ishaan Tharoor, 'The Pandemic's Chilling Effect on Free Speech', *The Washington Post* (April 21, 2021). Online: www.washingtonpost.com/world/2021/04/21/free-speech-pandemic/; Borzou Daragahi, 'A Pandemic of Repression: Governments Using Coronavirus to Crush Freedoms', *The Independent* (October 2, 2020). Online: www.independent.co.uk/news/world/coronavirus-democracy-rights-covid-sri-lanka-uk-france-freedom-house-b746988.html.
3. Elana Beiser, 'Record Number of Journalists Jailed Worldwide', *Committee to Protect Journalists* (December 15, 2020). Online: https://cpj.org/reports/2020/12/record-number-journalists-jailed-imprisoned/.
4. Vishwas Satgar, 'Trump May Be Gone, but Neofascism Remains', *Socialist Project* (February 7, 2021). Online: https://socialistproject.ca/2021/02/trump-gone-neofascism-remains/.
5. One of the best theorists alive writing about violence is Brad Evans. See his many columns, interviews in the *New York Times* and *Los Angeles Review of Books*, along with his history of violence website, and many books on the subject, including Brad Evans and Adrian Parr, eds, *Conversations on Violence* (London: Pluto Press, 2021); Brad Evans, *Atrocity Exhibition: Life in the Age of Total Violence* (Los Angeles: Los Angeles Review of Books, 2019); Brad Evans and Natasha Lennard, *Violence: Humans in Dark times* (San Francisco: City Lights Books, 2018).
6. Frank Rich, 'Mueller's Steady Stream of Russia Revelations Is Driving Trump Crazy', *New York Magazine* (November 29, 2018). Online: http://nymag.com/intelligencer/2018/11/mueller-revelations-drive-trump-crazy.html.
7. Patrick Cockburn, 'The Republican Party has Turned Fascist and is Now the Most Dangerous Threat in the World', *CounterPunch* (June 22, 2021). Online: www.counterpunch.org/2021/06/22/the-republican-party-has-turned-fascist-and-is-now-the-most-dangerous-threat-in-the-world/.
8. Vishwas Satgar, 'Trump May Be Gone, But Neofascism Remains'.

9   Ibid.
10 Eugene Robinson, 'Opinion: It Was Much More than Tulsa', *The Washington Post* (May 31, 2021). Online: www.washingtonpost.com/opinions/2021/05/31/it-was-much-more-than-tulsa/.
11 Rick Perlstein, 'The Long Authoritarian History of the Capitol Riot', *Intelligencer* (June 30, 2021). Online: https://nymag.com/intelligencer/2021/06/long-authoritarian-history-january-6-insurrection.html.
12 Maggie Aster, 'Michael Flynn Suggested at a QAnon-affiliated Event that a Coup Should Happen in the U.S.', *New York Times* (June 1, 2021). Online: https://www.nytimes.com/2021/06/01/us/politics/flynn-coup-gohmert-qanon.html.
13 Mary Papenfuss, 'Trump's Ex-National Security Adviser Michael Flynn Calls for Myanmar-Type Coup In U.S.', *HuffPost* (May 30, 2021). Online: www.huffpost.com/entry/michael-flynn-qanon-conference-myanmar-military-coup_n_60b424eee4b0ead2796a24a4.
14 Edward Helmore, 'Biden Warns US Democracy "in peril" as He Commemorates America's War Dead', *Guardian* (May 31, 2021). Online: www.theguardian.com/us-news/2021/may/31/joe-biden-memorial-day-speech-warns-democracy-in-peril.
15 Edward Helmore, 'Tulsa Massacre: Biden Urges Americans to Reflect on "deep roots of racial terror"', *Guardian* (May 31, 2021). Online: www.theguardian.com/us-news/2021/may/31/tulsa-race-massacre-biden-speech.
16 Sarah Grillo, '2022's War over Racism', *Axios* (June 2, 2021). Online: www.axios.com/republican-strategy-culture-war-racism-e0c6ce43-98c9-4fd7-8600-d4093ca980ed.html.
17 Michael S. Schmidt and Luke Broadwater, 'Officers' Injuries, Including Concussions, Show Scope of Violence at Capitol Riot', *New York Times* (February 11, 2021). Online: www.nytimes.com/2021/02/11/us/politics/capitol-riot-police-officer-injuries.html.
18 Chauncey DeVega, 'Today's Republican Party is a Political Crime Family—And We Know Who the Godfather Is', *Salon* (May 25, 2021). Online: www.salon.com/2021/05/25/todays-republican-party-is-a-political-crime-family–and-we-know-who-the-godfather-is/.
19 António Guterres, 'The World Faces a Pandemic of Human Rights Abuses in the Wake of Covid-19', *Guardian* (February 22, 2021). Online: www.

theguardian.com/global-development/2021/feb/22/world-faces-pandemic-human-rights-abuses-covid-19-antonio-guterres.

20 Cited in Report, '2020 Marked 15th Straight Year of Declining World Freedom: Report', *Aljazeera* (March 3, 2021). Online: www.aljazeera.com/news/2021/3/3/2020-15th-straight-year-declining-global-freedom-report.

21 Ishaan Tharoor, 'The "free world" Keeps Shrinking', *The Washington Post* (March 3, 2021). Online: www.washingtonpost.com/world/2021/03/03/democracy-declining-freedom-house-report/.

22 Editorial, 'Global Democracy Has a Very Bad Year', *The Economist* (February 2, 2021). Online: www.economist.com/graphic-detail/2021/02/02/global-democracy-has-a-very-bad-year.

23 See Zygmunt Bauman, *The Individualized Society* (London: Polity Press, 2001); Henry A. Giroux, *Public Spaces, Private Lives* (New York: Routledge, 2001); Ulrich Beck, *Individualization: Institutionalized Individualism and its Social and Political Consequences* (Thousand Oaks, CA: Sage, 2002); Edgar Cabanas and Eva Illouz, *Manufacturing Happy Citizens* (London: Polity, 2019).

24 Zygmunt Bauman, *In Search of Politics* (Stanford: Stanford University Press, 1999).

25 Coco Das, 'What Are You Going To Do about the Nazi Problem?' *refusefascism.org* (November 24, 2020). Online: https://revcom.us/a/675/refuse-fascism-what-are-you-going-to-do-about-the-nazi-problem-en.html.

26 Bill Moyers, 'Losing Reality: Can We Get the Truth Back?' *BillMoyers.com* (March 3, 2020). Online: https://billmoyers.com/story/losing-reality-can-we-get-the-truth-back/.

27 Cedric J. Robinson, *Black Marxism: The Making of the Black Radical Tradition*, revised and updated third edition (Durham: University of North Carolina Press, 2021).

28 Ibid.; see also Robin D. G. Kelley, 'Birth of a Nation', *Boston Review* (March 6, 2017). Online: http://bostonreview.net/race-politics/robin-d-g-kelley-births-nation.

29 Alberto Toscano, 'The Long Shadow of Racial Fascism', *Boston Review* (October 27, 2020). Online: http://bostonreview.net/race-politics/alberto-toscano-long-shadow-racial-fascism.

30 See, for instance, Ruth Ben-Ghiat, *Strongmen* (New York: Norton, 2020); Bill V. Mullen and Christopher Vials, eds, *The U.S. Anti-Fascism Reader*

(New York: Verso, 2020); Timothy Snyder, *On Tyranny: Twenty Lessons from the Twentieth Century* (New York: Tim Duggan Books, 2017); Jason Stanley, *How Fascism Works* (New York: Random House, 2018); Henry A. Giroux, *American Nightmare: Facing the Challenge of Fascism* (San Francisco: City Lights Books, 2018); Cal Boggs, *Fascism Old and New* (New York: Routledge, 2018).

31 James Baldwin, *No Name in the Street* (New York: Vintage; reprint edition (January 9, 2007), p. 87.

32 Frederick Douglass, 'If There Is No Struggle, There Is No Progress' (1857), *BlackPast* (January 25, 2007). Online: www.blackpast.org/african-american-history/1857-frederick-douglass-if-there-no-struggle-there-no-progress/.

33 Al Baker, J., David Goodman, and Benjamin Mueller, 'Beyond the Chokehold: The Path to Eric Garner's Death', *New York Times* (June 13, 2015). Online: www.nytimes.com/2015/06/14/nyregion/eric-garner-police-chokehold-staten-island.html.

34 Meagan Flynn, 'Another Black Man Who Died in Custody Told Officers, "I can't breathe." One Responded, "I don't care"', *The Washington Post* (June 11, 2020). Online: www.washingtonpost.com/nation/2020/06/11/derrick-scott-oklahoma-city-police/.

35 George Yancy, 'Chomsky: Protests Unleashed by Murder of George Floyd Exceed All in US History', *Truthout* (May 7, 2021). Online: https://truthout.org/articles/chomsky-protests-unleashed-by-murder-of-george-floyd-exceed-all-in-us-history/.

36 See, for instance, Elizabeth Hinton, *From the War on Poverty to the War on Crime: The Making of Mass Incarceration in America* (Cambridge, MA: Harvard University Press, 2016); Michelle Alexander, *The New Jim Crow: Mass Incarceration in the Age of Colorblindness* (New York: The New Press, 2010).

37 Toscano, 'The Long Shadow of Racial Fascism'.

38 On the birth of neoliberalism, see Quinn Slobodian, *Globalists: The End of Empire and the Birth of Neoliberalism* (Cambridge, MA: Harvard University Press, 2018).

39 Samir Amin, 'The Return of Fascism in Contemporary Capitalism', *Monthly Review* (September 1, 2014). Online: https://monthlyreview.org/2014/09/01/the-return-of-fascism-in-contemporary-capitalism/.

40 Ibid.
41 Ibid.
42 Jeremy Scahill, 'Scholar Robin D.G. Kelley on How Today's Abolitionist Movement Can Fundamentally Change the Country', *The Intercept* (June 27, 2020). Online: https://theintercept.com/2020/06/27/robin-dg-kelley-intercepted/; see also Robin D. G. Kelley, 'Why Black Marxism, Why Now?' *Boston Review* (February 1, 2021). Online: http://bostonreview.net/race-philosophy-religion/robin-d-g-kelley-why-black-marxism-why-now.
43 Jeremy Scahill, 'Scholar Robin D. G. Kelley on How Today's Abolitionist Movement Can Fundamentally Change the Country'.
44 Laura Flanders, 'David Harvey: Looking toward a Moneyless Economy and Sleeping Well at Night', *Truthout* (February 3, 2015). Online: www.truth-out.org/news/item/28879-looking-toward-a-moneyless-economy-and-sleeping-well-at-night.
45 Paul Street, 'We Have a Fascism Problem', *CounterPunch* (December 16, 2020). Online: www.counterpunch.org/2020/12/16/we-have-a-fascism-problem/; Paul Street, 'The Anatomy of Fascism Denial: 26 Flavors of Anti-Antifascism, Part 1', *CounterPunch* (February 7, 2021). Online: www.counterpunch.org/2021/02/07/the-anatomy-of-fascism-denial/; Sarah Churchwell, 'American Fascism: It Has Happened Again', *The New York Review of Books* (May 26, 2020). Online: www.nybooks.com/daily/2020/06/22/american-fascism-it-has-happened-here; Timothy Snyder, *On Tyranny: Twenty Lessons from the Twentieth Century* (New York: Tim Duggan Books, 2017); Jason Stanley, *How Fascism Works* (New York: Random House, 2018); Henry A. Giroux, *American Nightmare: Facing the Challenge of Fascism*; Cal Boggs, *Fascism Old and New* (New York: Routledge, 2018).
46 Drucilla Cornell and Stephen D. Seely, 'What Has Happened to the Public Imagination, and Why?' *Global-e* 10:9 (March 21, 2017). Online: www.21global.ucsb.edu/global-e/march-2017/what-has-happened-public-imagination-and-why; Rob Hopkins, 'Drucilla Cornell on the Power of the Public Imagination', *Resilience* (February 10, 2021). Online: www.resilience.org/stories/2021-02-10/drucilla-cornell-on-the-power-of-the-public-imagination/; Dmitri N. Shalin, 'Identity Politics and Civic Imagination', *Tikkun* (April 5, 2021). Online: www.tikkun.org/identity-politics-and-civic-imagination/.

47 Henry A. Giroux and Brad Evans, *Disposable Futures: The Seduction of Violence in the Age of Spectacle* (San Francisco: City Lights Books, 2015).
48 Zygmunt Bauman, *In Search of Politics* (Stanford: Stanford University Press, 1999), p. 12.
49 Frank B. Wilderson III, 'Introduction: Unspeakable Ethics', *Red, White, & Black* (London: Duke University Press, 2012), p. 20.
50 Judith Butler, *Precarious Life: The Powers of Mourning and Violence* (London: Verso Press, 2004), p. 34.
51 Thomas Piketty, *Capital in the Twenty-First Century* (Cambridge, MA: Belknap Press, 2017); Keith Payne, *The Broken Ladder: How Inequality Affects the Way We Think, Live, and Die* (New York: Penguin, 2018); Michael D. Yates, *The Great Inequality* (New York: Routledge, 2016).
52 Achille Mbembe, 'Necropolitics', trans. Libby Meintjes, *Public Culture* 15:1 (2003), p. 40.
53 Amy Goodman, 'GOP Criminalizes Dissent with Anti-Riot Laws Targeting Black Lives Matter & Anti-Pipeline Protests', *Democracy Now* (April 26, 2021). Online: www.democracynow.org/2021/4/26/anti_protest_bills.
54 Ibid.
55 Reid J. Epstein and Patricia Mazzei, 'G.O.P. Bills Target Protesters (and Absolve Motorists Who Hit Them)', *New York Times* (June 16, 2021). Online: www.nytimes.com/2021/04/21/us/politics/republican-anti-protest-laws.html.
56 Henry A. Giroux, *Neoliberalism's War on Higher Education*, 2nd edition (Chicago: Haymarket Books, 2019).
57 See, for instance, Matt Taibbi, *The Divide: American Injustice in the Age of the Wealth Gap* (New York: Spiegel & Grau, 2014); Virginia Eubanks, *Automating Inequality: How High-Tech Tools Profile, Police, and Punish the Poor* (New York: St. Martin's Press, 2017).
58 William I. Robinson, *The Global Police State* (London: Pluto Press, 2020).
59 Jill Lepore, 'The Invention of the Police', *The New Yorker* (July 13, 2020). Online: www.newyorker.com/magazine/2020/07/20/the-invention-of-the-police.
60 Tyler J. Pollard, 'Hardened Cultures and the War on Youth: A Conversation with Henry A. Giroux', *The Review of Education, Pedagogy, and Cultural Studies* (June 30, 2104), pp. 180–92. Online: www.

tandfonline.com/doi/abs/10.1080/10714413.2014.917901?journal Code=gred20<.

61 I explore this issue in detail in Henry A. Giroux, *Youth in a Suspect Society* (New York: Palgrave, 2010).

62 Aaron Morrison, 'Floyd's Death is Latest Suffered by Blacks over Trivial Activities', *Press Herald* (June 12, 2020). Online: www.pressherald.com/2020/06/12/floyds-death-latest-suffered-by-blacks-over-trivial-activities/.

63 Judith Butler, *Precarious Life: The Powers of Mourning and Violence*.

64 Aaron Morrison, 'Floyd's Death is Latest Suffered by Blacks over Trivial Activities'.

65 On the militarizing of the police on a global level, see the brilliant William I. Robinson, *The Global Police State* (London: Pluto Press, 2020); also see Nathaniel Lee, 'How Police Militarization Became an over $5 Billion Business Coveted by the Defense Industry', *CNBC* (July 9, 2020). Online: www.cnbc.com/2020/07/09/why-police-pay-nothing-for-military-equipment.html; see also Talib Visram, 'Eliminating This Federal Program Would Play a Major part in Demilitarizing the Police', *Fast Company* (June 8, 2020). Online: www.fastcompany.com/90513061/eliminating-this-federal-program-would-play-a-major-part-in-demilitarizing-the-police.

66 Ryan Welch and Jack Mewhirter, 'Does Military Equipment Lead Police Officers to be More Violent? We Did the Research', *The Washington Post* (June 30, 2017). Online: www.washingtonpost.com/news/monkey-cage/wp/2017/06/30/does-military-equipment-lead-police-officers-to-be-more-violent-we-did-the-research/.

67 Tom Nolan, 'Arming Our Police with More Powerful Weapons Has Led to More Violence Against Americans, Ex-Cop Says', *MarketWatch* (June 2, 2020). Online: www.marketwatch.com/story/ex-cop-militarization-of-local-police-leads-to-more-law-enforcement-violence-against-citizens-2020-06-02.

68 Mariame Kaba, 'Yes, We Mean Literally Abolish the Police', *New York Times* (June 12, 2020). Online: www.nytimes.com/2020/06/12/opinion/sunday/floyd-abolish-defund-police.html?referringSource=articleShare.

69 On the issue of militarism and the police, see Andrew Metheven, 'Militarism and the Police—How Our Streets Became Battlefields', *The*

Transnational Institute (May 16, 2021). Online: www.tni.org/en/article/militarism-and-the-police.

70 Radley Balko, *The Rise of the Warrior Cop* (New York: Public Affairs, 2013).
71 Frank Edwards, Michael H. Esposito, and Hedwig Lee, 'Risk of Police-Involved Death by Race/Ethnicity and Place, United States, 2012–2018', *American Public Health Association* (September 2018). Online: https://ajph.aphapublications.org/doi/10.2105/AJPH.2018.304559.
72 Francesca Mari, 'How Can We Stop Gun Violence?' *The New York Review of Books* (June 10, 2021). Online: www.nybooks.com/articles/2021/06/10/how-can-we-stop-gun-violence/.
73 See Jill Nelson, ed., *Police Brutality* (New York: Norton, 2000); A Truthout Collection, *Who Do You Serve, Who Do You Protect? Police Violence and Resistance in the United States* (Chicago: Haymarket, 2016).
74 See the ground-breaking work on this issue from Ruth Gilmore, *Golden Gulag: Prisons, Surplus, Crisis, and Opposition in Globalizing California* (Oakland: University of California Press, 2008).
75 Elizabeth Hinton, *From the War on Poverty to the War on Crime*, p. 332.
76 Elizabeth Hinton, *America on Fire: The Untold History of Police Violence and Black Rebellion since the 1960s* (New York: Liveright, 2021).
77 Angela Y. Davis, *Abolition Democracy: Beyond Empire, Prisons, and Torture* (New York: Seven Stories Press, 2005), pp. 40–1.
78 Kahilil Gibran Muhammad, *The Condemnation of Blackness: Race, Crime, and the Making of Modern Urban America* (Cambridge, MA: Harvard University Press, 2nd edition, 2019), p. xiii.
79 For a critique of so-called liberal reforms to prison, see Maya Schenwar and Victoria Law, *Prison by Any Other Name: The Harmful Consequences of Popular Reforms* (New York: The New Press, 2021).
80 Robert Barnes, 'Supreme Court Rules Against Juvenile Sentenced to Life Without Parole', *The Washington Post* (April 22, 2021). Online: www.washingtonpost.com/politics/courts_law/supreme-court-life-without-parole/2021/04/22/6a633136-a371-11eb-a774-7b47ceb36ee8_story.html.
81 Adam Liptak, 'Supreme Court Rejects Limits on Life Terms for Youths', *New York Times* (April 22, 2021). Online: www.nytimes.com/2021/04/22/us/supreme-court-life-terms-youths.html.
82 Anne-Marie Cusac, *Cruel and Unusual: The Culture of Punishment in America* (New Haven, CT: Yale University Press, 2009).

83 Virginia Eubanks, *Automating Inequality: How High-Tech Tools Profile, Police, and Punish the Poor* (New York: St. Martin's Press, 2017).

84 Michelle Brown, *The Culture of Punishment* (New York: NYU Press, 2009), pp. 10–11.

85 Jack Johnson, 'South Carolina Gov Signs "Inhumane" Bill Forcing Death Row Inmates to Choose Firing Squad or Electric Chair', *Common Dreams* (May 17, 2021). Online: www.commondreams.org/news/2021/05/17/south-carolina-gov-signs-inhumane-bill-forcing-death-row-inmates-choose-firing-squad?cd-origin=rss&utm_term=AO&utm_campaign=Daily%20 Newsletter&utm_content=email&utm_source=Daily%20 Newsletter&utm_medium=Email.

86 Sharon Zhang, 'South Carolina Can Now Execute People on Death Row by Firing Squad', *Truthout* (May 18, 2021). Online: https://truthout.org/articles/south-carolina-can-now-execute-people-on-death-row-by-firing-squad/.

87 Paul Street, 'No Time to Relax: Dark Clouds in Biden's America', *CounterPunch* (June 2021). Online: www.counterpunch.org/2021/06/04/no-time-to-relax-dark-clouds-in-bidens-america/.

88 Chris Boyette, Jay Croft, and Hollie Silverman, 'Gun Violence in 6 States This Weekend Brings US Mass Shootings to 272 So Far This Year', *CNN* (June 14, 2021). Online: www.cnn.com/2021/06/12/us/us-mass-shootings/index.html.

89 Ibid.

90 Paul Street, 'No Time to Relax: Dark Clouds in Biden's America'.

91 Report, 'Deaths of People of Color By Law Enforcement Are Severely Under-Counted', *UnidosUS* (May 2021). Online: http://publications.unidosus.org/bitstream/handle/123456789/2164/unidosus_specialadvancefactsheet.pdf?sequence=4. See also Saeed Ahmed, 'There Have Been, On Average, 10 Mass Shootings in The U.S. Each Week This Year', *NPR* (May 10, 2021). Online: www.npr.org/2021/05/10/995380788/there-have-been-on-average-10-mass-shootings-in-the-u-s-each-week-this-year. See also the Gun Violence Archive at www.gunviolencearchive.org/reports/mass-shooting.

92 Victoria Law, 'Gun Availability Worsens Domestic Abuse, but Gun Bans Don't Create Safety Either', *Truthout* (May 23, 2020). Online: https://

truthout.org/articles/gun-availability-worsens-domestic-abuse-but-gun-bans-dont-create-safety-either/?eType=EmailBlastContent&eId=3d3616de-5b79-4a0e-97de-d7d02d616fd1.

93 Gary Younge, 'The (Way Too Many) Kids Whose Lives Have Been Upended by Gun Violence', *New York Times* (March 25, 2021). Online: www.nytimes.com/2021/03/25/books/review/children-under-fire-john-woodrow-cox.html.

94 Dora Mekouar, 'The Other Pandemic: Violence Against Women', *Voice of America* (May 23, 2021). Online: https://learningenglish.voanews.com/a/the-other-pandemic-violence-against-women/5894017.html.

95 Dan Glaun, 'A Handful of States Fueled a National Increase in Domestic Violence Shooting Deaths as COVID-19 Spread', *Frontline* (June 2, 2021).

96 Rosanna Smart and Terry L. Schell, 'Mass Shootings in the United States', *Rand Corporation—Gun Policy in America* (April 15, 2021). Online: www.rand.org/research/gun-policy/analysis/essays/mass-shootings.html. See also Michael Luca, Deepak Malhotra, and Christopher Poliquin, 'The Impact of Mass Shootings on Gun Policy', *Harvard Business School* (August 2012). Online: www.hbs.edu/ris/Publication%20Files/16-126_f03b33c6-5698-41d2-8b8e-2f98120e3dbc.pdf.

97 Keeanga-Yamahtta Taylor, 'The Emerging Movement for Police and Prison Abolition', *The New Yorker* (May 7, 2021). Online: www.newyorker.com/news/our-columnists/the-emerging-movement-for-police-and-prison-abolition.

98 Alex Vitale and Scott Casleton, 'The Problem Isn't Just Police—It's Politics', *Boston Review* (July 1, 2020). Online: http://bostonreview.net/race-politics-law-justice/alex-vitale-scott-casleton-problem-isnt-just-police%E2%80%94its-politics.

99 Ibid.

100 Vitale fully develops this position in Alex Vitale, *The End of Policing* (London: Verso, 2018).

101 Jon Queally, 'Cornel West Says "Neo-Fascist Gangster" Trump Exposes America as a "failed social experiment"', *Common Dreams* (May 30, 2020). Online: www.commondreams.org/news/2020/05/30/cornel-west-says-neo-fascist-gangster-trump-and-neoliberal-democrats-expose-america.

102 Ibid.
103 Mark LeVine, 'Why Charlie Hebdo Attack is Not About Islam', *Al Jazeera* (January 10, 2015).Online: www.aljazeera.com/indepth/opinion/2015/01/charlie-hebdo-islam-cartoon-terr-20151106726681265.html.
104 The landscape of domestic terrorism and various movements that respond to it both in the US and abroad can be found in a number of books by Angela Y. Davis. See most recently, *Freedom Is a Constant Struggle: Ferguson, Palestine, and the Foundations of a Movement* (Chicago: Haymarket, 2016).
105 See, for instance, Marc Mauer, *Race to Incarcerate* (New York: The New Press, 2006).
106 Alex Vitale and Scott Casleton, 'The Problem Isn't Just Police – It's Politics'.
107 Zack Beauchamp, 'What the Police Really Believe', *Vox* (July 7, 2020). Online: www.vox.com/policy-and-politics/2020/7/7/21293259/police-racism-violence-ideology-george-floyd.
108 Adam Serwer, *The Cruelty is the Point: The Past, Present, and Future of Trump's America* (New York: One World, 2021).
109 Emma Rindlisbacher, 'Boot Camps for Crushing Democracy', *The Daily Poster* (March 25, 2021). Online: www.facebook.com/OurRevolutionSD/posts/4219066951450791.
110 Tom Engelhardt, *A Nation Made by War* (Chicago: Haymarket Books, 2020); Andrew Bacevich, *After the Apocalypse: America's Role in a World Transformed* (New York: Metropolitan Books, 2021). Also see the classic Chalmers Johnson, *The Sorrows of Empire: Militarism, Secrecy, and the End of the Republic* (New York: Metropolitan, 2004).
111 Jill Lepore, 'The Invention of the Police', *The New Yorker* (July 13, 2020). Online: www.newyorker.com/magazine/2020/07/20/the-invention-of-the-police.
112 Elizabeth Hinton, *America on Fire*.
113 Robert C. Koehler, 'Armed Racism Keeps No One Safe', *Uncommon Thought* (April 17, 2021). Online: www.uncommonthought.com/mtblog/archives/2021/04/17/armed-racism-keeps-no-one-safe.php.
114 Alfredo Saad-Filho, 'The Left Must Seize This Moment, or Others Will', *Jacobin Magazine* (April 23, 2020). Online: www.jacobinmag.com/2020/04/coronavirus-crisis-covid-economy-recession-pandemic.

115 Babriela Bucher, 'Six-fold Increase in People Suffering Famine-like Conditions since Pandemic Began', *Oxfam International* (July 9, 2021). Online: www.oxfam.org/en/press-releases/six-fold-increase-people-suffering-famine-conditions-pandemic-began.
116 Ibid.
117 Ibid.
118 Cited in Jon Queally, 'Cornel West Says "Neo-Fascist Gangster" Trump Exposes America as a "failed social experiment"', *Common Dreams* (May 30, 2020). Online: www.commondreams.org/news/2020/05/30/cornel-west-says-neo-fascist-gangster-trump-and-neoliberal-democrats-expose-america.
119 Sasha Abramsky, *Jumping at Shadows* (New York: Nation Books, 2017).
120 David Theo Goldberg, *Dread: Facing Futureless Futures* (London: Polity, 2021).
121 Mariame Kaba, 'Yes, We Mean Literally Abolish the Police', *New York Times* (June 12, 2020). Online: www.nytimes.com/2020/06/12/opinion/sunday/floyd-abolish-defund-police.html?referringSource=articleShare.
122 Abigail Weinberg, 'Georgia Sen. Raphael Warnock Eviscerates Republican Voter-Suppression Tactics', *Mother Jones* (March 17, 2021). Online: www.motherjones.com/politics/2021/03/georgia-sen-raphael-warnock-eviscerates-republican-voter-suppression-tactics/.
123 Report, 'The Corporate Sponsors of Voter Suppression', *Public Citizen* (April 5, 2021). Online: www.citizen.org/article/corporate-sponsors-of-voter-suppression-state-lawmakers-50-million/.
124 Ibid.
125 Igor Derysh, 'Conservative Groups Are Writing GOP Voter Suppression Bills—And Spending Millions to Pass Them', *Salon* (March 27, 2021). Online: www.salon.com/2021/03/27/conservative-groups-are-writing-gop-voter-suppression-bills—and-spending-millions-to-pass-them/.
126 Yannis Stavrakakis, in Cihan Aksan and Jon Bailes, eds, *One Question Fascism (Part One), Is Fascism Making a Comeback?* State of Nature Blog (December 3, 2017). Online: http://stateofnatureblog.com/one-question-fascism-part-one/.
127 Charlie Post, in Cihan Aksan and Jon Bailes, eds, *One Question Fascism (Part One), Is Fascism Making a Comeback?* State of Nature Blog

(December 3, 2017). Online: http://stateofnatureblog.com/one-question-fascism-part-one/.

128 Amy Goodman, '"Jim Crow in New Clothes": In First Senate Speech, Raphael Warnock Slams GOP Assault on Voting Rights', *Democracy Now!* (March 19, 2021). Online: www.democracynow.org/2021/3/19/raphael_warnock_first_senate_speech.

129 Rebecca Klapper, 'Mondaire Jones Says Manchin Op-Ed Might as Well Be Titled "Why I'll Vote to Preserve Jim Crow"', *Newsweek* (June 6, 2021). Online: www.newsweek.com/mondaire-jones-says-manchin-op-ed-might-well-titled-why-ill-vote-preserve-jim-crow-1597966.

130 Joe Manchin, 'Why I'm Voting Against the For the People Act', *The Charleston Gazette-Mail* (June 6, 2021). Online: www.wvgazettemail.com/opinion/op_ed_commentaries/joe-manchin-why-im-voting-against-the-for-the-people-act/article_c7eb2551-a500-5f77-aa37-2e42d0af870f.html

131 Paul Krugman, 'Policy in a Time of Political Madness', *New York Times* (June 8, 2021). Online: http://web.liyang-invest.com.tw/2021/06/policy-in-time-of-political-madness.html.

132 John Feffer, 'Twilight of the Pandemic?' *TomDispatch.com* (June 8, 2021). Online: https://tomdispatch.com/twilight-of-the-pandemic.

133 Fintan O'Toole, 'The Trump Inheritance', *The New York Review of Books* (February 25, 2021). Online: www.nybooks.com/articles/2021/02/25/trump-inheritance/.

134 James Baldwin, 'An Open Letter to My Sister, Miss Angela Davis', *The New York Review of Books* (January 7, 1971). Online: www.nybooks.com/articles/archives/1971/jan/07/an-open-letter-to-my-sister-miss-angela-davis/?pagination=false.

135 Ibid.

136 Wright Mills, 'Letter to The New Left' *The New Left Review* (September–October 1960), pp. 18–23. Online: www.marxists.org/subject/humanism/mills-c-wright/letter-new-left.htm.

137 Theodor W. Adorno, 'Appendix 1: Discussion of Professor Adorno's Lecture "The Working Through the Past"', trans. Henry W. Pickford, in *Critical Models: Interviews and Catchwords* (New York: Columbia University Press, 1998), p. 303.

Chapter 3

1. The full transcript of Trump's speech can be found at 'Trump's Speech that "incited" Capitol Violence: Full Transcript', *Aljazeera* (January 11, 2020). Online: www.aljazeera.com/news/2021/1/11/full-transcript-donald-trump-january-6-incendiary-speech.
2. Aaron Blake, 'Sarah Huckabee Sanders Says Trump Has Never "promoted or encouraged violence." She is Very Wrong', *The Washington Post* (June 29, 2017). Online: www.washingtonpost.com/news/the-fix/wp/2017/06/29/sarah-huckabee-sanders-says-trump-has-never-encouraged-any-form-of-violence-she-is-very-wrong/.
3. Fabiola Cineas, 'Donald Trump is the Accelerant', *Vox* (January 9, 2021). Online: www.vox.com/21506029/trump-violence-tweets-racist-hate-speech.
4. Mike Ludwig, 'The Trumps Have Fueled a Far-Right Media Monster that Is Not Going Away', *Truthout* (January 6, 2021). Online: https://truthout.org/articles/the-trumps-have-fueled-a-far-right-media-monster-that-is-not-going-away/.
5. Ed Pilkington, 'Incitement: A Timeline of Trump's Inflammatory Rhetoric before the Capitol Riot', *Guardian* (January 7, 2021). Online: www.theguardian.com/us-news/2021/jan/07/trump-incitement-inflammatory-rhetoric-capitol-riot.
6. Bess Levin, 'Trump Has Reportedly Been Telling People He's Going To Be President Again by August, Which Would Suggest He's Planning a Coup (or has fully descended into madness)', *Vanity Fair* (June 1, 2021). Online: www.vanityfair.com/news/2021/06/donald-trump-august-reinstatement.
7. Ed Pilkington, '"Stand back and stand by": How Trumpism Led to the Capitol Siege', *Guardian* (January 6, 2021). Online: www.theguardian.com/us-news/2021/jan/06/donald-trump-armed-protest-capitol.
8. Karissa Bell, 'Twitter Suspends Donald Trump', Yahoo.com (January 6, 2021). Online: www.nytimes.com/2021/01/06/opinion/trump-capitol-dc-protests.html?campaign_id=39&emc=edit_ty_20210107&instance_id=25742&nl=opinion-today&regi_id=51563793&segment_id=48622&te=1&user_id=ac16f3c28b64af0b86707bb1a8f1b07chttps://money.yahoo.com/twitter-suspends-donald-trump-001400097.html.

9   Editorial Board, 'Trump Is to Blame for the Capitol Attack', *New York Times* (January 6, 2020). Online: www.nytimes.com/2021/01/06/opinion/trump-capitol-dc-protests.html?action=click&module=Opinion&pgtype=Homepage.
10 Paul Street, 'Nine Points of Difference: A Response to Noam Chomsky on American Fascism', *CounterPunch* (June 25, 2021). Online: www.counterpunch.org/2021/06/25/nine-points-of-difference-a-response-to-noam-chomsky-on-american-fascism/.
11 Joan C. Williams, 'How Biden Won Back (Enough of) the White Working Class', *Harvard Business Review* (November 10, 2020). Online: https://hbr.org/2020/11/how-biden-won-back-enough-of-the-white-working-class; see also Anthony DiMaggio, 'Election Con 2016: New Evidence Demolishes the Myth of Trump's "Blue-Collar" Populism', *CounterPunch* (June 16, 2017). Online: www.counterpunch.org/2017/06/16/93450/; Anthony DiMaggio, *Rebellion in America: Citizen Uprisings, the News Media, and the Politics of Plutocracy* (New York: Routledge, 2020); Anthony DiMaggio, 'Election 2020: A Democratic Mandate or a Vote Against Trump?', *CounterPunch* (November 24, 2020). Online: www.counterpunch.org/2020/11/24/election-2020-a-democratic-mandate-or-a-vote-against-trump/.
12 Robert O' Paxton, 'I've Hesitated to Call Donald Trump a Fascist. Until Now', *Newsweek* (January 11, 2021). Online: www.newsweek.com/robert-paxton-trump-fascist-1560652.
13 Timothy Snyder, 'The American Abyss', *New York Times* (January 9, 2021). Online: www.nytimes.com/2021/01/09/magazine/trump-coup.html.
14 Samuel Farber, 'Trumpism Will Endure', *Jacobin* (January 3, 2021). Online: https://jacobinmag.com/2021/01/donald-trump-white-working-class-trumpism.
15 John Feffer, 'Twilight of the Pandemic?' *TomDispatch.com* (June 8, 2021). Online: https://mail.google.com/mail/u/0/#inbox/WhctKKWxTCSQgWdpVxVWGPdFMmpfqmjrfDRfTWShJBlNCfVnTgkshMnSfMlkHFCKRqcLkhl.
16 Farber, 'Trumpism Will Endure'.
17 Kenny Stancil, 'Poll Shows Nearly Half of GOP Voters—Lied to by Right-Wing Media—Approve of US Capitol Ransacking', *Common Dreams*

(January 7, 2021). Online: www.commondreams.org/news/2021/01/07/poll-shows-nearly-half-gop-voters-lied-right-wing-media-approve-us-capitol.

18 Carlie Warzel, 'The Pro-Trump Movement Was Always Headed Here', *New York Times* (January 6, 2021). Online: www.nytimes.com/2021/01/06/opinion/protests-trump-disinformation.html; Sarah Kendzior, *Hiding in Plain Sight: The Invention of Donald Trump and the Erosion of America* (New York: Flatiron Books, 2020).

19 David Theo Goldberg, 'On Civil War', *Talking Violence Podcast* (January 5, 2021). Online: https://talkingviolence.podbean.com/e/ep-7-on-civil-war-david-theo-goldberg/.

20 Anthony DiMaggio, 'The Coup in Washington: Why is Anyone Surprised by Trump's Fascist Politics', *CounterPunch* (January 7, 2021). Online: www.counterpunch.org/2021/01/07/the-coup-in-washington-why-is-anyone-surprised-by-trumps-fascist-politics/.

21 Don Evon, 'Was a Noose Hung across from the US Capitol?' *Snopes* (January 6, 2021). Online: www.snopes.com/fact-check/noose-hung-outside-capitol/.

22 Fintan O'Toole, 'The Trump Inheritance', *The New York Review* (February 25, 2021). Online: www.nybooks.com/articles/2021/02/25/trump-inheritance/.

23 William Barber II, Liz Theoharis, Timothy B. Tyson, and Cornel West, 'What the Courage to Change History Looks Like', *New York Times* (June 19, 2021). Online: www.nytimes.com/2020/06/19/opinion/floyd-protests-race-america.html.

24 Masha Gessen, 'Why America Needs a Reckoning with the Trump Era', *The New Yorker* (November 10, 2020). Online: www.newyorker.com/news/our-columnists/why-america-needs-a-reckoning-with-the-trump-era.

25 I take this quote from Slavoj Zizek's liberal translation of Gramsci, which can be found in Slavoj Zizek, 'A Permanent Economic Emergency', *New Left Review* (July/August 2010). Online: https://newleftreview.org/issues/ii64/articles/slavoj-zizek-a-permanent-economic-emergency.

26 Becky Z. Dernbach and Jeremy Schulman, 'The Shockingly Long List of Corrupt Officials and Political Allies Pardoned by Trump', *Mother Jones* (December 22, 2020). Online: www.motherjones.com/politics/2020/12/trump-pardons-hunter-collins-stockman-blackwater/.

27 Jennifer Evans, 'Trump Lost, but Racism is Alive and Infused in U.S. History', *The Conversation* (November 10, 2020). Online: https://theconversation.com/trump lost but racism-is-alive-and-infused-in-u-s-history-149249.

28 Jonathan D. Karl, 'Inside William Barr's Breakup With Trump', *The Atlantic* (June 27, 2021). Online: www.theatlantic.com/politics/archive/2021/06/william-barrs-trump-administration-attorney-general/619298/?utm_source=feedburner&utm_medium=feed&utm_campaign=Feed%3A+AtlanticPoliticsChannel+%28The+Atlantic+-+Politics%29.

29 Sophia Ankel, 'Trump Promises "wild" Protests in Washington, DC, on the Day Congress is Set to Finalize Election Results', *Yahoo! News* (December 20, 2020). Online: https://news.yahoo.com/trump-promises-wild-protests-washington-165055313.html.

30 Noam Chomsky, 'On Trump's Disastrous Coronavirus Response, WHO, China, Gaza and Global Capitalism', *Democracy Now* (May 25, 2020). Online: www.democracynow.org/2020/5/25/noam_chomsky_on_trump_s_disastrous.

31 Teo Armus, 'Unaccompanied Migrant Children Suffer "inhumane and cruel experience" in CBP Custody, Report Alleges', *The Washington Post* (October 30, 2020). Online: www.washingtonpost.com/nation/2020/10/30/migrant-children-border-unaccompanied/.

32 Susan Cornwell, 'Congress to Probe "Rogue" Actions of Trump's Justice Dept', *Reuters* (June 13, 2021). Online: www.reuters.com/world/us/congress-probe-rogue-actions-trumps-justice-dept-pelosi-says-2021-06-13/.

33 Sarah Kendzior, *Hiding in Plain Sight: The Invention of Donald Trump and the Erosion of America* (New York: Flatiron Books, 2020), pp. 201–2.

34 Masha Gessen, *Surviving Autocracy* (New York: Riverhead Books, 2020), p. 58.

35 William I. Robinson, *The Global Police State* (London: Pluto Press, 2020), p. 123.

36 Ashton Carter, Dick Cheney, William Cohen, Mark Esper, Robert Gates, Chuck Hagel, James Mattis, Leon Panetta, William Perry, and Donald Rumsfeld, 'All 10 Living Former Defense Secretaries: Involving the Military in Election Disputes Would Cross into Dangerous Territory', *The*

Washington Post (January 3, 2021). Online: www.washingtonpost.com/opinions/10-former-defense-secretaries-military-peaceful-transfer-of-power/2021/01/03/2a23d52e-4c4d-11eb-a9f4-0e668b9772ba_story.html. See also Jennifer Rubin, 'It's Impeachable. It's Likely Illegal. It's a Coup', *The Washington Post* (January 3, 2021). Online: www.washingtonpost.com/opinions/2021/01/03/its-impeachable-its-likely-illegal-its-coup/.

37 Edward-Isaac Dovere, 'How Joe Biden Watched the Capitol Assault', *The Atlantic* (January 6, 2021). Online: www.theatlantic.com/politics/archive/2021/01/joe-biden-responded-storming-capitol/617575/.

38 Tim Nichols, 'Worse than Treason', *The Atlantic* (January 4, 2021). Online: www.theatlantic.com/ideas/archive/2021/01/what-republicans-are-doing-worse-treason/617538/.

39 Federico Finchelstein, *A Brief History of Fascist Lies* (Oakland: University of California Press, 2020).

40 Masha Gessen, *Surviving Autocracy* (New York: Riverhead Books, 2020), pp. 17–18.

41 Stuart Hall, 'Subjects in History: Making Diasporic Identities', in Wahneema Lubiano, ed. *The House that Race Built* (New York: Pantheon, 1997), p. 295.

42 Ishaan Tharoor with Ruby Mellen, 'Trump Joins Dictators and Demagogues in Touting "patriotic education"', *The Washington Post* (September 21, 2020). Online: www.washingtonpost.com/world/2020/09/21/trump-patriotic-education-china-orban/; Aamer Madhani and Deb Riechmann, 'Trump Pushes "patriotic education" while Downplaying History of U.S. Slavery', *Global News* (September 17, 2020). Online: https://globalnews.ca/news/7342896/trump-patriotic-education-slavery/.

43 Ishaan Tharoor, 'Trump Joins Dictators and Demagogues in Touting "patriotic education"', *The Washington Post* (September 21, 2020). Online: www.washingtonpost.com/world/2020/09/21/trump-patriotic-education-china-orban/.

44 The Editorial Board, 'The Wreckage Betsy DeVos Leaves Behind', *New York Times* (January 2, 2021). Online: www.nytimes.com/2021/01/02/opinion/sunday/education-department-cardona-biden.html.

45 Jane Mayer, 'The Making of the Fox News White House', *The New Yorker* (March 4, 2019). Online: www.newyorker.com/magazine/2019/03/11/the-

making-of-the-fox-news-white-house; Michael I. Niman, 'Weaponized Social Media is Driving the Explosion of Fascism', *Truthout* (April 5, 2019). Online: https://truthout.org/articles/weaponized-social-media-is-driving-the-explosion-of-fascism/.

46 Amelia Mertha, 'Watch This Space: Spectacle and Speed on the Internet', *Honi Soit* (October 18, 2020). Online: https://honisoit.com/2020/10/watch-this-space-spectacle-and-speed-on-the-internet/.

47 Matt Taibbi, *Hate Inc.: Why Today's Media Makes Us Despise One Another* (New York: OR Books, 2019).

48 Guy Debord, *Society of the Spectacle* (New York: Black & Red, 2002).

49 One particularly egregious reading of this sort can be found in the work of Ross Douthat, 'Donald Trump Doesn't Want Authority', *New York Times* (May 2019). Online: www.nytimes.com/2020/05/19/opinion/coronavirus-trump-orban.html?smtyp=cur&smid=tw-nytopinion.

50 Norman Solomon, 'In 2021, the Best Way to Fight Neofascist Republicans Is to Fight Neoliberal Democrats', *Reader Supported News* (January 4, 2021). Online: https://readersupportednews.org/opinion2/277-75/67103-rsn-in-2021-the-best-way-to-fight-neofascist-republicans-is-to-fight-neoliberal-democrats.

51 Samuel Moyn, 'How Trump Won', *The New York Review of Books* (November 9, 2020). Online: www.nybooks.com/daily/2020/11/09/how-trump-won/.

52 Saharra Griffin and Malkie Wall, 'President's Trump's Anti-Worker Agenda', *Center for American Progress Action Fund* (August 19, 2019). Online www.americanprogressaction.org/issues/economy/reports/2019/08/28/174893/president-trumps-anti-worker-agenda/.

53 A brilliant analysis of this issue can be found in John Bellamy Foster, *Trump in the White House: Tragedy and Farce* (New York: Monthly Review Press, 2018).

54 Samuel Moyn, 'How Trump Won', *The New York Review of Books* (November 9, 2020). Online: www.nybooks.com/daily/2020/11/09/how-trump-won/; Jeet Heer, 'Even as a Weak President, Trump Has Undermined Democracy', *The Nation* (December 28, 2020). Online: www.thenation.com/article/politics/trump-weak-undermine-democracy/.

55 See especially, Sarah Churchwell, 'American Fascism: It Has Happened Again', *The New York Review of Books* (May 26, 2020). Online: www.

nybooks.com/daily/2020/06/22/american-fascism-it-has-happened-here/; see also Paul Street, 'We Have a Fascism Problem', *CounterPunch* (December 16, 2020). Online: www.counterpunch.org/2020/12/16/we-have-a-fascism-problem/; Timothy Snyder, *On Tyranny: Twenty Lessons from the Twentieth Century* (New York: Tim Duggan Books, 2017); Jason Stanley, *How Fascism Works* (New York: Random House, 2018); and Henry A. Giroux, *American Nightmare: Facing the Challenge of Fascism* (Chicago: City Lights Books, 2018).

56 Richard J. Evans, 'Why Trump's Isn't a Fascist', *New Statesman* (January 13, 2021). Online: www.newstatesman.com/world/2021/01/why-trump-isnt-fascist.

57 Timothy Snyder, 'The American Abyss', *New York Times* (January 9, 2021). Online: www.nytimes.com/2021/01/09/magazine/trump-coup.html.

58 Vishwas Satgar, 'Trump May Be Gone, but Neofascism Remains', *Socialist Project* (February 7, 2021). Online: https://socialistproject.ca/2021/02/trump-gone-neofascism-remains/.

59 Cited in Terry Eagleton, 'Reappraisals: What is the Worth of Social Democracy?" *Harper's Magazine* (October 2010), p. 78.

60 Ruth Ben-Ghiat, *Strongmen: Mussolini to the Present* (New York: Norton, 2020).

61 Robert Jay Lifton, *Losing Reality: On Cults, Cultism, and the Mindset of Political and Religious Zealotry* (New York: The New Press, 2019), p. 1.

62 Ibid.

63 Frank Bruni, 'We Still Don't Really Understand Trump—or America', *New York Times* (November 7, 2020). Online: www.nytimes.com/2020/11/07/opinion/sunday/trump-election-performance.html.

64 Coco Das, 'What Are You Going To Do about the Nazi Problem?' *Refuse Fascism* (November 24, 2020). Online: https://refusefascism.org/2020/11/24/what-are-you-going-to-do-about-the-nazi-problem/.

65 David Klion, 'Almost the Opposite of Fascism', *Jewish Currents* (November 26, 2020). Online: https://jewishcurrents.org/almost-the-complete-opposite-of-fascism/.

66 Ibid.

67 Richard A. Etlin, 'Introduction: The Perverse Logic of Nazi Thought', in Richard A. Etlin, ed., *Art, Culture, and Media under the Third Reich* (Chicago: University of Chicago Press, 2002), p. 8.

68 Fintan O'Toole, 'Trial Runs for Fascism are in Full Flow', *Irish Times* (June 26, 2018). Online: www.irishtimes.com/opinion/fintan-o-toole-trial-runs-for-fascism-are-in-full-flow-1.3543375.
69 Bill Dixon, 'Totalitarianism and the Sandstorm', *Hannah Arendt Center* (February 3, 2014). Online: www.hannaharendtcenter.org/?p=12466.
70 Lucia Graves, 'How Trump Weaponized "fake news" for His Own Political Ends', *Social Justice* (February 26, 2018). Online: https://psmag.com/social-justice/how-trump-weaponized-fake-news-for-his-own-political-ends; Donie O'Sullivan, 'Misinformed through social media, Trump supporters take to the streets to challenge election result', *CNN* (November 8, 2020). Online: www.cnn.com/2020/11/08/tech/trump-election-protest/index.html.
71 Robert Jay Lifton, *Losing Reality: On Cults, Cultism, and the Mindset of Political and Religious Zealotry* (New York: The New Press, 2019), p. 1.
72 Ruth Ben-Ghiat, 'Fascism Scholar: Strongman Trump Radicalized His Supporters; Turning This Back Will Be Very Hard', *Democracy Now* (January 11, 2021). Online: www.democracynow.org/2021/1/11/trump_impeachment_pelosi_pence?utm_source=Democracy+Now%21&utm_campaign=7c4a997b99-Daily_Digest_COPY_01&utm_medium=email&utm_term=0_fa2346a853-7c4a997b99-190213053.
73 Cited in Elisabeth Young-Bruehl, *Why Arendt Matters* (New York: Integrated Publishing Solutions, 2006), p. 149.
74 David Cohen, 'Trump on Jan. 6 insurrection: "These Were Great People"', *Politico* (July 11, 2021). Online: www.politico.com/news/2021/07/11/trump-jan-6-insurrection-these-were-great-people-499165.
75 Fintan O'Toole, 'Democracy's Afterlife', *The New York Review* (December 3, 2020). Online: www.nybooks.com/articles/2020/12/03/democracys-afterlife/.
76 Chauncey DeVega, 'Irish Author Fintan O'Toole Explains the "suspension of disbelief" that Made Trump's Destruction of America Possible', *Alternet* (May 26, 2020). Online: www.alternet.org/2020/05/irish-author-fintan-otoole-explains-the-suspension-of-disbelief-that-made-trumps-destruction-of-america-possible.
77 Judith Butler, 'Genius or Suicide' *London Review of Books* 41:20 (October 24, 2019). Online: www.lrb.co.uk/the-paper/v41/n20/judith-butler/genius-or-suicide.

78 Kali Holloway and Martin Mycielski, 'Increasingly a Necessity: A 15-Point Guide to Surviving Authoritarianism', *Moyers on Democracy* (December 15, 2017). Online: https://billmoyers.com/story/increasingly-necessity-15-point-guide-surviving-authoritarianism/.
79 Wendy Brown, *Undoing the Demos: Neoliberalism's Stealth Revolution* (New York: Zone Books, 2015), pp. 178–9.
80 Masha Gessen, 'Why America Needs a Reckoning with the Trump Era', *The New Yorker* (November 10, 2020). Online: www.newyorker.com/news/our-columnists/why-america-needs-a-reckoning-with-the-trump-era.
81 For different views on such accountability, see Jill Lepore, 'Let History, Not Partisans, Prosecute Trump', *The New Yorker* (October 16, 2020). Online: www.washingtonpost.com/outlook/truth-reconciliation-tribunal-trump-historians/2020/10/16/84026810-0e88-11eb-b1e8-16b59b92b36d_story.html and Elie Mystal, 'We're Going to Need a Truth and Reconciliation Commission to Recover From Trump', *The Nation* (October 20, 2020). Online: www.thenation.com/article/politics/trump-truth-reconciliation/.
82 George Will, 'Trump, Hawley and Cruz Will Each Wear the Scarlet "S" of a Seditionist', *The Washington Post* (January 6, 2021). Online: www.washingtonpost.com/opinions/trump-hawley-and-cruz-will-each-wear-the-scarlet-s-of-a-seditionist/2021/01/06/65b0ad1a-506c-11eb-bda4-615aaefd0555_story.html.
83 Peter Baker, 'An Insurgency from Inside the Oval Office', *New York Times* (January 4, 2020). Online: www.nytimes.com/2021/01/04/us/politics/trump-white-house.html?referringSource=highlightShare.
84 Cited in L. Robert Block Johannesburg, 'South Africa Begins Laying Ghosts to Rest', *Independent* (April 25, 1996). Online: www.independent.co.uk/news/world/south-africa-begins-laying-ghosts-to-rest-1305130.html.
85 Etienne Balibar, 'Outline of a Topography of Cruelty: Citizenship and Civility in the Era of Global Violence', in *We, The People of Europe? Reflections on Transnational Citizenship* (Princeton: Princeton University Press, 2004), pp. 115–32
86 Mie Inouye, 'Frances Fox Piven on Why Protesters Must "Defend Their Ability to Exercise Disruptive Power"', *Jacobin Magazine* (June 17, 2020).

Online: https://jacobinmag.com/2020/06/frances-fox-piven-protests-movement-racial-justice.
87 Rabbi Michael Lerner, *Revolutionary Love: A Political Manifesto to Heal and Transform the World* (Berkeley: University of California Press, 2019).

Chapter 4

1. C. J. Polychroniou, 'Chomsky: Republicans Are Willing to Destroy Democracy to Retake Power', *Truthout* (June 16, 2021). Online: https://truthout.org/articles/chomsky-republicans-are-willing-to-jeopardize-human-survival-to-retake-power/.
2. Ibid.
3. Paul Street, 'Nine Points of Difference: A Response to Noam Chomsky on American Fascism', *CounterPunch* (June 25, 2021). Online: www.counterpunch.org/2021/06/25/nine-points-of-difference-a-response-to-noam-chomsky-on-american-fascism/.
4. Amy Goodman, "'The United States of America Has Gone Mad': John le Carré on Iraq War, Israel & U.S. Militarism', *Democracy Now* (December 25, 2020). Online: www.democracynow.org/2020/12/25/the_united_states_of_america_has.
5. Peter Thompson, 'The Frankfurt School, Part 5: Walter Benjamin, Fascism and the Future', *Guardian* (April 21, 2013). Online: www.theguardian.com/commentisfree/belief/2013/apr/22/frankfurt-school-walter-benjamin-fascism-future.
6. See, especially, Stuart Hall, Chapter 1: 'The Neoliberal Revolution', *The Neoliberal Crisis*, eds, Jonathan Rutherford and Sally Davison (London: Lawrence Wishart 2012). Online: http://wh.agh.edu.pl/other/materialy/678_2015_04_21_22_04_51_The_Neoliberal_Crisis_Book.pdf; David Harvey: *A Brief History of Neoliberalism* (New York: Oxford University Press, 2005); Sheldon S. Wolin, *Democracy Incorporated: Managed Democracy and the Specter of Inverted Totalitarianism* (Princeton: Princeton University Press, 2008); Wendy Brown, '*Undoing the Demos: Neoliberalism's Stealth Revolution* (New York: Zone Books,

2015); George Monbiot, *Out of the Wreckage* (New York: Verso Press, 2017); Henry A. Giroux, *American Nightmare: Facing the Challenge of Fascism* (Chicago: City Lights 2018).

7   Charles Derber, *Welcome to the Revolution: Universalizing Resistance for Social Justice and Democracy in Perilous Times* (New York: Routledge, 2017). Heinrich Geiselberger, ed. *The Great Regression* (London: Polity, 2017).

8   I take this issue up in great detail in Henry A. Giroux, *Race, Politics and Pandemic Pedagogy: Education in a Time of Crisis* (London: Bloomsbury, 2021).

9   Yaryna Sekez, 'These Charts Show That Your Lockdown Experience Wasn't Just About Luck', *New York Times* (March 11, 2021). Online: www.nytimes.com/interactive/2021/03/11/opinion/covid-inequality-race-gender.html?campaign_id=93&emc=edit_fb_20210616&instance_id=33111&nl=frank-bruni&regi_id=51563793&segment_id=60804&te=1&user_id=ac16f3c28b64af0b86707bb1a8f1b07c.

10 Michael D. Yates, 'Can the Working Class Change the World?', *Truthout* (December 23, 2018). Online: https://truthout.org/articles/can-the-working-class-change-the-world/.

11 Howie Hawkins, 'The Case for an Independent Left Party', *International Socialist Review* Issue 107 (May 10, 2018). Online: https://isreview.org/issue/107/case-independent-left-party.

12 Michael D. Yates, 'Can the Working Class Change the World?'

13 Rafael Khachaturian and Sean Guillory, 'The American Left Resurgent: Prospects and Tensions', *Socialist Project: The Bullet* (February 7, 2019). Online: https://socialistproject.ca/2019/02/the-american-left-resurgent/.

14 Roberto Lovato, 'The Kids Are Reimagining International Solidarity', *The Nation* (June 9, 3022). Online: www.thenation.com/article/activism/millennial-genz-solidarity/.

15 See, for example, Jane Mayer, 'The Making of the Fox News White House', *The New Yorker* (March 4, 2019). Online: www.newyorker.com/magazine/2019/03/11/the-making-of-the-fox-news-white-house.

16 Jon Nixon, 'Hannah Arendt: Thinking Versus Evil', *Times Higher Education* (February 26, 2015). Online: www.timeshighereducation.co.uk/features/hannah-arendt-thinking-versus-evil/2018664.article?page=0%2C0.

17 Umberto Eco, 'Ur-Fascism', *The New York Review of Books* (June 22, 1995). Online: www.nybooks.com/articles/1995/06/22/ur-fascism/?pagination=false&printpage=true.

18 Hannah Arendt, *Origins of Totalitarianism* (New York: Harcourt Trade Publishers, New Edition, 2001).

19 Paul Gilroy, '*Against Race: Imagining Political Culture beyond the Color Line*', Chapter 4 in *Hitler in Khakis: Icons, Propaganda, and Aesthetic Politics* (Cambridge, MA: The Belknap Press of Harvard University Press, 2000), pp. 144–5, 146.

20 James Baldwin, *No Name in the Street* (New York: Vintage; reprint edition 2007), p. 149.

21 Pankaj Mishra, 'A Gandhian Stand Against the Culture of Cruelty', *The New York Review of Books* (May 22, 2018). Online: www.nybooks.com/daily/2018/05/22/the-culture-of-cruelty/.

22 Jean Seaton, 'Why Orwell's 1984 Could Be About Now', *BBC Culture* (May 7, 2018). Online: www.bbc.com/culture/article/20180507-why-orwells-1984-could-be-about-now.

23 John Berger, Hold Everything Dear: Dispatches on Survival and Resistance (New York: Vintage, 2008), p. 89.

24 Nicole Aschoff, 'The Smartphone Society', *Jacobin Magazine*, Issue 17 (Spring 2015). Online: www.jacobinmag.com/2015/03/smartphone-usage-technology-aschoff/.

25 Ruth Levitas, 'Introduction: The Elusive Idea of Utopia', *History of the Human Sciences* 16:1 (2003), p. 4.

26 Goldie Blumenstyk, 'How Higher Education can Help Repair our Democracy', *The Edge: Chronicle.com* (January 13, 2021). Online: www.chronicle.com/newsletter/the-edge/2021-01-13.

27 Roberto Lovato, 'The Kids Are Reimagining International Solidarity', *The Nation* (June 9, 3022). Online: www.thenation.com/article/activism/millennial-genz-solidarity/.

28 Ruth Ben-Ghiat, 'Liberal Democracy Is Losing the Image Wars', *Lucid* (June 1, 2021). Online: https://lucid.substack.com/p/liberal-democracy-is-losing-the-image.

29 Ronald Aronson, *We: Reviving Social Hope* (Chicago: University of Chicago Press, 2017).

30. Hannah Arendt, 'Personal Responsibility under Dictatorship', in Jerome Kohn, ed., *Responsibility and Judgement* (New York: Schocken Books, 2003). Online: https://grattoncourses.files.wordpress.com/2016/08/responsibility-under-a-dictatorship-arendt.pdf.
31. Nicola Bertoldi, 'Are We Living through a New "Weimar era"? Constructive Resolutions for Our Future', *OpenDemocracy* (January 3, 2018). Online: https://us1.campaign-archive.com/?e=d77f123300&u=9c663f765f28cdb71116aa9ac&id=367a142d39.
32. Henry A. Giroux, *The Terror of the Unforeseen* (Los Angeles: Los Angeles Review of Books, 2019).

Chapter 5

1. John Feffer, 'Twilight of the Pandemic?' Tom Dispatch.com (June 8, 2021). Online: https://tomdispatch.com/twilight-of-the-pandemic/.
2. Paul Basken, 'Florida Mandates Political Viewpoint Survey in Universities', *Times Higher Education* (June 25, 2021). Online: www.timeshighereducation.com/news/florida-mandates-political-viewpoint-survey-universities.
3. Ibid.
4. James Baldwin, *No Name in the Street* (New York: Vintage; reprint edition 2007), p. 87.
5. Adam Harris, 'The GOP's "Critical Race Theory" Obsession', *The Atlantic* (May 7, 2021). Online: www.theatlantic.com/politics/archive/2021/05/gops-critical-race-theory-fixation-explained/618828/.
6. Donald J. Trump, 'A Plan to Get Divisive & Radical Theories Out of Our Schools', *Real Clear Politics* (June 18, 2021). Online: www.realclearpolitics.com/articles/2021/06/18/a_plan_to_get_divisive__radical_theories_out_of_our_schools_145946.html.
7. Cited in Judd Legum, '1 Truth and 3 Lies about Critical Race Theory', *Popular Information* (June 28, 2021). Online: https://popular.info/p/1-truth-and-3-lies-about-critical.
8. Kate McGee, 'Texas' Divisive Bill Limiting How Students Learn about Current Events and Historic Racism Passed by Senate', Texas Public Radio (May 23, 2021). Online: www.tpr.org/education/2021-05-23/texas-

divisive-bill-limiting-how-students-learn-about-current-events-and-historic-racism-passed-by-senate.

9   Simon Romero, 'Texas Pushes to Obscure the State's History of Slavery and Racism', *New York Times* (May 20, 2021). Online: www.nytimes.com/2021/05/20/us/texas-history-1836-project.html.
10 Ibid.
11 Julie Carrie Wong, 'The Fight to Whitewash US History: "A drop of poison is all you need"', *Guardian* (May 25, 2021). Online: www.theguardian.com/world/2021/may/25/critical-race-theory-us-history-1619-project.
12 Nathan M. Greenfield, 'Why Are States Lining up to Ban Critical Race Theory?' *University World News* (June 12, 2021). Online: www.universityworldnews.com/post.php.
13 H.B. No. 237, press conference, June 15, 2021. https://ohiochannel.org/video/press-conference-6-15-2021-discussing-h-b-no-327?fbclid=IwAR00pKOucypIJcPKMYnOlmqg-i6uE8_OvKU9MjXyDNIUcmsBE6J1ndqTgXQ, time mark 1:50.
14 Timothy Messer-Kruse, 'Anti-Critical Race Theory and Neo-McCarthyism', *CounterPunch* (June 18, 2021). Online: www.counterpunch.org/2021/06/18/anti-critical-race-theory-and-neo-mccarthyism/.
15 Ibid.
16 David Theo Goldberg, 'The War on Critical Race Theory', *Boston Review* (May 7, 2021). Online: http://bostonreview.net/race-politics/david-theo-goldberg-war-critical-race-theory.
17 Adam Harris, 'The GOP's Critical Race Theory Obsession'.
18 Blair McClendon, 'To James Baldwin, the Struggle for Black Liberation was a Struggle for Democracy', *Jacobin* Magazine (June 19, 2021). Online: www.jacobinmag.com/2021/06/james-baldwin-civil-rights-struggle-democracy.
19 George Sanchez and Beth English, 'OAH Statement on White House Conference on American History', *Organization of American History* (September 2020). Online: www.oah.org/insights/posts/2020/september/oah-statement-on-white-house-conference-on-american-history/#:~:text=History%20is%20not%20and%20cannot%20be%20simply%20celebratory.&text=The%20history%20we%20teach%20must,slavery%2C%20exploitation%2C%20and%20exclusion.

20 Cited in Judd Legum, '1 Truth and 3 Lies about Critical Race Theory'.
21 Adam Harris, 'The GOP's Critical Race Theory Obsession'.
22 For a longer discussion of Rufo's views on critical race theory, see Christopher Rufo, '"White Fragility" Comes to Washington', *City Journal* (July 18, 2021). Online: www.city-journal.org/white-fragility-comes-to-washington.
23 Cited in Stephen Kearse, 'GOP Lawmakers Intensify Effort to Ban Critical Race Theory in Schools', *Stateline* (June 14, 2021). Online: www.pewtrusts.org/en/research-and-analysis/blogs/stateline/2021/06/14/gop-lawmakers-intensify-effort-to-ban-critical-race-theory-in-schools.
24 Editorial, 'Mission Goals and Objectives', *No Left Turn in Education* (2021). Online: https://noleftturn.us/.
25 Kali Holloway, 'White Ignorance Is Bliss—and Power', *Yahoo! News* (May 24, 2021). Online: https://news.yahoo.com/white-ignorance-bliss-power-080232025.html.
26 Michelle Goldberg, 'The Social Justice Purge at Idaho College', *New York Times* (March 26, 2021). Online: www.nytimes.com/2021/03/26/opinion/free-speech-idaho.html.
27 Selene San Felice, 'DeSantis Takes Aim at Student "Indoctrination" in Florida', *Axios* (June 24, 2021). Online: www.axios.com/ron-desantis-education-laws-florida-free-speech-f4f174bc-265c-492f-a75a-5d445a35c45d.html.
28 Governor's Press Office, 'Governor Ron DeSantis Signs Legislation to Set the Pace for Civics Education in America', *Florida Department of Education* (June 22, 2021). Online: www.fldoe.org/newsroom/latest-news/governor-ron-desantis-signs-legislation-to-set-the-pace-for-civics-education-in-america.stml.
29 Katie Robertson, 'Nikole Hannah-Jones Denied Tenure at University of North Carolina', *New York Times* (May 19, 2021). Online: www.nytimes.com/2021/05/19/business/media/nikole-hannah-jones-unc.html.
30 Andy Thomason, 'After Controversial Delay, UNC Awards Tenure to Nikole Hannah-Jones', *The Chronicle of Higher Education* (June 20, 2021). Online: www.chronicle.com/article/after-controversial-delay-unc-awards-tenure-to-nikole-hannah-jones.
31 Nikole Hannah-Jones, 'Statement on Decision to Decline Tenure Offer at University of North Carolina-Chapel Hill and to Accept Knight

Chair Appointment at Howard University', *NAACP Legal Defense and Educational Fund* (July 6, 2021). Online: www.naacpldf.org/press-release/nikole-hannah-jones-issues-statement-on-decision-to-decline-tenure-offer-at-university-of-north-carolina-chapel-hill-and-to-accept-knight-chair-appointment-at-howard-university/.

32 Michelle Goldberg, 'The Campaign to Cancel Wokeness', *New York Times* (February 26, 2021). Online: www.nytimes.com/2021/02/26/opinion/speech-racism-academia.html.

33 Henry A. Giroux, *Neoliberalism's War on Higher Education* (Chicago: Haymarket Press, 2020).

34 Silke-Marie Weineck, 'The Tenure Denial of Nikole Hannah-Jones Is Craven and Dangerous', *The Chronicle of Higher Education* (May 20, 2021). Online: www.chronicle.com/article/the-tenure-denial-of-nikole-hannah-jones-is-craven-and-dangerous.

35 Keith E. Whittington and Sean Wilentz, 'We Have Criticized Nikole Hannah-Jones. Her Tenure Denial Is a Travesty', *The Chronicle of Higher Education* (May 24, 2021). Online: www.chronicle.com/article/we-have-criticized-nikole-hannah-jones-her-tenure-denial-is-a-travesty?utm_source=Iterable&utm_medium=email&utm_campaign=campaign_2377858_nl_Afternoon-Update_date_20210524&cid=pm&source=ams&sourceId=11167.

36 See Judd Legum and Tesnim Zekeria, 'The Obscure Foundation Funding "Critical Race Theory" Hysteria', *Popular Information* (July 13, 2021). Online: https://popular.info/p/the-obscure-foundation-funding-critical.

37 David Theo Goldberg, 'The War on Critical Race Theory', *Boston Review* (May 7, 2021). Online: http://bostonreview.net/race-politics/david-theo-goldberg-war-critical-race-theory.

38 Cited in Nathan M. Greenfield, 'Why Are States Lining up to Ban Critical Race Theory?' *University World News* (June 12, 2021). Online: www.universityworldnews.com/post.php.

39 Thomas Klikauer and Catherine Link, 'Even if Fox Ever Went Down along with Murdoch, the Law of Media Capitalism Would Ensure the Right-Wing Chorus Would Continue Humming Along', *Buzzflash* (May 5, 2020). Online: https://buzzflash.com/articles/thomas-klikauer-and-catherine-link-for-buzzflash-even-if-fox-ever-went-down-along-with-murdoch-the-law-of-media-capitalism-would-ensure-the-right-wing-show-will-continue.

40 Noam Chomsky and Marv Waterstone, *Consequences of Capitalism: Manufacturing Discontent and Resistance* (Chicago: Haymarket, 2021); Zoe Carpenter, 'Misinformation Is Destroying Our Country. Can Anything Rein It In?' *The Nation* (April 23, 2021). Online: www.thenation.com/article/society/right-wing-media-misinformation/.

41 Amelia Mertha, 'Watch This Space: Spectacle and Speed on the Internet', *Honi Soit* (October 2020). Online: https://honisoit.com/2020/10/watch-this-space-spectacle-and-speed-on-the-internet/.

42 Marc Fisher, 'From Memes to Race War: How Extremists Use Popular Culture to Lure Recruits', *The Washington Post* (April 30, 2021). Online: www.washingtonpost.com/nation/2021/04/30/extremists-recruiting-culture-community/?utm_campaign=wp_main&utm_source=twitter&utm_medium=social.

43 Cited in Chauncey DeVega, 'Tucker Carlson Prepares White Nationalists for War: Don't Ignore the Power of his Rhetoric', *Salon* (June 30, 2021). Online: www.salon.com/2021/06/30/tucker-carlson-prepares-white-nationalists-for-war-dont-ignore-the-power-of-his-rhetoric/.

44 Luke O'Neil, 'Advertisers Recoil as Tucker Carlson Says Immigrants Make US "dirtier"', *Guardian* (December 18, 2018). Online: www.theguardian.com/media/2018/dec/18/tucker-carlson-immigrants-poorer-dirtier-advertisers-pull-out.

45 Paige Williams, 'Kyle Rittenhouse, American Vigilante', *The New Yorker* (June 28, 2021). Online: www.newyorker.com/magazine/2021/07/05/kyle-rittenhouse-american-vigilante.

46 Judd Legum, 'Tucker, Lachlan, and Subsidized Speech', *Popular Information* (April 26, 2021). Online: https://popular.info/p/tucker-lachlan-and-subsidized-speech.

47 Eric Kelderman, 'The Far Right's College Crusade', *Chronicle.com* (June 28, 2021). Online: www.chronicle.com/article/the-far-rights-college-crusade?utm_source=Iterable&utm_medium=email&utm_campaign=campaign_2520976_nl_Afternoon-Update_date_20210628&cid=pm&source=ams&sourceId=11167&cid2=gen_login_refresh.

48 Jake Lahut, 'Fox News Pushes Conspiracy Theory about "reeducation camps" on the Eve of Biden's Inauguration', *Business Insider* (January 19, 2021). Online: www.businessinsider.com/video-fox-news-reeducation-camps-conspiracy-theory-harris-faulkner-2021-1.

49 Eric Kelderman, 'The Far Right's College Crusade'.
50 Paul Blest, 'ICYMI Tucker Carlson Endorsed a Core Belief of White Supremacy Last Night', *Vice News* (April 9, 2021). Online: www.vice.com/en/article/4avgap/tucker-carlson-endorsed-a-core-belief-of-white-supremacy-last-night; see also Tucker Carlson 'Touts "Replacement" Conspiracy Theory; But His Own Ancestor Could Have Been Lynched', *Informed Comment* (April 10, 2021). Online: www.juancole.com/2021/04/replacement-conspiracy-ancestor.html.
51 Joe Heim, 'Recounting a Day of Rage, Hate, Violence and Death', *The Washington Post* (April 14, 2017). Online: www.washingtonpost.com/graphics/2017/local/charlottesville-timeline/.
52 Astead W. Herndon, 'How Republicans Are Warping Reality around the Capitol Attack', *New York Times* (January 17, 2021). Online: www.nytimes.com/2021/01/17/us/politics/Capitol-conspiracy-theories-blm-antifa.html.
53 Roger Sollenberger, 'Calls Grow for Tucker Carlson to be Fired from Fox News over Accusations of "inciting violence"', *Salon* (August 27, 2020). Online: www.salon.com/2020/08/27/calls-grow-for-tucker-carlsonto-be-fired-from-foxnews-over-accusations-of-inciting-violence/.
54 Michael Gerson, 'Elected Republicans are Lying with Open Eyes. Their Excuses are Disgraceful', *The Washington Post* (May 3, 2021). Online: www.washingtonpost.com/opinions/2021/05/03/trump-republicans-big-lie/.
55 Ibid.
56 Michael I. Niman, 'Weaponized Social Media Is Driving the Explosion of Fascism', *Truthout* (April 5, 2019). Online: https://truthout.org/articles/weaponized-social-media-is-driving-the-explosion-of-fascism/.
57 Ruth Ben-Ghiat, 'Why Do People Believe Liars?' *Lucid* (May 4, 2021). Online: https://lucid.substack.com/p/why-do-people-believe-liars; see also Federico Finchelstein, *A Brief History of Fascist Lies* (Oakland: University of California Press, 2020).
58 Jason Stanley, *How Propaganda Works* (Princeton: Princeton University Press, 2015), p. 3.
59 Andreas Inderwwildi, 'The Scathing Portrait of the Pro Fascist in "Disco Elysium: The Final Cut"', *Vice* (May 5, 2021). Online: www.vice.com/en/article/epnnbm/the-scathing-portrait-of-the-pro-fascist-in-disco-elysium-the-final-cut.

60 Etienne Balibar, 'Outline of a Topography of Cruelty: Citizenship and Civility in the Era of Global Violence', in *We, The People of Europe? Reflections on Transnational Citizenship* (Princeton: Princeton University Press, 2004), p. 128.
61 Patricia Ticento Clough and Craig Willse, 'Beyond Biopolitics: The Governance of Life and Death', in Patricia Ticento Clough and Craig Willse, eds, *Beyond Biopolitics* (Durham, NC: Duke University Press, 2011), p. 3.
62 Volker Weiss, 'Afterword', in Theodor W. Adorno, *Aspects of the New Right-Wing Extremism* (London: Polity, 2020), p. 61.
63 Brad Evans and Isaac Cordal, 'Histories of Violence: Look Closer at the World, There You Will See', *Los Angeles Review of Books* (December 28, 2020). Online: https://lareviewofbooks.org/article/histories-of-violence-look-closer-at-the-world-there-you-will-see/.
64 Jean Comaroff and John L. Comaroff, *The Truth About Crime* (Chicago: University of Chicago Press, 2016), p. x.
65 Henry A. Giroux, *Dangerous Thinking in the Age of the New Authoritarianism* (New York: Routledge, 2015).
66 Charlotte Klein, 'Mitch McConnell: Don't Teach Our Kids that America Is Racist', *Vanity Fair* (May 4, 2021). Online: www.vanityfair.com/news/2021/05/mitch-mcconnell-dont-teach-our-kids-that-america-is-racist; Michael Crowley, 'Trump Calls for "Patriotic Education" to Defend American History From the Left', *New York Times* (September 17, 2020). Online: www.nytimes.com/2020/09/17/us/politics/trump-patriotic-education.html.
67 Editorial, 'Trump's Crusade against the Media is a Chilling Echo of Hitler's Rise', *Las Vegas Sun* (August 14, 2017). Online: https://lasvegassun.com/news/2017/aug/14/trumps-crusade-against-the-media-is-a-chilling-ech/; for a larger examination of this issue, see Federico Finchelstein, *A Brief History of Fascist Lies* (Oakland: University of California Press, 2020).
68 David Graeber, 'Dead Zones of the Imagination', *HAU: Journal of Ethnographic Theory* 2 (2012), p. 105.
69 Chantal Mouffe, *For a Left Populism* (London: Verso, 2018), p. 37.
70 Institute for Critical Social Analysis, 'A Window of Opportunity for Leftist Politics?' *Socialist Project: The Bullet* (August 3, 2020). Online: https://socialistproject.ca/2020/08/window-of-opportunity-for-leftist-politics/.

71　Roger Berkowitz, 'Thoughts Amidst the Storm', *HAC Bard* (November 5, 2020). Online: https://hac.bard.edu/amor-mundi/thoughts-amidst-the-storm-2020-11-05.
72　Robin D. G. Kelley, 'Black Study, Black Struggle—Final Response', *Boston Review* (March 7, 2016). Online: http://bostonreview.net/forum/black-study-black-struggle/robin-d-g-kelley-robin-d-g-kelleys-final-response.
73　Audre Lorde, 'Learning from the 60s', *Black Past* (August 12, 2012). Online: www.blackpast.org/african-american-history/1982-audre-lorde-learning-60s/. This speech was first delivered on February 1982 as part of the Malcolm X weekend at Harvard University.
74　Mark Fisher, *Capitalist Realism: Is There No Alternative?* (Winchester, UK: Zero Books, 2009), p. 2. It would be useful on this issue to read the brilliant Stanley Aronowitz, especially *The Death and Rebirth of American Radicalism* (New York: Routledge, 1996).

Chapter 6

1　Roger Berkowitz, 'Can Moral Life Survive Dictatorship?' *HAC Bard* (February 4, 2021). Online: https://hac.bard.edu/amor-mundi/can-moral-life-survive-dictatorship-2021-02-04.
2　John Merrick, 'The Angel of History', *Boston Review* (September 4, 2020). Online: https://bostonreview.net/philosophy-religion/john-merrick-angel-history.
3　Walter Benjamin, *Walter Benjamin's Selected Writings, vol. 1: 1913–1926*, eds, Marcus Bullock and Michael W. Jennings (Cambridge, MA: Belknap Press, 1996), p. 356.
4　For an excellent source on intersectionality and education, see Patricia Hill Collins and Sirma Bilge, *Intersectionality* (London: Polity, 2016).
5　Bruce Robbins, 'A Starting Point for Politics', *The Nation* (October 27, 2016). Online: www.thenation.com/article/the-radical-life-of-stuart-hall/.
6　Stanley Aronowitz, 'Introduction', in Paulo Freire, *Pedagogy of Freedom* (Lanham: Rowman & Littlefield, 1998), p. 12.
7　Zygmunt Bauman and Keith Tester, *Conversations with Zygmunt Bauman* (Malden: Polity Press, 2001), p. 4.
8　Stanley Aronowitz, 'Introduction'.

9. Scott J. Peters, Hélène Grégoire, and Margo Hittleman, 'Practicing a Pedagogy Of Hope: Practitioner Profiles as Tools for Grounding and Guiding Collective Reflection in Adult, Community, and Youth Development Education', in M. Reynolds and R. Vince, eds, *Organizing Reflection* (Aldershot: Ashgate, 2004). Online: https://courses2.cit.cornell.edu/fit117/documents/Petersetal_final_.pdf.
10. John Dewey, *The Political Writings*, eds, D. Morris and I. Shapiro (London: Hackett Publishing, 1993), p. 122.
11. Mark Fisher, *Capitalist Realism: Is There No Alternative?* (Winchester, UK: Zero Books, 2009), p. 6.
12. Ibid., p. 9.
13. Alain Badiou, *Ethics: An Essay on the Understanding of Evil* (London: Verso, 1998), p. 11
14. Cited in Anson Rabinach, 'Unclaimed Heritage: Ernst Bloch's Heritage of Our Times and the Theory of Fascism', *New German Critique* (Spring 1977), p. 11.

Chapter 7

1. Lacino Hamilton, 'This is Going to Hurt', *The New Inquiry* (April 11, 2017). Online: thenewinquiry.com/this-is-going-to-hurt/.
2. Associated Press, 'Canadian Indigenous Group Says More Graves Found at New Site', *The Washington Post* (June 2021). Online: www.washingtonpost.com/world/indigenous-groups-in-canada-reports-more-bodies-at-school/2021/06/30/d40bd6fe-d9ce-11eb-8c87-ad6f27918c78_story.html.
3. See Robert Latham, A. T. Kingsmith, Julian von Bargen, and Niko Block, eds, *Challenging the Right, Augmenting the Left–Recasting Leftist Imagination* (Winnipeg, Canada: Fernwood Publishing, 2020).
4. Nico Block, 'Augmenting the Left: Challenging the Right, Reimagining Transformation', *Socialist Project: The Bullet* (August 31, 2020). Online: https://socialistproject.ca/2020/08/augmenting-the-left-challenging-the-right-reimagining-transformation/.
5. C. Wright Mills, *The Politics of Truth* (New York: Oxford University Press, 2008), p. 155.

6   Elisabeth Young-Bruehl, *Why Arendt Matters* (New Haven: Yale University Press, 2006), p. 155
7   Wendy Brown, '*Undoing the Demos: Neoliberalism's Stealth Revolution* (New York: Zone Books, 2015), p. 179.
8   The sheer stupidity of Cotton in his calling for the firing of a US Air Force Academy professor boggles the mind. See Greg Sargent, 'Tom Cotton's Slimy Attack on a "Critical Race Theory" Professor is Full of Holes', *The Washington Post* (July 8, 2021). Online: www.washingtonpost.com/opinions/2021/07/08/tom-cotton-critical-race-theory-professor-attack-holes/.
9   James Baldwin, *No Name in the Street* (New York: Knopf, 2007), p. 60.
10 Peter Uwe Hohendahl, *Prismatic Thought: Theodor Adorno* (Lincoln: University of Nebraska Press, 1995), p. 56.
11 Brad Evans and Vincent Brown, 'Histories of Violence: Violence, Power and Privilege', *LA Review of Books* (March 1, 2021). Online: https://lareviewofbooks.org/article/histories-of-violence-violence-power-privilege/.
12 Melvin Rogers, 'Democracy is a Habit: Practice It', *Boston Review* (July 25, 2019). Online: http://bostonreview.net/politics/melvin-rogers-democracy-habit-practice-it.
13 Conversation between Lani Guinier and Anna Deavere Smith, 'Rethinking Power, Rethinking Theater', *Theater* 31:3 (Winter 2002), pp. 34–5.
14 Roger Simon, 'Empowerment as a Pedagogy of Possibility', *Language Arts* 64:4 (April 1987), p. 375.
15 João Biehl, *Vita: Life in a Zone of Social Abandonment* (Los Angeles: University of California Press, 2005), p. 11.
16 Zoe Williams, 'The Saturday Interview: Stuart Hall', *Guardian* (February 11, 2012). Online: www.guardian.co.uk/theguardian/2012/feb/11/saturday-interview-stuart-hall.
17 See, for instance, Leon Botstein, 'What Does It Mean to Educate Citizens?' *HAC Bard* (November 20, 2019). Online: https://hac.bard.edu/amor-mundi/what-does-it-mean-to-educate-citizens-2019-11-20.
18 James Baldwin, 'Strangers in the Village', in *Baldwin: Collected Essays* (New York: Literary Classics, 1998), p. 129.
19 Eric Blanc, 'Nina Turner: "Good Ideas Are Not Enough, We Need to Marry Our Ideas to Power"', *Jacobin* (March 2021). Online: www.jacobinmag.com/2021/03/nina-turner-congress-progressive-policy.
20 Ibid.

21 'Naomi Klein, 'Sandy's Devastation Opens Space for Action on Climate Change and Progressive Reform', *Democracy Now* (November 15, 2012). Online: www.democracynow.org/2012/11/15/naomi_klein_sandys_devastation_opens_space.
22 Hannah Arendt, *Thinking Without a Banister: Essays in Understanding, 1953–2021*, ed. Jerome Kohn (New York: Shocken, 2021).
23 Robin D. G. Kelley, 'Black Study, Black Struggle', *Boston Review* (March 7, 2016). Online: https://bostonreview.net/forum/robin-d-g-kelley-black-study-black-struggle.
24 James Baldwin, 'An Open Letter to My Sister, Miss Angela Davis', *The New York Review of Books* (January 7, 1971). Online: www.nybooks.com/articles/archives/1971/jan/07/an-open-letter-to-my-sister-miss-angela-davis/?pagination=false.
25 Alfredo Saad-Filho, 'The Left Must Seize This Moment, or Others Will', *Jacobin Magazine* (April 23, 2020). Online: www.jacobinmag.com/2020/04/coronavirus-crisis-covid-economy-recession-pandemic.

Index

A
Abolish Democracy 76
accountability 31, 35, 83, 106, 121, 123, 141
activism 152, 203, 209
activists 172, 201, 207, 209
   American Nazism 60, 88
   fascism 133, 144
Adorno, Theodor 33, 40, 53, 93
agency *see also* fascism
   American Nazism 63, 69, 74–5, 86–8, 93
   ignorance and public imagination 23–4, 45, 47, 49, 52
   Pedagogy of Hope 179, 181–2, 185–7, 192–3
   resistance, towards a pedagogy of 198–9, 202–5, 207, 210
   Trumpism 109–10, 115, 118, 120
alienation 24, 48, 204
American Enterprise Institute, The 159
American Legislative Exchange Council 90
amnesia, historical 33–41, 42, 45, 51, 111, 136
anti-Semitism 39, 43
anxiety 179
apartheid 149–161
   disinformation in age of spectacle 161–7
   social imagination 169–73
   spectacle of violence 167–9
Arbery, Ahmaud 72, 82
Arendt, Hannah 134, 139, 147
Aronowitz, Stanley 184, 191–2
authoritarianism 199 *see also* Trumpism
   American Nazism 56–7, 65, 86, 91
   apartheid 165, 170

   fascism 130, 134, 137
   ignorance and public imagination 21–2, 31, 34
   Pedagogy of Hope 177, 180, 187, 195
authority 66, 165
   Pedagogy of Hope 182, 186–7, 189, 193
   Trumpism 105–6, 111

B
Baker, Peter 122–3
Baldwin, James 134, 150, 199, 206, 210
   American Nazism 63, 79, 92
   ignorance and public imagination 26, 51
Bauman, Zygmunt 61, 186
Ben-Ghiat, Ruth 33, 36–7, 122, 145
Biden, Joe 140
   American Nazism 58, 69, 78, 84
   ignorance and public imagination 25, 27, 39, 52
   Trumpism 95, 100, 104, 108, 110, 120–1
Birth of a Nation 43
Black Lives Matter movement 37, 61, 65, 160, 172, 195–6
Bloch, Ernst 134, 193
bombings 82
Breitbart 162
Brown, Vincent 32, 200
Brown, Wendy 49, 198
Bruni, Frank 115–16

C
capitalism *see also* Nazism, America; resistance, towards a pedagogy of
   apartheid 168, 170–3

fascism 129–34, 136, 139, 141–2, 147–8
ignorance and public imagination. *see* ignorance
Pedagogy of Hope 178–9, 181
Trumpism 102, 105, 107, 112–14, 124–5
Carlson, Tucker 37, 38, 39, 162–5, 166
celebrities 27
censorship 153–4, 159, 199
children 195
   American Nazism 59, 71, 77, 79, 89
   apartheid 150, 156, 170
   ignorance and public imagination 43–5, 50
   Trumpism 96, 102, 105, 107
Chomsky, Noam 65, 129–30
citizenry 120
citizenship 142, 168, 187, 205
   American Nazism 61, 67, 87, 90–1
   ignorance and public imagination 22–3, 44, 46, 48
   Trumpism 111, 120
civic culture 118, 193
   American Nazism 68, 91
   apartheid 155, 171
   ignorance and public imagination 27, 33
civil rights 92, 100, 113, 129, 152, 172
class 154, 196
   American Nazism 68–9, 74, 81
   fascism 131–3, 148
   ignorance and public imagination 22, 30
   Pedagogy of Hope 178, 181, 190–1
   Trumpism 99, 108, 113, 124
classrooms 35, 149, 152, 157, 183, 188
Clavey, Charles H. 121–2
climate change (crisis) 25, 131, 156, 160, 177, 190, 207
COINTELPRO 82
collective consciousness 28–31
commodification 47, 61, 198, 202
Common Dreams 100

communities 23, 115, 147, 202
   American Nazism 64, 86
   apartheid 154, 162
competition 33, 138, 204
complicity 59, 196
Condemnation of Blackness: Race, Crime, and the Making of Modern Urban America, The 76
conformity 4, 7, 64, 150, 169, 190, 199
conspiracy theories 165–6, 178
   American Nazism 57, 61, 87
   ignorance and public imagination. *see* ignorance
   Trumpism 95–6, 100–1, 105–6, 108, 116
consumerism 138
   American Nazism 67, 86
   ignorance and public imagination 22, 44–5, 47–8, 51
   Trumpism 111, 120
consumption 23, 46, 57, 137, 162, 189
contexts 52
control 37, 196
   American Nazism 71, 76, 81–2, 89
   apartheid 149, 152, 155, 157, 167
   fascism 136, 142
   Trumpism 105–6, 111, 114
corporations 52, 90
corruption *see also* Trumpism
   American Nazism 56, 59, 81, 87
   ignorance and public imagination 27, 45
coups 121
COVID-19 177–178 *see also* ignorance
   American Nazism 79, 86
   fascism 130–1, 134
   Trumpism 105, 109
crises 177
critical pedagogy 63, 124–5, 199, 203–5 *see also* fascism
   apartheid 149, 151, 155
   Pedagogy of Hope 181, 183, 185, 187, 193

Index

critical race theory 33-4, 151-2, 153, 155, 159, 160
critical thinking 111, 141-3, 198
  American Nazism 57, 93
  apartheid 153-155, 159
  ignorance and public imagination 27, 35, 46-7, 50, 52
  Pedagogy of Hope 177, 182, 187-8
cruelty 196, 210
  American Nazism 56, 59, 68, 77, 86
  fascism 133, 137, 141
  ignorance and public imagination 24, 27-9, 33, 45
  Trumpism 100, 103-5, 116
Cruz, Ted 96, 121, 151
cultism 22, 109
Culture of Punishment, The 78
cultures 47-8, 135, 165, 184-5, 205
  see also civic culture; fascism
  politics 202-4
  Trumpism 109-12, 114, 116-19
curricula 137, 150, 153, 199

D

Daily Stormer, The 163
Davis, Angela Y. 76, 134, 153, 202
dehumanization 166
  ignorance and public imagination 24, 28, 31-2
  Trumpism 107, 113-14, 117, 125
democracy 196, 197-200, 202-8, 210-11 *see also* apartheid; fascism; ignorance; Nazism, America; Trumpism
  Pedagogy of Hope 177-80, 183, 185-7, 190-4
demonstrators 107, 133
denial 88, 155
  ignorance and public imagination 26, 42, 51
  Trumpism 100, 113-15, 117, 121, 124
depoliticization 23, 40-1, 45, 124, 163, 198

deregulation 29, 32, 47, 131, 133, 137-8
Desantis, Ron 150, 152, 157
Dewey, John 26, 198, 202
dignity 49, 109, 194, 200, 202, 209
  American Nazism 68, 86-7
discrimination 154
  American Nazism 60, 71, 89
  ignorance and public imagination 30, 48
  Trumpism 113, 121
disinformation 24-6, 52, 110-11, 155
  in age of spectacle 161-7
disposability 166-7, 196
  American Nazism 67-70, 77, 82, 87-8
  ignorance and public imagination 31-2, 48
  Trumpism 107, 114, 117
dissenters 100, 119
diversity 66, 149, 156-7, 163
domination 168
  fascism 129, 134-5, 144
  ignorance and public imagination 47, 53
  Pedagogy of Hope 180 1, 188, 193
Douglas, Frederick 63-4, 153, 180

E

economic rights 62, 85, 124, 201, 208
education *see also* ignorance; resistance, towards a pedagogy of
  American Nazism 63, 75, 86, 88, 93
  apartheid 149-55, 164-6, 168-9, 171, 173
  as depoliticizing machine 41-6
  fascism 131-2, 134-6, 141, 143, 145-6
  Pedagogy of Hope 177, 179-89
  public imagination 46-8
  Trumpism 104, 110, 123

educators 56, 199, 204 *see also* teachers
 apartheid 157, 172
 fascism 135, 138–9, 142–4, 146–7
 Pedagogy of Hope 180, 183, 186–7, 194
elections 37, 57–8, 89, 108, 121–3, 161
elections, presidential 84, 90, 95, 103, 140, 165
elites 30, 57, 131
 American Nazism 69, 87
 apartheid 167, 169
 Trumpism 99, 111, 113–14, 120–1
entertainment 111, 141, 187
 apartheid 161–2, 166, 168
 ignorance and public imagination 24, 27–8, 45, 47–8
equality 125, 202, 206–8
 American Nazism 86, 92
 apartheid 154, 160, 165, 167, 172–3
 fascism 132, 135, 137, 147
 ignorance and public imagination 25, 46
 Pedagogy of Hope 181, 190, 192, 194
Evans, Richard 42, 114
experts 43, 110, 178
extremism 39, 43, 163, 177, 194

F
fake news 24, 51, 107, 112, 141, 169
falsehoods 38, 87, 138–9, 200
 apartheid 150, 155, 159, 165–6
 Trumpism 110, 121
fascism *see also* ignorance
 American Nazism 56–7, 62, 66, 87, 89–91
 apartheid 166, 168, 172
 neoliberal 48–54
 Trumpism 98–9, 112–14, 119, 123–5
fascism, culture
 agency, vision, identity, and politics 147–8
 America under siege 129–31
 beyond critical thinking 142–4
 gangster capitalism 131–3
 manufactured ignorance 140–2
 pedagogy and politics 138–40
 politics in image-based society 144–7
 social abandonment 136–8
 thinking the unthinkable 133–6
fear, culture of 91, 103, 111
Feffer, John 99, 149
feminism 191
Floyd, George 64, 71, 82, 86, 179
food 85, 97
Fox News 150, 162
freedom 200–2, 206, 209–10
 American Nazism 63–4, 92
 apartheid 152, 154, 157–60, 173
 fascism 135, 141–2, 148
 ignorance and public imagination 29, 41, 44, 47, 53
 Pedagogy of Hope 181–2, 186
 Trumpism 111–12, 116–17, 120, 125
Freedom House 55, 60
Freire, Paulo 134, 177–94, 198, 202
Fromm, Erich 23, 181

G
gangster capitalism 114, 196–7, 199, 207
 American Nazism 56, 69, 85–6
 apartheid 168, 171, 173
 fascism 131–3, 147
 ignorance and public imagination 22–3, 32, 44, 53
Garner, Eric 64, 70
Gessen, Masha 102, 106, 120
Giuliani, Rudy 77, 96
globalization 76, 85, 99, 130, 180
Goldberg, David Theo 88, 100, 160
Golden Gulag: Prisons, Surplus, Crisis, and Opposition in Globalizing California 75
Gramsci, Antonio 103, 202
groups, extremist 30, 45, 100

guns 44, 57, 72
  reform failures 80–4
  reforms 78–80
Guterres, Antonio 59–60

H
Hall, Stuart 109, 205
Hannah-Jones, Nikole 157–9
hardship 68, 103, 114, 137
health 91
health care 56, 87, 97, 132, 207–9
healthcare 27, 32, 75, 131–3
Hedges, Chris 50, 51
Heritage Foundation 90
higher education 69, 110, 203
  apartheid 156–9, 169
  fascism 129, 134, 137–40, 148
Holloway, Kali 119, 156
Holocaust 33
Homeland Security Grant Program 73
hosts, media 161
human rights 29, 49, 124, 194, 203 see also Nazism, America
humiliation 24, 136

I
I Alone Can Fix It 36
identity 182, 199, 203
  American Nazism 86, 88–9
  apartheid 149, 164, 168
  fascism 132, 144, 147–8
  ignorance and public imagination 45–7, 49
  Trumpism 98, 109
ignorance
  education and public imagination 46–8
  education as depoliticizing machine 41–6
  historical amnesia 33–41
  neoliberal fascism 48–54
  past histories 21–6
  pedagogical plagues and collective consciousness 28–31
  public imagination and Trumpism 26–8
  Republican Party 31–3
ignorance, manufactured 196–8, 209–11 see also ignorance
  American Nazism 62, 64, 67, 87
  apartheid 149, 155, 165–6, 168
  fascism 140, 144
  Trumpism 98, 114
immigration (immigrants) 163–164, 181 see also Nazism, America; Trumpism
  fascism 129, 136
  ignorance and public imagination 25, 36–7, 40–1, 44
impeachment 121
indigenous peoples 72, 195
individual freedom 29, 44, 47, 112
individualism 111, 138, 202
  American Nazism 61, 69, 88
  ignorance and public imagination 23, 53
  Pedagogy of Hope 172, 190
indoctrination 151, 153, 155–7, 186–7, 199
inequalities 137, 200
  American Nazism 69, 85, 87
  ignorance and public imagination 22, 31, 33, 49
  Pedagogy of Hope 178, 181
  Trumpism 114, 125
Infowars 162
insecurity 23, 46, 55
institutions 196, 199, 201–2, 205, 209 see also ignorance; Nazism, America
  apartheid 159, 163, 165, 167
  fascism 129, 132–3, 148
  Pedagogy of Hope 178, 180–1, 188–9, 194
  Trumpism 102, 106, 110, 120
intellectualism 189
  American Nazism 57, 67
  apartheid 156, 169

ignorance and public imagination 22, 25, 51
isolation 22, 178, 190

J
journalists 110, 150
   American Nazism 56, 60
   fascism 141, 146
   ignorance and public imagination 25, 36
   justice 121, 123

K
Kaba, Mariame 74, 88
Kelley, Robin D. G. 31, 67, 209
King, Martin Luther Jr. 79, 170
Klein, Naomi 49, 209
knowledge 111, 198, 203, 205, 210
   apartheid 153, 161
   fascism 139–40, 142–4, 146
   ignorance and public imagination 34, 48, 52
   Pedagogy of Hope 180, 182–5, 187–8

L
language 95, 139, 195, 200–1, 204, 209–10 see also ignorance; Trumpism
   American Nazism 58, 63, 67, 69, 89
   apartheid 161–3, 166, 170–3
   Pedagogy of Hope 183–4, 186, 188–9, 191
Language of the Third Reich, The 25
Law Enforcement Assistance Act (1965) 73
leadership 31, 105, 131, 158
learning 123, 200, 202–3
   fascism 142, 144, 146, 148
   ignorance and public imagination 35, 42
   Pedagogy of Hope 182–4, 187
literacy 173, 206
   fascism 135, 138, 142–5
   ignorance and public imagination 27, 30, 32, 45, 51

Pedagogy of Hope 181–2, 185, 193–4
Trumpism 97, 110, 124
Lorde, Audre 153, 172
Los Angeles Review of Books 32

M
Manchin, Joe 91–2
Manhattan Institute 159
manipulation 57, 98
manufactured ignorance 196–8, 209 *see also* ignorance
   American Nazism 62, 64, 67, 87
   apartheid 149, 155, 165–6, 168
   fascism 140–2, 144
   Trumpism 98, 114
marginalization 184
Marxism 186
mass consciousness 45
mass entertainment 24, 141
mass shootings 79
Mbembe, Achille 44, 68
McCarthyism 129, 153, 157, 161
McConnell, Mitch 34, 150
media 188, 197 *see also* ignorance; social media
   American Nazism 57, 62, 65, 68–9, 81
   apartheid 150, 161–9
   digital 24–5
   fascism 129–30, 140–1, 143–5
   Trumpism 95, 100–1, 110, 117, 120–1
Mercieca, Jennifer 162–3
Mewhirter, Jack 73–4
militarism 82, 170–3, 201
   fascism 132, 145
   ignorance and public imagination 22, 33
   Trumpism 116, 121
Mills, Charles W. 156
Mills, C. Wright 93, 181, 197, 202
misinformation 24–5, 37, 111, 145, 178
   apartheid 161, 164–5, 169, 171
moral agency 117

morality 22, 206
MOVE 82
movements, social 195, 197, 205–8
   American Nazism 56, 62, 65, 68, 93
   apartheid 161, 171–3
   fascism 130, 134, 143, 145, 148
   Pedagogy of Hope 192, 194
   Trumpism 100–1, 108, 120, 125
Moyn, Samuel 112–14, 117
Muhammad, Khahil Gibran 70, 76

N
nationalism 162, 201 *see also* Nazism, America
   fascism 130, 135
   ignorance and public imagination 29, 31, 40, 46, 50–1
   Trumpism 102, 107–8, 114, 117
nativism 42
   American Nazism 59, 70, 89
   Trumpism 102, 107, 116
Nazism, America 61–4
   capitalism and racial hierarchies 64–7
   democracy in crisis 55–61
   disposability 67–70
   domestic spaces 72–6
   guns and reforms 78–80
   gun violence and reform failure 80–4
   punishment and youth 76–8
   racial violence 70–1
   violence beyond policing 84–8
   voters and white supremacy 89–93
neoliberal fascism 48–54
neoliberalism 172, 196, 207 *see also* Nazism, America
   fascism 131, 138, 140, 148
   ignorance and public imagination 23, 27–8, 32, 43
   Pedagogy of Hope 180–1, 190–1
   Trumpism 99, 108, 113
Newsmax 162

New York Times 115, 122, 152, 156
9/11 attacks 74

O
One America News 162
oppression 138–9, 195, 204, 207, 210
   American Nazism 63, 67, 81, 88
   apartheid 150, 154, 164, 170–1
   Pedagogy of Hope 181–3, 185, 187, 189–91, 193
   Trumpism 109, 111
Oxfam 85

P
pandemics 105, 177–8
   American Nazism 79, 85, 91
   fascism 131, 134
   ignorance and public imagination 27, 43
past histories 21–6, 33–41
patriarchy 131, 201
Paxton, Robert O. 98, 113
Pedagogy of Freedom 182
Pedagogy of Hope 177–94
Pedagogy of the Oppressed 182, 188, 191
people of colour 129, 163 *see also* ignorance; Nazism, America
   Trumpism 103, 108–9
Perlstein, Rick 21, 58
pessimism 179
Pitt, William Rivers 38–9
Piven, Francis Fox 125
platforms, media 162
policing 64–5, 70, 72–5, 81, 84–8, 97
political rights 124, 134
politics 147–8, 202–4
   image-based society 144–7
   pedagogy 138–40
Poor People's Campaign 171–2
poverty 201, 207–8 *see also* Nazism, America
   apartheid 168–70, 172–3
   fascism 131, 133
   Trumpism 102, 117

power 195–6, 198–200, 202–3, 205, 207–8, 210 *see also* apartheid; fascism; ignorance; Trumpism
Pedagogy of Hope 177–83, 185–9, 191–4
press 205
    apartheid 153, 169
    ignorance and public imagination 37, 41
    Trumpism 114, 122
privatization 169, 189–90, 197
    American Nazism 64, 69
    fascism 131, 137–8
    ignorance and public imagination 23, 27, 29, 32, 47
problem-solving 183
propaganda 129
    American Nazism 56, 87
    apartheid 161–2, 165–6, 169
    ignorance and public imagination 24–5, 40
    Trumpism 95, 103, 111, 114, 119–20
protesters 72, 74, 117–18, 163–4
protest groups 130
Public Citizen 90
public consciousness 106, 110, 112
public health 29, 43, 56, 97, 105, 178–9
public imagination 26–8, 46–8
    education as depoliticizing machine 41–6
    historical amnesia 33–41
    neoliberal fascism 48–54
    past histories 21–6
    pedagogical plagues and collective consciousness 28–31
    Republican Party 31–3
    Trumpism 26–8
public schools
    American Nazism 72, 76
    apartheid 151–3, 156
    fascism 133, 137
punishments 76–8

Q
QAnon 25, 45, 92, 164

R
racial imagination, recasting of 197–200
racism 201, 208 *see also* ignorance; Nazism, America
    apartheid 149–57, 159–60, 162, 169–73
    fascism 130–1, 133
    hierarchies 64–7
    Pedagogy of Hope 177, 179, 190, 194
    Trumpism 98–99, 102, 108, 116, 125
reforms, gun 78–80
    failures 80–4
religious fundamentalism 49–51
remembrance, historical 123
repression 42, 137, 199
    American Nazism 61–3, 65, 69, 76, 87
    apartheid 150, 154, 159, 169
    Pedagogy of Hope 180, 182
    Trumpism 102–3, 106, 111, 116, 123
Republican Party 31–3
resistance, towards a pedagogy of
    beyond manufactured ignorance– education and social change 209–11
    beyond neoliberal capitalism 200–2
    critical education in a democracy 204–6
    education and racial imagination 197–200
    madness and hope 195–6
    politics follows culture 202–4
    rethinking the future 206–9
responsibilities 52–3, 141, 160, 179, 194
    American Nazism 82, 91
    Trumpism 103, 112, 118
responsibilities, individual 23, 64, 115, 190, 193
responsibilities, social 210 *see also* ignorance
    American Nazism 61, 64

apartheid 156, 165-6
  fascism 134, 136, 142, 148
  Pedagogy of Hope 180, 182, 187-8
  Trumpism 113, 125
Rich, Frank 56-7
Robin, Corey 114, 116, 117
Rufo, Chris 155-6
Rushdie, Salmon 30, 49
Russo, Bill 52-3

S
schools 195, 199, 206, 209
  American Nazism 62, 70-1, 77, 81-2, 86-8
  apartheid 149, 156-7, 160
  fascism 129, 140-1, 143, 146
  ignorance and public imagination 34-5, 49-50
  Pedagogy of Hope 180, 183
segregation 152, 154-5
selfishness 27, 61
self-reflection 93, 98, 181
self-responsibility 190
sexism 22, 157, 199, 201
slavery 130, 200
  American Nazism 65, 71-2, 77, 90
  apartheid 149, 151-2, 154-5, 157, 161
  ignorance and public imagination 32, 34-5, 41
  Trumpism 110, 116
Snyder, Timothy 99, 113-14
social abandonment 184
social atomization 33, 87-8, 136, 190
social bonds 115, 181
social change 145, 204-5, 207, 209-11
  American Nazism 63, 88, 93
  apartheid 171, 173
  Pedagogy of Hope 177, 183, 187-8
social imagination 169-73
socialism 47, 97, 196, 204, 206-11
  apartheid 152, 161, 171, 173
  fascism 130, 132-4, 139, 146, 148

social media 200
  American Nazism 63, 69
  apartheid 144-5, 161-2, 169
  ignorance and public imagination 25, 28, 38, 47, 52
  Trumpism 99, 106, 109
social responsibilities 210 *see also* ignorance
  American Nazism 61, 64
  apartheid 156, 165-6
  fascism 134, 136, 142, 148
  Pedagogy of Hope 180, 182, 187-8
  Trumpism 113, 115, 125
Society of the Spectacle 111
solidarity 110, 134, 198, 202
  American Nazism 70, 84
  apartheid 162, 171
  ignorance and public imagination 26, 29
  Pedagogy of Hope 181, 190
spaces, domestic 72-6
spectacle, age of 41-6, 70-1
spectacles
  disinformation 161-7
  violence 167-9
Sperling, Joshua 40
Stanley, Jason 113, 166
Stop the Steal campaign 165
Street, Paul 78, 113
strikes 171
students 35, 203
  apartheid 150-2, 154-5, 157-9, 171
  fascism 137, 140, 142-3, 146-7
  Pedagogy of Hope 181-5, 187-90
subjectivity 23, 47-8, 114, 183, 204
Sunrise movement 171-2
Sunstein, Cass 113-14
suppression, voter 140
  American Nazism 65, 69, 86-7, 89-93
  ignorance and public imagination 31, 50
  Trumpism 96-7, 104, 108, 117

T

Taylor, Breonna 71, 82
teachers 52, 199 *see also* educators
    apartheid 150-2, 154, 171
    fascism 137, 143, 146
    Pedagogy of Hope 181, 183, 189
technologies 24, 28, 73, 82, 143
1033 Program 73
tenures 157-9
terrorism 57-59
    American Nazism 65, 82
    apartheid 165, 167
    Trumpism 97, 101, 107
Thomas W. Smith Foundation 159
Trump, Donald 138 *see also* ignorance; Trumpism
    American Nazism 56-, 60-61, 65, 68-9, 84
    apartheid 161, 163-5, 168-9
Trumpism 95-125, 141, 198-9, 201 *see also* ignorance
    American Nazism 77, 89
truth 123
truth-telling 123
Tucker Carlson Tonight 38
Tulsa 57
tyranny 183, 207, 210
    American Nazism 55, 63
    apartheid 154, 166
    fascism 143, 148
    Trumpism 104, 106, 123-4

U

unemployment 85

V

violence 84-8, 184 *see also* Nazism, America
    spectacle of 167-9
vision 147-8
Vitale, Alex 81, 83

voters 31, 89-93, 100 *see also* suppression, voter

W

wages 99
Wallbuilders 90
Washington Capital, attack (storming) 164
    American Nazism 57, 58, 61
    ignorance and public imagination 30, 39, 41, 43
    Trumpism 95, 101, 104, 108
Washington Post 36, 73
weapons, military-grade 73
weapons of mass destruction 71
websites 163
Welch, Ryan 73-4
West, Cornel 82, 86, 102
white supremacy 135
    American Nazism. *see* Nazism, America
    apartheid 149, 154-5, 161-2, 164, 168
    ignorance and public imagination 31-3, 36-9, 42-3, 46, 52
    Trumpism 96-7, 102, 116
women 79, 109
workers 56, 159, 180, 200, 204-5, 208
    fascism 129, 135, 146
    Trumpism 99, 113, 124
Wright, Duante 71, 72

Y

young people
    American Nazism 71, 77
    apartheid 152, 162, 172
    fascism 130, 133-4, 137-8, 143-4, 146
    ignorance and public imagination 28, 31, 34
    Pedagogy of Hope 179, 193
youth 76-8

Intro — both child & society → two strands

school as replicating social anxieties + fears, eg. book banning in the US. Site of populism, conspiracy theory. Race, social justice, sexism, etc.

Also — do schools have role in pushing back on damaging ideas? Critical thinking — in truest sense — so vital.

Teacher teaching children about poverty, capitalism etc — may get fired!